MAKING THE CASE

RHETORIC AND PUBLIC AFFAIRS SERIES

- *Eisenhower's War of Words: Rhetoric and Leadership,* Martin J. Medhurst, editor
- *The Nuclear Freeze Campaign: Rhetoric and Foreign Policy in the Telepolitical Age,* J. Michael Hogan
- *Mansfield and Vietnam: A Study in Rhetorical Adaptation,* Gregory A. Olson
- *Truman and the Hiroshima Cult,* Robert P. Newman
- *Post-Realism: The Rhetorical Turn in International Relations,* Francis A. Beer and Robert Hariman, editors
- *Rhetoric and Political Culture in Nineteenth-Century America,* Thomas W. Benson, editor
- *Frederick Douglass: Freedom's Voice, 1818–1845,* Gregory P. Lampe
- *Angelina Grimké: Rhetoric, Identity, and the Radical Imagination,* Stephen Howard Browne
- *Strategic Deception: Rhetoric, Science, and Politics in Missile Defense Advocacy,* Gordon R. Mitchell
- *Rostow, Kennedy, and the Rhetoric of Foreign Aid,* Kimber Charles Pearce
- *Visions of Poverty: Welfare Policy and Political Imagination,* Robert Asen
- *General Eisenhower: Ideology and Discourse,* Ira Chernus
- *The Reconstruction Desegregation Debate: The Politics of Equality and the Rhetoric of Place, 1870–1875,* Kirt H. Wilson
- *Shared Land/Conflicting Identity: Trajectories of Israeli and Palestinian Symbol Use,* Robert C. Rowland and David A. Frank
- *Darwinism, Design, and Public Education,* John Angus Campbell and Stephen C. Meyer, editors
- *Religious Expression and the American Constitution,* Franklyn S. Haiman
- *Christianity and the Mass Media in America: Toward a Democratic Accommodation,* Quentin J. Schultze
- *Bending Spines: The Propagandas of Nazi Germany and the German Democratic Republic,* Randall L. Bytwerk
- *Malcolm X: Inventing Radical Judgment,* Robert E. Terrill
- *Metaphorical World Politics,* Francis A. Beer and Christ'l De Landtsheer, editors
- *The Lyceum and Public Culture in the Nineteenth-Century United States,* Angela G. Ray
- *The Political Style of Conspiracy: Chase, Sumner, and Lincoln,* Michael William Pfau
- *The Character of Justice: Rhetoric, Law, and Politics in the Supreme Court Confirmation Process,* Trevor Parry-Giles
- *Rhetorical Vectors of Memory in National and International Holocaust Trials,* Marouf A. Hasian Jr.
- *Judging the Supreme Court: Constructions of Motives in* Bush *v.* Gore, Clarke Rountree
- *Everyday Subversion: From Joking to Revolting in the German Democratic Republic,* Kerry Kathleen Riley
- *In the Wake of Violence: Image and Social Reform,* Cheryl R. Jorgensen-Earp
- *Rhetoric and Democracy: Pedagogical and Political Practices,* Todd F. McDorman and David M. Timmerman, editors
- *Invoking the Invisible Hand: Social Security and the Privatization Debates,* Robert Asen
- *With Faith in the Works of Words: The Beginnings of Reconciliation in South Africa, 1985–1995,* Erik Doxtader
- *Public Address and Moral Judgment: Critical Studies in Ethical Tensions,* Shawn J. Parry-Giles and Trevor Parry-Giles, editors
- *Executing Democracy: Capital Punishment and the Making of America, 1683–1807,* Stephen John Hartnett
- *Enemyship: Democracy and Counter-Revolution in the Early Republic,* Jeremy Engels
- *Spirits of the Cold War: Contesting Worldviews in the Classical Age of American Security Strategy,* Ned O'Gorman

MAKING THE CASE

ADVOCACY AND JUDGMENT IN PUBLIC ARGUMENT

EDITED BY

Kathryn M. Olson, Michael William Pfau, Benjamin Ponder, and Kirt H. Wilson

MICHIGAN STATE UNIVERSITY PRESS • *East Lansing*

♾ The paper used in this publication meets the minimum requirements of ANSI/NISO Z39.48-1992 (R 1997) (Permanence of Paper).

Michigan State University Press
East Lansing, Michigan 48823-5245

Printed and bound in the United States of America.

20 19 18 17 16 15 14 13   1 2 3 4 5 6 7 8 9 10

LIBRARY OF CONGRESS CATALOGING-IN-PUBLICATION DATA
Making the case : advocacy and judgment in public argument / edited by Kathryn M. Olson . . . [et al.].
p. cm. — (Rhetoric and public affairs series)
Includes bibliographical references.
ISBN 978-1-61186-052-8 (pbk. : alk. paper) 1. Political oratory—United States—Case studies. 2. Communication in politics—United States—Case studies. 3. Persuasion (Rhetoric)—Political aspects—Case studies. 4. Rhetoric—Political aspects—Case studies. 5. Rhetorical criticism. I. Olson, Kathryn M.
JA85.2.U6M372 2012
320.97301'4—dc23
2011050519

ISBN 978-1-61186-052-8 (paper) / 978-1-60917-344-9 (e-book)

Book design by Charlie Sharp, Sharp Des!gns, Lansing, MI

green press INITIATIVE Michigan State University Press is a member of the Green Press Initiative and is committed to developing and encouraging ecologically responsible publishing practices. For more information about the Green Press Initiative and the use of recycled paper in book publishing, please visit *www.greenpressinitiative.org*.

Visit Michigan State University Press on the World Wide Web at *www.msupress.org*

For David Zarefsky
—peerless mentor, valued friend, and model scholar—
who inspired a discipline.

Contents

PREFACE · · · ix

ACKNOWLEDGMENTS · · · xv

Reflections on Making the Case | *David Zarefsky* · · · 1

The Beginnings of Oratorical Consciousness: Restarting Time in Homer's *Odyssey*, The Telemachy | *G. Thomas Goodnight* · · · 17

Lysander Spooner's *The Unconstitutionality of Slavery*: A Case Study in Constitutional Hermeneutics, Ethical Argument, and Practical Reason | *James Jasinski* · · · 45

Kind Persuasion: Lincoln's Temperance Address and the Ethos of Civic Friendship | *Michael Leff* · · · · · 75

Andrew Johnson's Fight for States' Rights on the Battlements of the Constitution | *Karlyn Kohrs Campbell* · · · · · 95

No End Save Victory: FDR and the End of Isolationism, 1936–1941 | *John M. Murphy* · · · · · 127

Iraq as a Representative Anecdote for Leadership: Barack Obama's Address on the Fifth Anniversary of the Iraq War | *Denise M. Bostdorff* · · · · · 161

Barack Obama's 2009 Inaugural Address: Narrative Signature and Interpretation | *Martin J. Medhurst* · · · · · 191

To Exist, You Need an Ideology: Alan Greenspan on Markets, Crisis, and Democracy | *Robert Asen* · · · · · 231

CONTRIBUTORS · · · · · 257

Preface

Case studies may be said to reveal a distinctively Aristotelian rhetorical epistemology. By privileging the specificity, timeliness, and granularity of texts, the case study as a critical method displays a productive bias toward judgment, particular knowledge, historical context, and situated discourse. In this important respect, this volume is more than a collection of well-conceived, well-executed rhetorical case studies. It also is an exploration of the means by which the case study, as a critical method grounded in particularity, isolates and extracts meanings from a given text and context. To call case studies "distinctively Aristotelian" is not to subscribe to the so-called neo-Aristotelian critical method of a previous era, which has been rightly condemned by many as a rote approach that often denied a rhetorical text's particularity by applying to it a kind of formulaic cookie cutter. Rather, each of these essays contributes to a broader, variegated "theory of the case," reflecting Aristotle's definition of rhetoric as "the faculty of observing in any given case the available means of persuasion."[1] According to David Zarefsky, such a "theory of the case," when executed effectively, produces "a better understanding of a specific instance of rhetorical practice achieved through close reading of the text and careful grounding of the text in its historical context." From this perspective, the varied theoretical orientations, historical contexts, and authorial perspectives recede in favor of an overarching vision that unites text with context and the particular moment of a discourse's articulation to the larger rhetorical art.

This collection is united not only by its focus on case studies per se, but also, and more importantly, by the theme of *making the case,* a more elaborate and challenging standard. As Zarefsky's introductory essay argues, this phrase operates in both a technical and a public sense with respect to rhetoric. Both require centering not merely on a distinct case, but also on the rhetor's or critic's rhetorical choices and how well they clarify and make persuasive his or her interpretation of that case's meaning and implications for a particular audience. Expert readings are important because, as Zarefsky contends,

> These [public] arguments, and the cases of which they are a part, do not announce themselves, but they are present nevertheless. . . . The nature of the case is seldom self-evident. Just as conversational analysts have suggested that informal interactions must be reconstructed in order to reveal their underlying argumentative dynamics, public argument must be reconstructed to make clear the cases that are being advanced. And reconstruction is a task not for the arguer but for the scholar of argumentation—the analyst, the historian, the critic.

Each essay in this volume exhibits the work of an expert trained in reconstructing, evaluating, and explaining the larger importance of a public argument in a specific historical case. Furthermore, each expert critically examines and evaluates a situated instance in which a rhetor used argument in an attempt to build a case in the public sphere for *phronesis,* or practical wisdom about what we should do or how we should act. Of course, each public rhetor is trying to influence a relevant audience under particular constraints in a specific historic episode by making his argumentative case; nevertheless, in the course of each careful investigation, these specialists extract larger lessons to make their own cases about how rhetoric operates more generally.

Given the outstanding quality of each of these case studies, scholars in several disciplines and fields of inquiry will no doubt mine this volume for the unique contributions that individual essays make to ongoing scholarly questions, problems, and pursuits. In addition, the combined studies in this volume participate in larger conversations that include scholars of rhetoric and history, argumentation, and political communication. For those interested in rhetorical history, this collection extends the perspective articulated by the editor of and contributors to *Doing Rhetorical History: Concepts and Cases.*[2] Presented in chronological order, the essays within this volume develop a sense of history in which rhetoric plays a crucial part. That is, the interpretive claims of each essay bleed into adjacent essays and enable readers to construct a coherent narrative about the development of public discourse.

G. Thomas Goodnight's essay "The Beginnings of Oratorical Consciousness" calls attention to Homeric sketches of rhetorical concepts that would later be formalized in classical Greek civilization and that continue to inform rhetorical theory and practice into the twenty-first century. As such, this essay's reading of Homer and classical oratorical culture provides an outstanding entry point into the subsequent meditations on rhetorical practice.

Michael Leff's piece on Lincoln's "Kind Persuasion" commences the larger sequence of essays focused on public discourse and public argument in the United States. Leff's essay explores how even an orator of Lincoln's caliber struggled to encapsulate both conflicting and deeply entwined views on temperance and slavery through a dialectical speech structure that negotiated stability and innovation on complex public problems. Leff's essay also points toward issues that inform the next two essays concerning slavery: the Constitution and presidential leadership.

Whereas Leff's reading of Lincoln emphasizes the manner in which temperance arguments are tightly connected with arguments concerning slavery, it also potentially informs—both topically and contextually—James Jasinski's neighboring essay on Lysander Spooner's constitutional arguments against slavery. Readers who consider the essays in order may also appreciate how Leff's and Jasinski's essays concerning Lincoln, slavery, and the Constitution provide a context for Karlyn Kohrs Campbell's reading of President Andrew Johnson's interpretive use of the Constitution. Whereas Spooner used the Constitution to argue in favor of black civil rights, President Johnson used the same text to explain his veto of Reconstruction civil rights legislation. In addition, Jasinski and Campbell each engage the recurring issue of how to foreground some shared rhetorical groundings and to background others without forsaking either. Likewise, the two essays address the perennial problem of negotiating stability and innovation in persuasive public appeals.

As a case study in the rhetorical dimensions of presidential leadership, John M. Murphy's "FDR and the End of Isolationism" is appropriately read in proximity to both Campbell's essay on Johnson and the subsequent essays by Denise M. Bostdorff and Martin J. Medhurst concerning the rhetorical discourse of Barack Obama. Murphy shows how FDR's efforts to draw parallels between the brewing world war and his earlier success in addressing the 1930s economic disaster were essential to overcoming American isolationism, pressing the metaphor of capitalism and its evils into the service of democracy. Readers with the mettle to read the volume in one sitting will no doubt recognize how the rhetoric of FDR and Obama are both shaped by the institutional opportunities and constraints of the presidency, as well as the exigencies of war and economic crisis. The Bostdorff and Medhurst essays are united by more than their focus on Barack Obama's late-campaign and early-presidential rhetoric. Both authors address, though from significantly different angles, how one uses rhetoric to establish credentials as a leader and how publics can or should evaluate such attempts.

Then, readers of Robert Asen's essay on the context of economic crisis as characterized by Alan Greenspan will recall the challenges faced by FDR and his responding rhetorical turn to an economic paradigm as justification, even as the immediate historical context will conjure further images of Obama's presidential rhetoric in a time of economic crisis. Reversing the move from economics to other ideological goals that Murphy identified in FDR's wartime rhetoric, Asen demonstrates how Greenspan's "market talk" not only revealed and "de-naturalized" the logic behind the current economic crisis but also linked and leveraged the notion of democracy in the ideological service of protecting capitalism and ultimately touting its resilience.

As profitable as this chronological rhetorical history may be, it is only one way to read the collection. The volume highlights several ongoing rhetorical problems across multiple chapters. Furthermore, the historical problems, figures, and contexts emphasized in one particular essay inform a reader's engagement with neighboring essays.

For readers interested in public argument, this collection's focus on evaluating public reason-giving is reminiscent of Edward Schiappa's *Warranting Assent: Case Studies in Argument Evaluation*,[3] which presented a provocative set of evaluative critiques of situated public arguments. As in *Warranting Assent,* each study in this volume explicitly abstracts and assesses its larger implications for understanding and evaluating rhetoric and public argument beyond the particular case.

For readers interested in exploring how the critical boundaries of a rhetorical case inflect its findings, this book might call to mind Patricia A. Sullivan and Steven R. Goldzwig's *New Approaches to Rhetoric*.[4] That volume takes up rhetorics from the approaches of ethics and values, institutions and contexts, and cultures and ideologies. This one likewise exemplifies how to construct persuasive, situated rhetorical analyses of cases defined by a variety of boundary choices by the critic: single speeches or writings (Jasinski, Leff, Bostdorff), a trajectory of rhetorical practices regularly associated with a particular rhetor across time and occasions (Campbell, Murphy, Medhurst, Asen), and the establishment of new rhetorical traditions at the point of a noticeable break with the past (Goodnight).

Finally, readers interested in rhetoric's intersection with public morality will detect similarities between this volume and Shawn J. Parry-Giles and Trevor Parry-Giles's *Public Address and Moral Judgment*.[5] That collection focuses on how political discourse can (re)constitute the moral identity of a community in a way that carries moral imperatives. Likewise, the chapters in *Making the Case* all examine how public rhetoric builds or breaks communities and does so in ways that have practical and moral implications for evaluating both the case and the broader rhetorical processes at work.

Each case study contained herein is a valuable contribution that can be appreciated by interdisciplinary audiences ranging from rhetorical studies to history, political science, English, and beyond. Rhetorical scholars sympathetic to a nuanced Aristotelian conception of rhetoric in particular will appreciate the manner in which each author elucidates the means of persuasion exhibited in the discourse of his or her respective rhetor, as deployed in particular cases and situations. And it is to be hoped that any reader taking the time to read the essays together will quickly come to value the richness and suppleness of the case study approach for analyzing and evaluating public argument; the rhetors, topics, and contexts animating this volume are mutually reinforcing and enlightening. The editors believe that the multiple, inventive ways that "making the case" through both public argument and professional rhetorical analyses intersect within these pages offer insights into key and timeless struggles of humankind and nations: human rights; war, peace, and the transition between them; foreign policy; economic policy; and leadership. In this last iteration, the influence of David Zarefsky's scholarship is plain. He has inspired scholars whose interests range widely, but whose focus on public argument as it intersects history in well-chosen, situated cases informs readers—through lively and thoughtful rhetorical analyses—on larger theoretical and critical issues, as well as about the particular "case."

NOTES

1. Aristotle, "Rhetorica," in *The Basic Works of Aristotle*, ed. by Richard McKeon and trans. by W. Rhys Roberts (New York: Random House, 1941), 1355b.
2. Kathleen J. Turner, ed., *Doing Rhetorical History: Concepts and Cases* (Tuscaloosa: University of Alabama Press, 2003).
3. Edward Schiappa, ed., *Warranting Assent: Case Studies in Argument Evaluation* (Albany: State University of New York Press, 1995).
4. Patricia A. Sullivan and Steven R. Goldzwig, eds., *New Approaches to Rhetoric* (Thousand Oaks, CA: SAGE Publications, 2004).
5. Shawn J. Parry-Giles and Trevor Parry-Giles, eds., *Public Address and Moral Judgment* (East Lansing: Michigan State University Press, 2009).

Acknowledgments

With a single exception, the essays in this volume are based on papers originally presented at the conference "Justification, Reason, and Action: Tradition and Innovation in Public Argument" held at Northwestern University in May 2009. The occasion of the conference was the retirement from full-time teaching of David Zarefsky, former dean of the School of Speech at Northwestern and longtime leader in the field of rhetorical and communication studies. Though held in honor of Zarefsky, the conference itself was focused on specific topics of enduring interest in the field of rhetorical studies, since Zarefsky had given explicit instructions that the conference was not to be "about me." Long a leader in such areas as rhetorical history, rhetorical criticism, argumentation theory, and intercollegiate debate, Professor Zarefsky's work has inspired not only his own students but also scholars throughout North America, Europe, and the Middle East.

The conference organizers—Kathryn M. Olson, Michael William

Pfau, Benjamin Ponder, and Kirt H. Wilson—chose to invite scholars who represented the broad range of Professor Zarefsky's interests. Instead of including just Zarefsky's former students or colleagues, the organizers sought out scholars working on the cutting edge of those issues that had occupied Zarefsky's career for decades—the rhetoric of the Civil War and Reconstruction, the discourse of Abraham Lincoln, the rhetoric of war, presidential rhetoric, and the functioning of argument in particular situations. The conference thus featured noted scholars from across the nation.

Two of the conference presentations—one by Edward Schiappa of the University of Minnesota and one by Gordon Mitchell and Kathleen M. McTigue of the University of Pittsburgh—were unavailable for inclusion in this volume. Their contributions to the conversation at the conference were significant, and we thank them for their participation. In their stead, we are pleased to include the chapter by G. Thomas Goodnight of the Annenberg School for Journalism and Communication at the University of Southern California. Professor Goodnight was in attendance at the conference but did not present this research as part of the conference program because he had been invited to be a banquet speaker.

The idea for the conference originated with Robert Hariman, chair of the Department of Communication Studies at Northwestern University. We are indebted to Professor Hariman, the Department of Communication Studies, and the School of Communication at Northwestern not only for the original idea, but also for financially supporting and hosting the conference. We also extend our thanks to all those who served as panel chairs, discussants, or respondents, as well as to those whose attendance and lively discussions made the conference a success—and this book a reality. Special thanks are due to Martin J. Medhurst for his advice and encouragement on this project, to the anonymous reviewers, and to the staff at Michigan State University Press.

Reflections on Making the Case

David Zarefsky

Making the case is what arguers do. And they often do it in public. The most common understanding of *case* is that it is a set of reasons and supporting evidence used by an advocate to support or to oppose a claim. A definition similar to this can be found in most textbooks on argumentation and debate. One thinks, for example, of a prosecutor's case in a criminal proceeding or of the briefs by opposing lawyers outlining their respective cases in a civil suit. Within the realm of science, one can imagine a case being made for or against a disputed hypothesis or theory. In a Talmudic disputation, one would expect to find the proffering of competing doctrines and proof texts as scholars make the case for one or another interpretation of sacred scripture. And in the competitive debate context, one regularly finds the affirmative case and the negative case, structures of reasoning for or against a stated resolution.

These examples have at least two features in common. First, they are modeled on a dialogic encounter, an exchange between interlocutors in order to determine what is probably true or what is the best action to take. The exchange might not consist of questions and answers, as in a Socratic dialogue, but it is interactive. An advocate puts forward a claim. If it is not accepted by the antagonist, he or she will be expected to provide the reason for doubting either the truth of the evidence, or the link between the evidence and the claim, or both. Once this is done, the original advocate now has the responsibility to defend the original claim against the doubts and challenges. This may involve buttressing the original evidence and inferences or else adding new ones. The challenger then will seek to reinstate and strengthen the grounds for doubt or rejection of the claim. And so it will go until one arguer realizes that he or she is in error and capitulates, or until the two disputants arrive at some common understanding or compromise, or until time runs out and a third party acts as an arbitrator and reaches a decision. To say that the argument is interactive means that it is both sequential and adaptive. It does not spring forth all at once but evolves through a series of communication moves, whether orally or in writing. And each of these moves takes into account the preceding moves and responds to them. Neither repeating one's original position without responding to the interlocutor, nor making comments that are irrelevant to what the interlocutor has said, will be deemed acceptable. To put this another way, arguers must fulfill what lawyers call the production burden, or what argument theorists call the burden of going forward with the debate.[1]

The second characteristic of each of my examples is that it takes place in a context that is conventional. Whether stated explicitly or not, there are norms of procedure and standards of judgment that all parties implicitly accept. In the legal setting, these might include such disparate matters as the norm of civility in the courtroom, the presumption of innocence, and the rules against hearsay testimony. In science they might include the commitment to replicability in experimentation, the importance of control groups, and the standard order of topics in a write-up of research results. The disputing theologians work with principles of hermeneutics and a hierarchy of authoritative texts. And the competitive debaters rely on assumptions about what makes expert testimony compelling, what counts as effective refutation, and how to determine whether the benefits of a proposal outweigh its costs.

While the norms and conventions are understood by the arguers making their case, they may be unknown or even meaningless to outsiders. It requires special training and experience in order to gain the competence to make the case. To be able to make the case meaningfully is a sign that one has been admitted to the guild, as it were, and to be admitted to the guild is a sign that one has the expertise to make the case. To say all this is to say that the examples above fall squarely within what G. Thomas Goodnight has labeled the technical sphere of argument.[2]

Making the Case in Public Argument

Public argument is different. In principle it is open to all, and its subject matter is potentially of interest to anyone. No particular training or expertise is required in order to participate, and technical expertise is not necessarily valued. There usually are no clearly defined starting or ending points to the argument, and there are no universally accepted rules of procedure. There may be no consensually accepted standards for what counts as evidence or inference. For that matter, there often is no stated claim that marks the focus of the controversy, although it is usually possible to tease one out from the general topic. And that topic involves the uncertain and contingent, since, as Aristotle wrote, we do not deliberate about matters that are certain. Accordingly, the goal of public argument is *phronesis,* practical wisdom about what we should do or how we should act. The arguers seek probable truth, but not in the same sense as the participants in a dialectical encounter. Rather, they seek to determine whether a statement embodying a proposed action—"We should do X"—is true.

Along with these differences in genre, there are several contextual differences between the public sphere and the technical sphere. First, public argument is often one-to-many. A lecturer addressing a large audience; a president addressing the nation by radio, television, and the Internet; a business executive giving motivational speeches to employees or explaining the company's performance to stockholders; and the writer of an op-ed column for or against the government's intervention in the economy all illustrate this aspect of argument in the public sphere. The arguer is known but the audience is large, possibly even anonymous. Consequently, the discussion cannot be sequential in the sense described above. The arguer cannot determine the interlocutor's standpoints and respond specifically to them. Instead, the arguer makes assumptions about what the standpoints are, taking them for granted and using them as premises for arguments. This is what the classical theorists called the *enthymeme,* an argument that looks incomplete because some of its parts are derived from beliefs the arguer attributes to the audience and does not state explicitly.[3] When a speaker addresses an audience about the best way to close the deficit or the need to prepare for war, he or she has employed an enthymeme. That big government does not work, that politics is corrupt, and that terrorists pose a mortal threat to the United States are examples of premises that contemporary audiences largely take for granted and that arguers rely upon in building enthymemes. A culture's store of such premises is an index of its values and hence of what its members deem to be persuasive.

The arguer does not have the luxury, however, of validating what the audience's implicit premises are. Since the audience is vast and its exact membership unknown, it is not possible to put individual audience members "on the record" in the manner of a Socratic dialogue. Instead, the arguer must make judgments about premises that are attributed to rather than actually derived from them. These judgments could be wrong—opponents often will be ready to maintain that they *are* wrong—and if they are, then the argument will not persuade the public. But the arguer will improve the chances of making correct judgments by being both well grounded in the subject matter of the argument and an astute observer of the culture of the audience.

To complicate matters further, a second characteristic of public argument is that the audience is heterogeneous. Or, to put it another way, there often are several audiences for the same message. This is especially likely to happen when an argument concerns and is addressed to a very broad public, such as a society, a culture, a nation, or an international or global community. The argument may be heard by, and its success may depend upon, both liberals and conservatives, or Northerners and Southerners, or Whigs and Democrats, or secularists and people of faith, or Europeans and Americans. This list of binaries could be extended without limit, and not all the divisions with an audience are as simple as binaries! It is in the nature of public argument that, in order to succeed, arguers must find support from a coalition whose interests and commitments might well be in tension.

Accomplishing this task often will require that the case be made with a certain degree of strategic ambiguity or polysemy. This is nothing new. During the 1850s Stephen A. Douglas was able to hold the Democratic Party together only by adopting a policy of "popular sovereignty," which could be understood *either* as granting the inhabitants of a territory the opportunity to decide for or against slavery at the inception of their territorial government *or* as denying them that prerogative until they applied for admission as a state. Douglas failed to choose between these two interpretations. (The Democratic Party divided when this strategic ambiguity no longer could be maintained.) In like fashion, the theme of "human rights" has been used since the 1970s both to reward and to challenge authoritarian governments with whom we have common political interests,[4] and the concept of a "culture of life" has sometimes been effective in eliciting support from both pro-life and pro-choice groups for certain social service programs. In these and other examples, language is used by arguers to transcend political and other divisions in an attempt to fashion a coalition of supporters. It is in the nature of public argument that advocates will need to do that.

Third, because public argument normally has no defined initial or terminal point, the case will be made in fragmentary fashion by individual arguers and will take its complete shape only over an extended period of time. The case against officially sanctioned racial discrimination, for example, began during the antebellum era and was not concluded until the mid-1960s. Only in retrospect can one see the contours of the case and recognize later claims as repetition, refinement, elaboration, or refutation of earlier ones. The case for guaranteed health care was initiated 100 years ago by Theodore Roosevelt, and, as of this writing, has not been settled yet. The cases for foreign policy guided by idealism and by realpolitik have been made in different guises but have been little changed since the early days of the republic. What these examples suggest is that public arguments lack the clarity of structure that more typically can be found in the technical sphere. The relevant unit of analysis may be the controversy,[5] but the structure of a case in a controversy is hardly self-evident. The case must be *found,* and sometimes it must be reconstituted.

Fourth, a characteristic often attributed to argumentation is reasonableness, but public arguments often appear to be unreasonable, at least by conventional standards of reason. They can be based on premises that have been shown to be false, such as the belief that Saddam Hussein orchestrated the terrorist attacks of September 11, 2001, or that Medicare is not a government program. They can rely on seemingly unreasoned rhetorical moves such as the use of terms like "liberal," "sexist," "traditional," or "socialist" as terms of opprobrium without justifying the value judgment that the epithets are meant to convey. They can be based on seemingly inconsistent positions, such as simultaneous advocacy of tax cuts or government spending that will increase budget deficits and a balanced-budget amendment to bring deficits under control or support for the general claim that government spending should be cut and opposition to any particular cut that might be proposed. It is harder to see in such discourse the site of cases for or against public policies. But argument in the public sphere can be messy. A charitable reading of such discourse is necessary in order to see it as argument, but charity may be rewarded by recognition of the case that may lie beneath the surface of seemingly unreasoned discourse.

Finally, public argument is not always verbal. It also takes the form of editorial cartoons, iconic photographs, the massing of bodies, graphic presentations, and symbolic actions. There was an argument in the blocking of troop trains carrying conscripts bound for Vietnam during the 1960s, and it was part of a broader case against the war. There is an argument in the "tea party" protests, from Boston in 1773 to the present, and it is part of a case against what is seen as oppressive government taxation. Similarly, there is argument in the pictures of aborted fetuses distributed by pro-life organizations, in the photo of the Marines raising the flag at Mount Suribachi, and in the emptiness of the site in lower Manhattan where the World Trade Center once stood. These arguments, and the cases of which they are a part, do not announce themselves, but they are present nevertheless.

What all these characteristics of public argument suggest is that its shape is far more amorphous than that of the interactive dialectical encounters of the technical sphere. The nature of the case is seldom self-evident. Just as conversational analysts have suggested that informal interactions must be reconstructed in order to reveal their underlying argumentative dynamics,[6] public argument must be reconstructed to make clear the cases that are being advanced. And reconstruction is a task not for the arguer but for the scholar of argumentation—the analyst, the historian, the critic.

Making the Case through Analysis of Discourse

It is not only the advocate who makes a case; the analyst of discourse does so as well. In an essay on understanding history as argument, E. Culpepper Clark puts the matter succinctly: "Documents do not speak, they must be spoken for."[7] In speaking for a text, the analyst introduces his or her own voice. What the text means or signifies, and why it matters, is not self-evident. The analyst seeks to explain such matters and, in explaining them, makes a case for his or her point of view. And what is true of historical texts in Clark's example is true of any kind of discourse, as well as for symbolic action understood as discourse. The interaction of the analyst (with his or her experience and predispositions) and the text leads to a particular point of view about the text. Explaining that point of view is intertwined with making a case for it. The analyst is saying simultaneously, "Here is how the text looks to me," and "You should see the text this way as well." Just as the discourse being examined is developed with an audience in mind, so is the analysis and criticism of that discourse.

These general insights can be applied specifically to rhetorical criticism. The term "criticism" can be misleading if it is taken to mean attacking or finding fault with discourse. Most critics see themselves as analysts, and rhetorical criticism offers accounts of rhetorical works, whether they are products, artifacts, or processes. The central task is to explain the relationships among the rhetor, the text, and the audience. Doing so involves answering two general questions: (1) What's going on here? And (2) So what? The first question asks the analyst to make clear the underlying dynamics of the rhetorical work, how it might be seen as operating to influence people. The second question asks why the text and its dynamics matter; it relates the particular work to some consideration beyond itself.

In an essay written thirty-five years ago but which has received far too little attention, Wayne Brockriede maintains that strong answers to those questions involve argument, and that of course involves making a case.[8] The questions are hermeneutic, calling for understanding and meaning rather than prediction and causality. They cannot be answered solely by reference to the text, and they cannot be proved conclusively. It does not follow, though, that any account of the text is just as good as any other. Analysts and critics can miss the mark; they can make far-fetched or outlandish statements about the text that no one will take seriously. The accounts and explanations that analysts offer are claims on the judgment and belief of their readers and listeners. And like any claim, their strength is determined by the case they make for it. A strong claim will be one that is supported by good reasons, those that would convince a reasonable person exercising critical judgment.[9] Good reasons are those that will withstand critical scrutiny and give the claim a stronger hold on the audience's beliefs than would the statement of the claim alone.

The questions that the reader or listener should ask of any example of rhetorical analysis or criticism are (1) Does it meet appropriate tests of evidence and inference? (2) Is there a competing explanation that is stronger or more convincing? These are the very same questions that would be raised about any effort to make the case for a claim.

These observations suggest a parallel between the rhetor and the analyst. The rhetor makes claims about a topic with one or more audiences in mind, and the claims must withstand the scrutiny of those audiences in order to be convincing. So, too, the rhetorical analyst or critic makes claims about what the rhetor is doing. These claims also are made with one or more audiences in mind and will be convincing only if they withstand audience scrutiny. Since the arguments of rhetorical analysts are interpretive and hence not subject to empirical verification, they are tested by their conformity to norms and procedures of argumentation. The rhetorical analyst who satisfies these tests is said to have made a strong case.

To be sure, not every act of commentary on a text involves argumentation. Brockriede acknowledges that some responses to the text can be nonargumentative. Simple description (such as summarizing the content of a speech or offering a chronological account of the development of a persuasive campaign) contains no inference going beyond the work itself; it is merely reporting. Simple classification (identifying the genre of which the work is a case) says little about the work and more about the reach of the genre. By some definitions, even these acts could be seen as making a case: that events happened in one sequence and not another or that the work belongs in this category and not that. These usually would not be robust inferences or ambitious cases, however. The rhetorical critic who wants to convince an audience that his or her view of the text matters usually will aim higher.

Making the Case through Case Studies

Thinking about the kinds of argument rhetorical critics deploy brings to mind yet another meaning of "making the case." Aristotle understood rhetoric as the faculty of discovering the available means of persuasion *in a given case*,[10] and rhetorical critics often are concerned with the particularity of specific (perhaps even unique) situations. Studies of this type (of which the essays in this book are strong examples) are called *case studies*. But what sort of case does a case study make?

It sometimes is assumed that a case study is an application or illustration of a more general theory: one takes the theory and applies it to a particular case, demonstrating the power of the theory to account for the case. The purpose of such a study is to make apparent the utility of the theory, and it can be particularly valuable when the theory is new, when there are competing theories, or when the theory has been derived deductively from abstract propositions or models rather than built inductively from observation of empirical conditions. But it is of less value when the theory is well established or when it is sufficiently vast in scope to be essentially nonfalsifiable. Precisely because theories of this sort—such as Kenneth Burke's dramatism or Richard Weaver's insight that the only sound rhetoric is grounded in a preceding dialectic—offer such broad perspectives on human nature and on how discourse works, one would expect them to apply to virtually all cases.[11] So to take the theory, map its terms and categories onto the particular case, and then conclude that the theory applies to the case is not to yield a profound or interesting result.

Moreover, to insist that the sole value of the case study is in its contribution to theory is to underestimate the potential value of studying the particular, as well as to place the work of the historian, analyst, or critic in a subordinate position to that of the theorist.[12] Sometimes there is value in producing what lawyers call a "theory of the case," a better understanding of a specific instance of rhetorical practice achieved through close reading of the text and careful grounding of the text in its historical context. The analyst who proceeds in this fashion is making a case through abductive reasoning—inference from the facts of the case to what is put forward as the best explanation for them.[13]

The difference between a study relating a case to a theory, arguing by example, and a study giving primacy to the case itself, arguing abductively, is largely one of audience. In the former situation, the study will be of interest to a broad community whose members share disciplinary identity or commitment to a particular theoretical perspective (such as Marxism or utilitarianism) and who take from the study enhanced insight about their shared commitment. In the latter case, the audience is a broad community, quite likely interdisciplinary, of people who are interested in the case itself, who bring different insights to bear upon the case, and who value the contribution of the rhetorical critic in accounting for the *interaction* between the text and its historical context. Of course, such a community is easier to assemble with regard to texts already well known and regarded as paradigmatic or canonical than it is for obscure or newly discovered texts. In the former situation, though, there is the burden of contributing "news," of adding to what already is known or understood about the work. In the latter situation, the burden is to justify the interest of the audience in the unfamiliar.

Even if the focus of the case study is the case, however, the analyst should relate the text to something beyond itself, in order to make an inference to support some claim about it. Otherwise it will be very hard to answer the "so what?" question. The claim might be that the case suggests normative standards or models of rhetorical practice, or that its insight might apply analogically to other specific cases, or that it offers perspective by incongruity that aids the understanding of more typical or quotidian cases. It might furnish an explanatory sketch that an analyst could regard as a presumption when exploring new cases. Or it might offer a new point of view about its own meaning, significance, or value. It is important to recognize, though, that the function of the case study is not exclusively to serve as data supporting a larger or grander theoretical claim. It is also valuable in its own right. One can make a case about the case study, just as the case study can make a case.

Making the Case through Historical Inquiry

One function of the case study that has received too little attention in recent years is its contribution to rhetorical history—a contribution that is superbly exemplified by the essays in this volume. The term "rhetorical history" is variously understood, sometimes as the history of rhetorical theory, sometimes as the idea that history itself is a rhetorical construction. Neither of those understandings is employed here. Rather, rhetorical history is understood both as the historical study of rhetorical events and the study from a rhetorical perspective of historical forces, trends, processes, and events.[14]

The historical study of rhetorical events embraces studies in which rhetorical discourse is seen as a force in history, altering prevailing understandings, as well as studies in which it is seen as an index or mirror of historical or cultural forces. The latter sense may be more productive, if only because it is very rare that any individual rhetorical act by itself will effect significant change in an audience's attitudes or understanding. It is the latter sense that Ernest Wrage characterized when he wrote of public address as a repository of history's intellectual substance, revealing how ideas were affected by the process of sharing them in attempts to influence others.[15] An excellent example of a study employing this sense of "rhetorical history" is the investigation by Celeste Michelle Condit and John Louis Lucaites of the evolution of Americans' understanding of the term "equality." The shifting meanings of this term in public discourse, they argue, mirror the historical development of race relations in the United States.[16] Work of this sort demonstrates how historical scholarship enhances our understanding of the particular rhetorical case and how that understanding furthers a larger purpose.

Even more productive than historical studies of rhetorical events, however, may be the study of historical events and processes from a rhetorical perspective. This approach views history as a series of rhetorical problems—situations that call for public persuasion to advance a cause or to overcome an impasse. The goal of any case study is to examine how, and how well, people deployed rhetorical resources in a historical moment that called for them.[17] These case studies are valuable to the scholar of public discourse because they reveal patterns and variations in rhetorical exigencies and responses. They are of value to the rhetorical theorist because they provide rich accounts of how communication works in society. These accounts undergird broad theoretical claims about such topics as framing, collective memory, and the public sphere. And they are of value to the historian because they provide a different lens through which to view historical events and trends, and hence a different grounding for historical accounts than other perspectives can provide. Each case study reveals not just discrete events, but a moment in "the transcript of a continuing conversation."[18]

With one exception, the essays in this volume concern moments in the rhetorical history of the United States. This history reveals that American culture is both dialectical and rhetorical. It is dialectical in that it is constituted through a series of relationships between seeming opposites, such as liberalism and civic republicanism, dedication to the individual and to the group, realism and idealism, freedom and equality, diversity and community. American culture does not choose between these terms but embraces them both, enshrining a state of dialectical tension. And the culture is rhetorical in that it is public discourse that keeps these oppositions in productive tension, sustaining and also advancing understandings of the relationships. Case studies of public discourse are studies of individual moments, but they also make the case that the moments fit into this larger pattern. Examining public discourse from the perspective of argumentation is particularly valuable because it draws attention to the controversies among ideas and values that constitute these tensions, because it focuses on the competing rationales underlying these controversies, and because it counts as good reasons those that will sustain productive tensions, supporting an individual's claim in a particular situation while not seeking finality or certainty with respect to underlying principles. Sustaining these general tensions while reaching conclusions about specific matters enables a culture to change while remaining cohesive.

The one essay in this volume from outside the U.S. experience is drawn from the classical age. This is not so far removed from the other essays as it might seem. The American founders were steeped in the literature of the classics, and they saw themselves in part as replicating the classical experience. Of course, there was not just one classical experience. Many of the dialectical tensions that undergird American culture resulted from the attempt to incorporate into the new nation the competing traditions of both Greece and Rome.

It is both a strength and a weakness of rhetorical history that its scholars have focused so strongly on the United States, and both that strength and that weakness are evident in these essays as well. On the positive side, the accumulating scholarship yields increasingly sophisticated insight into the origins, development, and current state of U.S. political culture—insight that can contribute powerfully to public discussion and collective decision-making about where we go from here. On the negative side, such a heavy emphasis on one culture easily could fuel either the misperception that the American experience is universal or the misperception that it is utterly exceptional. Were there enough scholars and enough time, there would be case studies of other rhetorical traditions, comparative studies of different rhetorical cultures, and more emphasis on public argument in a global context. To say the least, the body of scholarship in U.S. rhetorical history makes the case by example that much could be learned from such a broadening of scope. At the same time, each case study is a reminder that there is always new perspective to be gained by renewed attention to the study of any particular case. The tension between breadth and depth is itself a productive tension. Embracing both of these seeming opposites is what enables scholarship to thrive.

In all the senses discussed here, the studies in this volume are about making the case. And, it hardly need be added, these studies make very good cases themselves.

NOTES

1. See, for example, Douglas Ehninger and Wayne Brockriede, *Decision by Debate* (New York: Dodd, Mead, 1963), 85–87, on the burden of going forward with the debate.
2. G. Thomas Goodnight, "The Personal, Technical, and Public Spheres of Argument: A Speculative Inquiry into the Art of Public Deliberation," *Argumentation and Advocacy* 18 (Spring 1982): 214–227. At the time, the title of the journal was *Journal of the American Forensic Association.*
3. An excellent discussion of the enthymeme is an essay by Lloyd F. Bitzer, "Aristotle's Enthymeme Revisited," *Quarterly Journal of Speech* 45 (1959): 399–408.
4. On the use of "strategic ambiguity" with respect to the issue of human rights, see Mary E. Stuckey, *Jimmy Carter, Human Rights, and the National Agenda* (College Station: Texas A&M University Press, 2008).
5. See G. Thomas Goodnight, "Controversy," in *Argument in Controversy,* ed. Donn W. Parson (Annandale, VA: National Communication Association, 1991), 1–13. The NCA was known at that time as the Speech Communication Association.
6. For example, Frans H. van Eemeren, Rob Grootendorst, Sally Jackson, and Scott Jacobs, *Reconstructing Argumentative Discourse* (Tuscaloosa: University of Alabama Press, 1993).
7. E. Culpepper Clark, "Argument and Historical Analysis," in *Advances in Argumentation Theory and Research,* ed. J. Robert Cox and Charles Arthur Willard (Carbondale: Southern Illinois University Press, 1982), 300.
8. Wayne Brockriede, "Rhetorical Criticism as Argument," *Quarterly Journal of Speech* 60 (1974): 165–174.
9. This position is developed more fully in David Zarefsky, "Knowledge Claims in Rhetorical Criticism," *Journal of Communication* 58 (2008): 629–640.
10. Aristotle, *The Rhetoric of Aristotle,* trans. Lane Cooper (New York: Appleton Century Crofts, 1932), 6 (emphasis added).
11. Kenneth Burke, "Dramatism," in *International Encyclopedia of the Social Sciences,* ed. David L. Sills (New York: Macmillan, 1968), 445–452; Richard Weaver, *The Ethics of Rhetoric* (Chicago: Henry Regnery, 1953), esp. 3–26.
12. The ideas in this and the preceding paragraph are discussed more extensively in David Zarefsky, "Public Address Scholarship in the New Century: Achievements and Challenges," in *The Handbook of Rhetoric and Public Address,* ed. Shawn J. Parry-Giles and J. Michael Hogan (New York: Wiley-Blackwell, 2010), 67–85.

13. See Douglas Walton, *Abductive Reasoning* (Tuscaloosa: University of Alabama Press, 2004). Walton credits the concept of abductive reasoning to the nineteenth-century pragmatist philosopher Charles Sanders Peirce.
14. These different meanings of "rhetorical history" are discussed in more detail in David Zarefsky, "Four Senses of Rhetorical History," in *Doing Rhetorical History: Concepts and Cases,* ed. Kathleen J. Turner (Tuscaloosa: University of Alabama Press, 1998), 19–32.
15. Ernest J. Wrage, "Public Address: A Study in Social and Intellectual History," *Quarterly Journal of Speech* 33 (1947): 451–457.
16. Celeste Michelle Condit and John Louis Lucaites, *Crafting Equality: America's Anglo-African Word* (Chicago: University of Chicago Press, 1993).
17. The notion that historical circumstances can "call for" rhetorical discourse is adapted from the analysis of Lloyd F. Bitzer, "The Rhetorical Situation," *Philosophy and Rhetoric* 1 (1968): 1–14.
18. I use this phrase as a description of the significance of individual cases in David Zarefsky, "The Roots of American Community," *The Carroll C. Arnold Distinguished Lecture, 1995* (Boston: Allyn & Bacon, 1996), 10.

The Beginnings of Oratorical Consciousness: Restarting Time in Homer's *Odyssey*, The Telemachy

G. Thomas Goodnight

The *Iliad* and the *Odyssey* are celebrated as generative works in the development of Western culture.[1] The epics are the end-product of a performative oral tradition transforming itself into discourse, the medium of written form; as a result, each exhibits the beginnings of a time where the practices of communication are no longer taken for granted and are changing.[2] A return to the beginnings of this cultural moment invites the study of oratorical consciousness, the reflexive quality of mind that shapes human agency within the social contingencies of an emergent rhetorical culture.[3] Thus, Quintilian identifies the distinction of Homer as "supreme not merely for poetic, but for oratorical power as well"—in fact, an indispensable resource for all those "who are ambitious of becoming orators."[4] Just as the might of rivers and the courses of springs take their rise from the ocean, Quintilian continues, so Homer "has given us a model and an inspiration for every department of eloquence."[5] J. F. Dobson observes: "Homer was studied with such devout references not only by the Athenian orators themselves but by their immediate literary predecessors, the cosmopolitan Sophists and the rhetoricians of Sicily."[6]

While the epics have been the source of study and imitation, each presents a singular face to speech. The *Iliad* treats great deeds as gestures of desire and honor enacted by heroes engaged in mortal combat. The *Odyssey,* by contrast, presents audiences with a comedy of manners, according to Longinus.[7] The practices of address in the *Iliad* gather, mount, and sharpen in war rhetoric. In contrast, postwar culture of the *Odyssey* is saturated with tentative speeches awkwardly voicing identity, reconciliation, and renewal. Unlike the heroic, violent gestures of war, shared communicative norms cannot be presupposed in domestic transitional moments. For some, the trauma of fighting will not pass; for others, it never really began. In such a moment, rhetoric must cross thresholds for beginning anew communication within a community. Following the ancient discipline to its inspired source, this essay poses the question: What can be learned from Homer's poetic speech activities in the *Odyssey* as a formative moment of rhetorical culture?[8]

Attention to arguments in the situated intrigues of speaking is key to understanding Homer's epic of transition. As Ernst Curtius notes, "Almost half the *Iliad* and more than two-thirds of the *Odyssey* are devoted to speeches by the characters, often quite long speeches."[9] George Kennedy observes "vitality" among these formal and vernacular "speeches delivered in assemblies or small meetings, as well as addresses to troops or groups of men, personal appeals, and shrewd attempts to persuade, deceive, or beguile someone divine or human."[10] In these addresses, Brian Vickers finds "all the basic forms of communication that exist in oral cultures."[11] Truly, "the leading characters in the Homeric poems are already fluent orators, able to debate intelligently on any concrete subject and, moreover, to seek guidance from general principles" in time of war.[12] The context of peace disturbs the fluency of cultural form, however. Speakers pose difficult questions of attachment to the dead, the missing, and the newly emergent generation in the context of intimate family and public relations.

The *Odyssey* models rhetoric that labors to restart time. The narrative contrasts and couples the rhetorical dilemmas of an older war vet trying to make it home against those of his son trying to make a start in the world. The Telemachy, constituting the first four chapters of the *Odyssey*, are the story of Odysseus's son, Telémakhos, who makes a turn from "a sniveling ineffectual boy to a commanding young man."[13] Importantly, C. M. H. Millar and J. W. S. Carmichael find him to be "the only character in Greek literature who shows any development."[14] The *Odyssey*'s adults generally speak in character when trying to negotiate "a set of dilemmas and hard choices" as the culture presents each "not with a coherent set of instructions, but with a structured problematic."[15] The dramatized case spurs invention in the exchange of communicative gambits and reposts. "Homer does not simply show us people in action; he gives them speech as well, the better to convey their living presence," Jacqueline de Romily concludes.[16] Thus, audiences have performed in the Telemachy precisely the thinking in action required to call into being an oratorical world and thereby ignite a rhetorical culture.[17]

Literary critics generally find these chapters to be *pro forma* and of lesser interest. The Telemachy is regarded often as a problematic, even artificial, addition to the epic. Indeed, most authors see Odysseus himself as the only character of worth. He is a user of lies, deceptions, and other tricks to get home and reclaim his house.[18] In this context, the Telemachy is but an extra moral tale enhancing the epic narrative. The chapters are interpreted to function as a plot device useful for introducing the main character and themes.[19] Some critics even claim that the chapters constitute a later add-on to what is in the main a sea saga.[20] In these readings, the core of the *Odyssey* is its transformation of folk tales into epic form.[21] Thus, the story of Telémakhos is interpreted as but a pedagogic effort for inculcating family piety among the young.[22] The present study joins with scholars who see the initial chapters as an essential, not an extra, part of the work. Gilbert Rose finds in Telémakhos's quest a "nexus of motifs" that provoke thinking.[23] W. J. Woodhouse similarly finds the parallel tales of the son (Books I through IV) and the father (Books V through XVI) to be a "brilliant" idea and the key source of "illumination" for Homer.[24] Deep-sea yarns were all too familiar, after all, but the coupling of travels of father and son was inspired. "Without Telémakhos, no *Odyssey*," he concludes.[25]

The Telemachy performs anew the beginnings of a rhetorical culture. Classical Greece was a highly verbal arena with "small numbers, concentrated in small residential groups and living the typically Mediterranean out-of-doors life"—a model "face-to-face society."[26] In such a "living oral tradition, people are exposed to verbal art constantly, not just on specific entertainment occasions, which can happen every night in certain seasons. When they work, eat, drink, and do other social small-group activities, myth, song, and saying are always woven into their talk," Richard Martin says. Consequently, he finds a bilingual situation where Homeric Greeks are both "fluent in their natural language but also in *Kunstprache* of their local verbal art forms."[27] Thus, Homer, by presenting Telémakhos's "development," dramatizes basic thresholds necessary to initiate a rhetorical culture when war has left customs in disuse, household norms uncertain, and the practice of hospitality in doubt. Therefore, in this essay all speech engagements will be revisited as models unfolding an oratorical consciousness, a series of cases where individuals begin to speak through the unspoken gaps, disguises, and repetitions into discourses of cooperation and competition that animate fresh possibilities of communication.

One "noticeable change" Telémakhos undoubtedly undergoes is the development of a capacity "for deception, or if we prefer for artful invention," Norman Austin concludes.[28] Like his father, the *polytropic* offspring discovers in himself "a preference for keeping silent while others talk for him or, if forced to make a statement, for giving an outright lie or a discreet circumlocution, truthful but not revealing," when forced by the situation.[29] Yet, communicate members of the household do through the partisanship of an unfolding new time. The speeches then are to be read as the conditions generating such discovery of the capacity, place, work, evaluation, and necessity of oratorical thinking.

An orator-in-the-making, Telémakhos speaks on five distinct occasions. First, the boy is coaxed through dialogue out of a daydreamed world of self-constraining anxieties to embrace his own and the community's potential capacity for action. Second, the youth disturbs the routine of the house by speaking back to a parent, voicing questions of hospitality openly for the first time. Third, a wider quarrel breaks out when host and guests fall out over household rules and resources. Fourth, Telémakhos calls a public assembly to air and to rectify the situation. Finally, in subsequent partisan give-and-take, the youth's private thoughts are concealed from opponents, divided from friends, and developed into a strategic practice that negotiates dangers and pursues ends. Thus, oratorical consciousness emerges within (1) capacity-building moments of situated reflection on identity and possibility, (2) speech that unsettles relationships within the private sphere, (3) the striking of a community-wide controversy, (4) the give-and-take of debate within a public forum, and (5) ongoing partisan speech acts and silences shaping strategic advocacy. Oratorical consciousness is interactive, generative, and contingent—jolting self and community out of repetition and putting conditional vectors of speech into playful reflection and exchange. The qualities of oratorical consciousness are recoverable only if the epic is interpreted by a close reading of *arguments in the making,* where the uncertainties and contingencies of the actors engaging with others are appreciated as communicative gambits and reposts. Thus, criticism reconstructs the intrigue and dangers of a liminal postwar culture. Rhetorical consciousness is illustrated most fully by Homer in these in-between times—if one but pays attention to the exchanges as they unfold.

Anxiety to Action

The story opens in the midst of a boisterous courtyard banquet at Odysseus's palace. Many guests frolic at the home of the absent host. Athena swoops down on this scene, assumes the appearance of a "stranger," and surveys the goings-on. A bard might engage the sympathies of the audience by speaking about what Athena sees: a gaggle of youths playing dice, lying about on oxen hides, drinking wine, and butchering cattle for roasting. The self-indulging swains are oblivious to the goddess (who appears as but an unknown old man). These youths, having known neither war nor peace, remain indifferent to all but the pleasures of gaming. In a few lines, Homer both suggests troubling conditions for a household and sets presumption against the suitors, who are shown by their actions to be voracious, graceless, thoughtless, and impious.

In this crowd appears alone a lad who "was sitting there unhappy among the suitors, a boy, daydreaming. What if his great father came from the unknown world and drove these men like dead leaves through the place, recovering honor and lordship in his domains: Then he who dreamed in the crowd gazed out at Athena."[30] The structure of private thought plays anxiety into a wish, into a fantasy; Telémakhos's thinking traffics in the what-ifs that could resolve his troubles. Personal longing is cathected on one highly improbable event that would have to drop felicitously out of the sky, from some "unknown world," to reverse fortune—the return of an absent father. Fantastically, *out of the blue does drop Athena*. At a glance, the dreaming boy connects with the stranger, the goddess of reason disguised as an uninvited guest. From this moment onward, the world begins to change. Telémakhos begins to learn to act through engagement in a provocative and imperfectly rational dialogue prompting his journey toward oratorical consciousness.

After brief eye contact, Telémakhos moves quickly to engage and offer the "old man" the hospitality of the house. The disguised goddess and boy sit down. Food and drink are consumed; song and music follow; a private discussion ensues. Telémakhos speaks of his sad situation with the newcomer. If Odysseus were to return home, things would be set right; but since his white "bones are rotting somewhere," it is sure that he is dead (1.167–1.168). Telémakhos's heartfelt complaint unwinds in the presence of disguised Athena, who is carrying forward the will of the gods. She initiates through him the success of the very return that the boy sees as hopeless. The dialogue perhaps yields much comic irony for an audience already familiar with the epic, since the young man's worries are whiny and misplaced. However, the conversation also illustrates the threshold moment of a deliberative encounter, of an exchange between the wisest of the gods and the most inexperienced and uncertain of mortals. The boy begins a conversation with reason.

Telémakhos requests that the stranger disclose his relationship to the household and business of the day. Athena identifies herself as Mêntes, a lord and metals trader, whose ship is moored nearby. Further, she says that she is a longtime friend of Telémakhos's father, which his grandfather could verify. The fictive self-identification crafts credibility, the goddess claiming to be a person of substance, a friend, and an outsider to the scene. Mêntes, the credible stranger, can bring fresh views, and so can utter almost blandly what otherwise would be an incredulous assertion: Odysseus is not dead, rather "the gods delay him" (1.194–1.196). Mêntes reports that the absent king is even now "plotting a way to journey home at last." There is no immediate response by Telémakhos. The dramatic revelation leaves him speechless. A first line of argument forms: the inference that time passed is a sign that Odysseus is dead becomes countered through a credible source that Odysseus's absence is but a sign of fortune delayed, a mutable constraint because "he'll scheme a way to come; he can do anything" (1.205). Deliberation originates in moments where the hemming of fate twists around to the prospects of fortune.

Hope is pressed with two further self-capacitating assertions. First, Athena makes the argument that since she (Mêntes) took meals with Odysseus, albeit long ago, she can judge resemblances, and Telémakhos looks like his father. This arouses the expression of a "wish" by the boy: that he might have known his father but, bitterly, he had never had that chance. Indeed, Telémakhos frets, people are never entirely certain about their "own engendering" (1.216). Despite this pessimistic repost, the wall of self-doubt has been breached by reliable, contrary evidence. Second, in Socratic fashion, Mêntes provides another outlet for anxiety by feigning not to know what the suitors are doing. Again, doubts wind out. Telémakhos complains of the suitors' habits and ways and that he is not strong enough to resist the suitors, who grow ever bolder the longer Odysseus is away. The overstayed guests think the king dead and thus do not fear his return. His mother is frozen in this intractable situation as well. She will not marry because "she cannot bring herself to choose among them," but she cannot "spurn" them because of their power; thus, while she delays "they eat their way through all we have, and when they will, they can demolish me" (1.253–1.256).

The predicaments amount to enduring and growing jeopardy. As resources diminish and constraints tighten, no good course of action appears on the horizon. Denunciation risks injury; marriage is odious; delay, ruinous. Absent the means of resistance, the situation grows steadily worse. Daydreams are a refuge for passions which dare not be summoned. Anxiety cannot be released into indignation, nor anger transformed to action, because no choices appear that do *not* become entangled in a web of dangerous options.

> Pallas Athena was disturbed, and said: "Ah, bitterly you need Odysseus, then! High time he came back to engage these upstarts. I wish we saw

> him standing helmeted there in the doorway, holding shield and spear,
> looking the way he did when I first knew him." (1.257–1.262)

She recounts a story when she (as Mêntes) visited their home long ago, adding that now it "lies upon the gods' great knees" whether or not Odysseus can return and "force a reckoning." The vivid image: Odysseus—king, father, hero—standing there in a fictional present and in an actual past creates a space for presence in an imagined future, a possibility that identifies and connects as a plan. If I were you, she says, I should take steps to make these men disperse. She recommends a flock of activities: that Telémakhos call an assembly to get the suitors "scattering to their homes." Then proposes "a course for you, if you agree," which involves sailing abroad "for news of your lost father." The trip involves a deadline and contingency: after a year, if you have found news, then hold out; if not, conclude that he is dead and give your mother away. Then, at some point mete out justice to the rascals by figuring out "how you should kill them, outright or by guile. You need not bear this insolence of theirs," she says, adding crucially: "You are a child no longer." Flatteringly, she confirms that Telémakhos is tall and brave and "men in times to come will speak of you respectfully" (1.271–1.300).

Commentators have remarked that the advice given by Athena is marvelously incoherent. It ignores probable constraints by imagining a host of vivid actions. The counsel appears to "jar, confuse," and get the boy thinking beyond his enervating predicaments, rather than to instruct logically.[31] Homer seems to be telling us that in first deliberations, opening lines of thinking are more important than finished planning. All the parts of the plan respond to the net of anxieties that have trapped the boy in a world of daydreams: his father's unknown fate, his mother's indecisiveness, the suitors' intransigence, the remoteness of the gods, and his own inactivity. All these conditions have been turned into moves that create scenes of choice. The discussion models how thinking, linked to acting, begins with the right words. Constraints are reversed and transformed into possibility by awakening the imagination to potential acts. Sorting and shaping are later to come. The assortment is neither the elegant deception nor divinely inspired plan of the gods. The reasons constitute a prompt for Telémakhos to think for himself.

Athena's counseling is couched as advice, not commands. The point of the dialogue is that Telémakhos sorts out issues, acts, and thereby develops into an agent by making decisive choices. Thus, the prince is not merely to obey a flawlessly articulated, divine plan. Refiguring the world as one of choice and action, rather than of absences and constraints, is what self-creates the deliberating agent who can respond with acumen to situations, modify plans on the fly, and sustain purposes in the face of setbacks. The coherence of rational planning is subordinate to the acts of reimagining a world where possibilities abound and thinking matters. Athena (as Mêntes) concludes with an analogical, transcending parable characteristic of what now is called "conductive argument," or "reasoning from cases." She tells Telémakhos that just as Orestês earned fame restoring a household, so you will too. This argument both characterizes the suitors' transgressions as in a league with Aigísthos's evil work (suggesting what may transpire should they not be stopped) and fits Telémakhos out with a heroic role to play and the prospect of respect and even fame. When the dialogue begins, the boy can't figure out what is the use in trying; when the coaching is finished, it is hard for him to see how he can fail. Thus, a "new spirit" infuses the young prince. As Mêntes (Athena) leaves, Telémakhos divines that the "new spirit in him" was put there by a god. "Then godlike in his turn, he joined the suitors" (1.323).

A Public Threshold Is Crossed

The feast continues, with its murmurs, shouts, and laughing; the play of human voices compete and blend with a musician's art. Up wells a "holy song" of "the Homecoming of Akhaians" from the Trojan War, up to the apartments of the Queen of Ithaca. What is but a historic tale, put to music before the feasting crowd of young swains by the bard, Phêmios, is to the queen a sad reminder of her own war-tossed life and disrupted, time-lost existence. She descends to admonish the poet: "Phêmios, other spells you know, high deeds of gods and heroes, as the poets tell them let these men hear some other; let them sit silent and drink their wine. But sing no more this bitter tale that wears my heart away" (1.377–1.382).

Penélopê's demand to stop such play is based on a two-pronged justification. First, the artist has a repertoire of alternative performances. Since the crowd is not quiet anyway, perhaps the hard-drinking youths would "appreciate" riotous entertainment. Switch songs. Tactfully, Penélopê appears to make an argument that the audience of suitors is unworthy of Phêmios's performance.[32] If the tale means too little to the youths who have known only the privilege of peace, it means too much to the queen, for whom the war has not ended. Life experiences cannot be turned to art because the events are still too raw, too unfinished and disturbing to be properly distanced as song. The beauty of music and greatness of theme swell painful memories that, for her, can find no release in song. Whichever way Phêmios takes it, the queen argues, whether from an indifferent or sympathetic view, the song is out of place. Penélopê's trauma models unsettled communicative norms constraining a postwar world that finds issues of mortality too difficult to address and so a new time impossible to begin.

Telémakhos transforms the discrete hint into an open argument. He confronts his mother, in public, shifting the private issue of absence to question a household norm of hospitality. The assembled audience of the banquet is completely startled at the novel exchange. Telémakhos defends the minstrel by differentiating art from life, celebration from what is celebrated. Respect the song "wherever his thought may lead," he tells Penélopê, because "poets are not to blame, but Zeus who gives what fate he pleases to adventurous men" (1.347–1.349). The distinction between the trauma of life's travails and the sadness of song is an endorsement of the independence of art. Telémakhos argues for the untrammeled freedom of poets to bring up even the freshest and most painful personal memories, if art plays on a landscape sufficiently large to address the community: "How many others lost their lives!" the prince interjects. Thus, Penélopê is advised that she must "nerve herself and try to listen." The arguments carry as Penélopê demurs and returns to her chambers, but the pain of grief raised by the music is not diminished as she falls to weeping—and sleep. Despite Telémakhos's winning argument, the crowd remains unmoved, and the queen, moved too deeply.

Homer daringly tests and defends the propriety of performing tales of war, singing songs among the inattentive or those thrilling to heroic adventure. The argument does double-duty. Telémakhos's confrontation explicitly serves the development of the plot as it initiates his first brief entry into the give-and-take of public culture. Additionally, oratorical consciousness appreciates the artists who perform the *Odyssey* and its conversions of suffering and loss, primarily by differentiating the suffering induced by art from the grief produced by life. The invitation to let poets speak—where they may—to permit the audience to hear of loss and triumph in its mixtures that affect the entire community opens a common space where grief can enter into the public realm by the bardic performance of the *Odyssey* itself. Poetry is a realm that may open public discussion to deal with personal and political issues left by the debris of war. With daring brilliance, Homer shows his audience the other side of the coin, too; in the uncontrollable grieving of Penélopê is the painful process of enduring an irreconcilable situation triggered by the accidental reach of a musician's lyre. The "doubleness" of the work as storied performance and as a prompt for public discussion pushes the edges of debate about the complex dealings of deliberation in this postwar world. Oratorical consciousness begins in private reflection, but with poetic provocation it invites the community to speak on issues where feelings run deep and remain unsettled.

A Quarrel Starts

Penélopê departs. The guests party on, woofing and boasting about bedding the queen. Telémakhos has had enough. The king's son pronounces a double command: first, guests must be quiet now to hear the minstrel; second, suitors must come to the assembly tomorrow, where he will tell them publicly to get out of the house: "Go feasting elsewhere, consume your own stores. Turn and turn about, use one another's houses," he says. The justification? "If you choose to slaughter one man's livestock and pay nothing, this is rapine; and by the eternal gods I beg Zeus you shall get what you deserve: a slaughter here, and nothing paid for it" (1.372–1.378)! The argument from definition is an indictment of rude behavior and complaint that the suitors are violating hospitality; more, the statement invokes a rhetorical logic of "what goes round comes around" in a twist: since you (parasites) "haven't paid for your slaughter, we shan't pay for ours"—when justice is meted out finally. Hospitality furnished a core ethic of Greek society, and the charge of a breach of manners on the part of host or guest raises a serious issue.[33] The impassioned Telémakhos reflexively tells the large group to "take it as you will," I am going to order you out—on the morrow, before the whole community—a stunning announcement (1.371).

Antínoös, a senior suitor, responds to the outburst. Gentling anger with humor, he treats the outburst as youthful petulance. "Zeus forbid you should be king," he jests. The angry threat and foretelling of the future is nothing less than a pronouncement that could only be made by trafficking with "the gods themselves," he facetiously jokes (1.382–1.384). Unbeknownst to Antínoös or other suitors, this is precisely the case of what has happened. The twist twists around to catch the suitor, whose deflecting joke is indeed funny, but at his own expense.

Telémakhos neither demurs nor becomes distracted but sticks to the issue *he* has raised. In a balanced reply, the son of Odysseus both seizes his rightful status as one who would some day be king by virtue of his birth, even while he admits that a number of eligible candidates (as possible husbands) may also be in the running. "All I insist on is that I rule our house and rule the slaves my father won for me" (1.395–1.396). The reply evidences the maturity of mind requisite to deal with a contested issue, by standing firm and thinking publicly in a balanced way. Eurýmakhos, another suitor, hears something new in the prudently fortified argument. He suspects the stranger's visit to be implicated in the child's newfound confidence. In soothing tones, the suitor feigns agreement while inquiring as to the identity of the unknown visitor.

Telémakhos's reply to the suitor is a first public instance of an argument made with some true premises, key facts elided, and a false conclusion. "There's no hope for my father," Telémakhos lies. "I would not trust a message, if one came, nor any forecaster my mother invites." My guest was a family friend, Mêntes, he reports. While Telémakhos does *not* in fact trust his mother's diviners, he conceals his suspicion that Mêntes is a god, that he has been counseled into a good plan of action, and that his mother did *not* bring the old friend in as a diviner. The conclusion *appears* true on its face, especially to the suitors, who are acting as if there is no hope of Odysseus return, but the adumbration of partial facts is wholly misleading. As Athena's private counsel involved an admixture of true and false premises marshaling reasons in the service of confrontation with the truth, public opposition finds a not entirely dissimilar strategic mixture responding to probing questions with evasion. Oratorical consciousness initiates a dangerous critical-productive game evolving a matrix for reading truth and appearance.

At the banquet's end, a song is played, and the gathering is transformed into an opposition of wills. Telémakhos's resentment is fired to outrage by the coaxing and confirmation of an old friend of the household, Mêntes/Athena. Argument is first occasioned by the inappropriate or rude treatment of a poet at the banquet. Further, Telémakhos inaugurates a quarrel when he names the offense of the suitors, lodges a complaint, and anticipates a full statement of objection at public assembly. The young speaker receives the "pity" of the crowd and generates enmity and suspicion from the suitors; he secures neither a mandate to remove the guests from his house nor resources for a nautical journey.[34] Nevertheless these initial efforts are a success in launching a controversy, which is not an inconsiderable achievement given that he was trapped in his own anxieties and fantasies at the beginning of the day. The arguments here start a postwar culture on the uncertain road to change.

The public quarrel breaks consciousness into doubly sealed, contesting positions. The pretense of false civic friendship by Eurýmakhos is met by Telémakhos's dissembling. Faked civic friendship consists of offers of identification in the interests of extracting information useful for oppositional ends. Dissembling itself appears as an admixture of deliberative elements, deployed to conceal aims and divert attention, while creating the impression of being open and direct. So suspicion and partisanship become insinuated into comic gestures providing time for actors to calm down and the outburst to blow over. The suitors return to dice and games for the remainder of the day.

The Public Assembles

A meeting of the Ithacan township opens. Lord Aigýptios—for whom the survival of three young sons in the Trojan War offered bare compensation for the unknown fate, and eventual loss of his fourth, Ántiphos—calls the community to its public forum. Tears welling in his eyes, he opens a public meeting not held since his long-absent king sailed for Troy. The lord asks who "finds occasion" for this assembly and calls those interested to rise and speak, whether old or young, with fresh news or new grievance. Notably, the community's deliberative field is thin because, as Clarke notes, "Ithaca is trapped in the weakness of its leaders, the weakness of old age [infirmed and withdrawn Laërtês] and the weakness of youth, senility and adolescence."[35] The full quarrel between the house of Odysseus and the community explodes in a central speech: the young prince "appeals to the Agora of the Ithacans to vindicate his rights, and a debate takes place." Thus, "an effective organ of civic discussion" is brought to life.[36]

Glowing with confidence, Telémakhos rises and accepts a "staff" from Peisênor, the old master of debate. Boldly, he announces the matter at issue. He calls the community to hear out "only my need, and the trouble of my house—the troubles" (2.47–2.48). His private troubles are transformed to a public question through an oration. He claims: (1) "My home and all I have are being ruined," because the suitors will neither woo Penélopê properly by requesting paternal approval nor surrender to her wishes to go away, but spend their time eating, drinking, and "not caring what they do." (2) The family cannot take care of this because he, unlike his father, does not have the strength to expel by force those who will not leave by request. (3) This situation constitutes a sustained "shame" by being a substantial breach of hospitality (2.247–2.269). Since the older generation feels no indignation at the situation and refuses to rein in its youthful parasites, Telémakhos predicts harm to the public. As gossip goes around, the weakness of Ithaca will become known, whether among rapacious enemies or angered gods. Nor can the blame for the situation be shared, for the young prince asks rhetorically, did my father do you wrong? If the answer is no, why do you not control your offspring and permit me to grieve his absence in peace? In mock irony, he invites the older members of the community to come and lead the same idle lives as their sons because at least *they* have household assets and would be honest enough to make restitution. Thus, Telémakhos transforms a personal quarrel to a public issue by illuminating the communal risks as well as injustices of younger and older generations implicated in the ruin of his household and the reputation of Ithaca.[37] George Kennedy concludes that the speech fails because the youth has "no model of oratory" available.[38] Homer's point, however, is not to model oratorical consciousness in its perfection, but to bring to the audience through public debates its full scope and varied range in a postwar culture.

Antínoös rises to speak in opposition. The advocate, surprisingly, makes no denials. The household is being drained, suitors are not going to leave, repayment is not likely, and the guests remain neither respectful of either Telémakhos's grief nor committed to the absent king. Much is conceded. What is contravened, however, is whether Telémakhos is giving a genuine account as to who, really, is responsible for the troubles. Rightly seen, the cause of the situation is not the suitors, Antínoös contends, but the beautiful and devious queen, Penélopê.

The heart of the suitor's case is a story of frustrated desire. As proof that he and his friends have been led on and left "dangling about," Antínoös offers a single, compelling illustration: the loom. The theme of the narrative is deception. Nearly four years ago, Penélopê had said, "Now my lord is dead, let me finish my weaving before I marry" (2.99). Generously, Penélopê was allowed to weave a shroud for her father-in-law, but what was done by day was undone by night, until a disloyal maid betrayed the ruse. The queen is conceded to possess a "talent in handicraft and a clever mind," without peer, but "well, she made poor use of them," the advocate for the suitors concludes, and so he advises Telémakhos either to kick his mother out of the house or to make her marry whomever her father picks. Either way, the issue is solved. If not, well: "She makes a name for herself, but you can feel the loss it means for you"—insinuating both that the gods' will and his mother's vanity are the root cause of the predicaments of the household (2.126–2.127).

As a forensic rebuttal, the speech leaves much to be desired. Antínoös does not explain why no one has yet to ask the queen's father for her hand, why the grocery bills have not been paid, much less why the issue of marriage is timely absent the knowledge of Odysseus's fate. Further, no proof is offered that Penélopê has been sending "promises to each man privately," and the shroud episode on its face offers only equivocal proof that the queen's bargain to wed is genuine. What the speech lacks in forensic scope, however, it regains in deliberative strategy, as it follows narrowly the single plausible course of reply open: to show Penélopê as the cause of delay—and ruin. So, unable to deny most allegations, which are in fact true, Antínoös must speak to redirect, and thus deflect, the frustrations and anger in the audience onto Penélopê and away from him and his friends.

"Clear-headed" Telémakhos is not fooled by this effort to shift the blame and denies the advisability of the proffered alternative. Even should one grant that the suitors are not at fault, he responds, if he sends his mother away, he himself will undoubtedly suffer either at the hands of Ikários, her father, or the Furies. The solution is not prudent for him personally and so not supportable publicly as a viable redress for his plaint. Thus, he rejects Antínoös's alternative and, again, publicly orders the overstayed guests out. Judged from the standpoint of changing the minds of the audience, one might find the oratory abortive and feeble; but the suitors already were committed and the older generation indifferent. The measure of powerful rhetoric is not always opinion change. Indeed, in public deliberation the first of order of business is often to get one's personal concerns heard as a public matter. On this score, the oration and counter-rebuttal are an unqualified success.

At this point, the debate ripples into the heavens. Eagles streak down from the blue and, flying low, ruffle the assembly. This raises the spiritual antennae of ancient Halithersês, who has something of a reputation for prophecy. Reading the event as a sign from Zeus, the man from the older generation warns of a "black wave towering" over the suitors and the imminent return of Odysseus, "carrying in him a bloody doom for all these men." "Let us think how to stop it," he cautions and for good measure recollects his prophecy of nineteen years past of the king's return (2.169). A sign from the heavens may provoke effective deliberation, prompting a space for timely thought, Homer seems to be saying; however, this thread is cut short by one of the young hotbloods who raises an interpretative objection, mocking his elder. "Old man, go tell the omens for your children at home, and try to keep them out of trouble. I am more fit to interpret this than you are," Eurýmakhos asserts without justification. He argues that the eagle is merely a bad bird buzzing the crowd, a coincidence, not a portent. Further, the old man is pegged as a fraud who is egging on the outraged prince because he hopes for a reward. "Here it is what I foretell," the suitor sarcastically jokes; if you keep it up we will "fix a penalty on you" that will outweigh your reward and will "make you groan to pay" (2.179–2.194). Of course, the dismissal of a sign and the shameless threat is predicated on the dangerous assumption that Odysseus is dead, which is inferred as probable from long absence. And even if he isn't, "we fear no one," Eurýmakhos darkly boasts. Besides, echoing Antínoös's main argument, "we have been waiting in rivalry for this beauty" as "she delays and maddens us." After all these years, the suitors are not about to give up the suit.

Unlike Antínoös, whose argumentation is sharply drawn, Eurýmakhos models careless deliberation. What should create pause is ridiculed; while the older speaker is known for competent judgment, brazen self-assertion is preferred by the youth; the motives of the opponent are slurred without self-examination; and the ultimate position rests upon an assumption whose lethal implications are waved away by a boast. Not good thinking. One thing he says is true, however: the suitors' reasoning is desire-driven and, within that narrow compass, determined. The weaving and unweaving of a shroud are entwined with the suspended life of postwar culture, a time of reciprocally sustained, self-elaborating, unsatisfied longings. Neither Penélopê nor the suitors can get on with their lives. Together they remain mired in these interminable days and can go no further absent *shared* action to get over the war.

At this point, Telémakhos intervenes for the third time, conceding that "appeals and arguments" appear to be going nowhere. The prince not willing to give up, nor the suitors to get out, a third alternative arises, consistent with an element of the plan hatched the day before. If he would be given a ship to sale to Pylos and Sparta to seek news of his father, then within the year the prince could discover his proper course of action. The postwar time would end then, either with Odysseus's return or with a proper funeral and marriage. Introduced into the divided oratorical consciousness of adversarial debate is the prospect of a third way to which both sides can lend support—but for very different reasons. Oratorical consciousness thus evolves into a thin consensus that buys time in the ongoing struggle for advantage. The public forum subsequently thins to side issues, name-calling, and jesting. A call to dinner ends the day.

Wit, Sap, and Prudence

The debate committed Telémakhos and the suitors publicly to a course of action and privately to a plan of opposition. Though open conflict was avoided, heated argument had accelerated the daily drift of private life into action-packed partisanship. The resulting oratorical consciousness features a triple-turning, strategically embedded awareness: (1) there are the internal commitments, plans, and appraisals of speakers who argue in opposition to (2) adversaries who maneuver strategically to sponsor counterarguments, diversions, and threats. Finally, (3) the broader community constitutes audiences that grant or withhold standing and lend support. Parties speak with passion of injustice and peaceful redress with full knowledge that outbreaks of violence are near, especially when the barbed and lively public exchanges arouse anger.

Alone the morning after, down by the sea, the troubled orator walks after the assembly. Telémakhos recollects the good reasons that had so filled his resolve, yet he was still unable to carry the day. Athena, again disguised as Old Mêntes, appears and with a "warm voice" looses "a lucid flight of words" (2.267). Intelligent encouragement ensues, not with the addition of more complicated plans, for the course is initiated, nor with naive estimates of success, for truly the situation is dire. Rather, the advice drives straight to the core of what is needed to shore up the prince: a confirmation of identity. This is not an easy thing for an adviser to accomplish in a situation where a youth does not know who he is, or how he will fare, or whom he can count on for support—and has just engaged in stinging debate before the community.

Mêntes's argument runs thus: your father was a great hero. He accomplished all that he set his mind to do. If you are his son, you are likely to have a successful voyage. Further, to your father's sagacity is added your mother's qualities, so your chances are even better (it is implied). Flattery is utilized here to equate identity with power to overcome the odds. "The son is rare who measures with his father, and one in a thousand is a better man, but you will have the sap and wit and prudence—for you get that from Odysseus—to give you a fair chance of winning through" (2.275–2.279). The argument is circular: because Telémakhos is the son of

Odysseus, he has qualities that enable him to persevere, and because he has a unique combination of qualities, he is certain to be the offspring of Odysseus. Rhetorically, such mentoring discourse incubates a consciousness that circulates around a tightly wound core: one is persuaded to do what one must because of who one is, and convinced to be secure in knowing who one is because of what one is doing.

Athena tells Telémakhos directly, the qualities that unite father and son—constituting his own core: "*wit*" and "*sap*" and "*prudence.*" Without *sap,* wit and prudence would result in a timorous adult, able to see possibilities in a situation and measure alternatives, but without the courage requisite to take risks or face adversity. Without *prudence,* wit and sap would condition a bold, reckless individual who would take more risks than necessary or wise. Finally, without *wit,* sap and prudence would lack traction, the capacity to appraise a situation and turn it to advantage, whether besting a debater, beast, or god. The three form the core of archaic character (as stubbornness, weakness, and excess are dangerous opposites) and ultimately shape the tripartite character of consciousness that brings each resource into the contingent, situated turns of speaking.[39] These virtues are at the heart of the character of father and of son (there is no reason to doubt Athena's argument here). Since Odysseus is the model rhetorician, as he has been celebrated throughout the ages, and since Telémakhos finds his identity as a quality of such character, then in this versed equation arguably appears nothing less than the wellsprings of Western rhetorical culture. Father and son, returning veteran and rising prince, speak in situations where these virtues are put into play and tested against humans and gods who alike and all play the games of speech with equal verve, risk, and challenge. Oratorical consciousness can shape actions to enhance odds of success, but it cannot determine outcomes when in times of contention slippery fortune intervenes. After counseling, Athena proceeds rapidly to flesh out a plan, suggesting to Telémakhos that he go home and get some sleep while she finds sailors willing to catch the morning tide.

Tests of Resolve

Though determination may be fortified in private reflection, personal resolve must withstand social challenges. Before sleep comes, three tests occur. Telémakhos meets revelers back at the house. Just as Antínoös tried to blunt and turn the emotional thrust of Telémakhos's original pronouncement, so he attempts to turn the lad's resolve by discounting the morning's speech as an act of temper. Offering a hearty clasp of the hand to the "dauntless orator," he invites his one-time young friend to "feast and drink with me, the way you used to" and suggests that he need not travel because the Achaeans can just as well gather news about his absent father (2.305–2.308). Unconfused, Telémakhos flatly rejects the gesture of friendship: "I cannot see myself again taking a quiet dinner in this company," and turns Antínoös's offer around.[40] It was bad enough, he says, to have taken advantage of the child; it is foolish or worse to try to turn him from his purpose "having grown." In fact, Telémakhos declares, "I'll bring black doom upon you if I can," and withdraws his hand. Partisan enmity is fully announced, if specific plans are not disclosed (2.310–2.320). It might have been easy to return to the familiar world, to forgive and forget, rather than to confront one's fears, risk a watery grave, and leave home; but for the boy-turned-orator the awareness of injustice was driven too deeply and the possibilities of action lit too brightly.

The angry response ignites a round of ridicule. One suitor imagines far-fetched plots, where Telémakhos uses an effeminate weapon, poison, to kill everyone. Another raises a core anxiety with an insult: "He might be lost at sea, just like Odysseus, knocking around in a ship, far from his friends. And what a lot of trouble that would give us, making the right division of his things! We'd keep his house as dowry for his mother and the man who marries her" (2.333–2.339). It would seem that the identity formation guided by Mêntes permitted Odysseus's son not to be deterred by such remarks or the genuinely dangerous prospects they anticipate. Telémakhos does not respond to the gibes, nor is he deterred from his purpose, but goes to request provisioning from his nurse, who guards the storeroom.

If Telémakhos confronts the difficulties of his decision in public ridicule, so he is attacked through intimate doubts in an argument with his nurse who argues that he should stay at home. First, there is a prudent obligation to the family. Your father died at sea. You are all we have. Stay home. There is a risk that the disaster of the household will be complete, a sense of double loss. Second, when you leave, the men will plot to kill you. This is the first time the explicit threat is brought up, and it becomes a genuine tactical issue. Finally, self-interest is involved. The sea brings suffering for you, "hardship and homelessness." This assertion is similar to Antínoös's argument, but whereas the lead suitor is insincere, the nurse's expression is a genuine concern, born of personal attachment. The nurse's arguments are a further testing of Telémakhos's resolve because they raise genuine doubts about the course of action illustrating the high stakes, tactical risks, and personal costs of taking to the sea.

Dramatically, the arguments double the danger. Doubts voiced by the ridicule of the suitors are duplicated unintentionally by the caring questions of the nurse. Internal deliberation is prompted by both, the ethos of respective sources not withstanding. Telémakhos does not reply to the individual arguments of the nurse, but trumps her concerns, stating "there's a god behind this plan" (2.372). He asks the nurse to keep mum or else Penélopê will weep—a motive that both reflects genuine concerns of the son and plays on the familial duties of the nurse. Further, the departure is to be kept secret, a prudential consideration. Athena gets the suitors suitably drunk, the crew recruited, and the departure scene is high adventure! Telémakhos is launched. Interestingly, in this scene collaboration crosses generations, genders, and social station in coming to a strategic resolve. Too often oratory is reduced to a speech genre that focuses on the success of a single discourse to move opinion. In contrast, Homer shows that oratorical consciousness is not exhausted by a speech, but the speech act is generative, guiding the speaker across the arguments of friends and foe alike into changing social relationships. The prince leaves Ithaca on the morning tide. He visits kingdoms ruled by the former heroes of war, Priam and Menelaus, talks of old days that are finished, even while a new time harkens across the horizon.

Oratorical Consciousness and the Cases of Rhetorical History

Generally, Homer is said to influence the development of Western culture, even while the serious work of the verbal arts, including rhetoric, are attributed to the powerful cast of thinkers, orators, poets, historians, and dramatists of the Greek Enlightenment. Donald Lemen Clark, for example, clearly states that he is not going to deal with the poetic tradition but only the rhetoric of Greece and Rome.[41] Thomas Cole believes that "rhetoric was established as an art (techné) of speaking when Plato and Aristotle combined the study of manner with that of matter."[42] Similarly, Edward Schiappa distinguishes between "traditional rhetoric," which is putatively "old as civilization itself" and "coextensive with the history of society," and rhetoric as a specialized discipline engineered by Plato and Aristotle. Of Homer and his times, it can be said at most that "the essential cultural and intellectual elements of rhetoric were present within the archaic and early classical periods."[43] These conventions, according to Carol Thomas and Edward Webb, furnish a "proto-rhetoric" awaiting the right democratic moment to be realized.[44] So, Andrew J. Karp believes he finds "a sketchy theory of persuasion" implicit in Homer whose characters, "when speaking, frequently employ rhetorical figures and techniques for the purpose of persuading one another" and who "often explicitly talk of persuading one another."[45]

My reading of Homer initiates a different interpretation, following Peter Toohey, who finds that the speaking is "not formless, but quite deliberately shaped," because the speeches in their "oral, paradigmatic, paratactic nature, betray a mind-set" of an oral culture.[46] A close reading of the engaged arguments of the Telemachy captures the "mind-set" in the development of an oratorical consciousness that arises first in the realization of agency in the half-formed plans of an actor and subsequently proceeds to envelop a community through informal quarrels, public speeches, and gestures of opposition and conciliation. The opening chapters of the *Odyssey* offer a first case where oratorical consciousness emerges for a set of characters that cannot rely upon the taken-for-granted norms, purposes, and prospects of communication due to the aimless, fragmenting repetition of postwar life. In these addresses, Homer models nothing less than the emergence of rhetoric, of human consciousness that seizes and interprets, reads and produces the complicated, interlacing gestures that restart communication in the uncertain mixtures of truth and appearances. Crucially, the consciousness is double: (1) thinking that unfolds individually and on a community-wide basis through communicative arguments within the story over time, and (2) interpretive gambits that may be brought near the surface by a bard addressing an audience in a given performance. Together with the questions of heroism and civil society raised by the *Iliad,* it was these rhetorical materials, featuring the doubling predicaments of communication, that fueled the subsequent intellectual debates of the Greek Enlightenment.

Scholars who give high praise to the *Odyssey* are interested, most generally, not in its cultivation of rhetorical consciousness but in its poetic form and aesthetic achievement, rendering a dramatic epic tale as a clear moral message. From a literary standpoint, the speeches are a vehicle for unfolding the drama of plot that succeeds or fails in terms of formal criteria for unity and coherence, cultivating piety. Rhetorical readings of the oratory of the epic offer an alternative view. Read as communicative exchange between performer and audience and as a controversy within an older postwar community, the speeches of the *Odyssey* roil across predicaments of consciousness in the humanly bounded interactions of a rhetorical culture. The counterpulls of wit, sap, and prudence swirl and reconfigure in the stresses between one's talents, social expectations, consequential choices, and cultural ideals among actors, thereby rendering communication a lively art with unpredictable outcomes.

Together the stories of Odysseus and Telémakhos unfold the temporal emergence of a rhetorical culture in a time of transition between war and peace. Odysseus speaks rhetorically with the voice of a sly, battle-seasoned veteran traveling an unknown world, while his son opens a dispute much closer to home.[47] Oratorical consciousness spreads across both domains, where people and gods find themselves in the middle of a story with an outcome yet to be determined fully. The lad's plans, though hard argued and fully embraced, are, as it turns out, wasted from a practical standpoint. Priam and Menelaus have nothing new to say. Yet, it is the emergence of rhetorical consciousness that readies the actors for moments to come in which the case finds resolution. "If tragic irony means blindness to coming evil," John H. Finley writes, then "comic irony means blindness to coming good."[48] Analogously, Homer's own modeling of rhetorical culture gestures toward inexhaustible human spaces. Oratorical consciousness arises to take up the predicaments of communication, which continually arise in the challenging personal and public traumas of life.

The speeches of the Ithacan community model fundamental dilemmas in restarting a post-traumatic peacetime culture. There have been many other wars, other moments of reinitiating the pacific duties of communication, of course. These furnish cases for inquiry into the polytropic dimensions of oratorical consciousness. Rhetorical history is vested in strategies of understanding that appreciate bounded human communication in all its experiments and predicaments. The Telemachy offers a valuable window into a postwar, dynastic, rural, archaic culture. The study of rhetorical history offers other cases where the threshold between anxiety and speech, repetition and development, civic disturbance and partisanship cross thresholds of engagement. The study of oratorical consciousness offers multiple windows into the unfolding of the vast, yet-unfathomed range of human communication.

NOTES

1. K. W. Grandsen, "Homer and the Epic," in *The Legacy of Greece: A New Appraisal*, ed. M. I. Finley (Oxford: Clarendon Press, 1981), 75.
2. Jasper Griffin, *Homer: The Odyssey* (Cambridge: Cambridge University Press, 1987), 24.
3. Thomas B. Farrell, *The Norms of Rhetorical Culture* (New Haven, CT: Yale University Press, 1993). Farrell begins rhetorical culture with a rendering of the philosophical arguments of Aristotle and Plato. This study examines the oratorical vectors that animate the trouble of communicative norms while Ancient Greece was undergoing transition to new communicative forms. Homer finds in postwar culture a model context for performers to vary interpretations and for audiences to appreciate communicative predicaments and dilemmas characteristic of beginning moments in the making or renewal of a rhetorical culture.
4. Quintilian, *Institutes of Oratory Vol. IV*, H. E. Butler, trans. (Cambridge, MA:

Harvard University Press, 1998), 10.1, 45–47.

5. Ibid., 36–40.
6. J. F. Dobson, *The Greek Orators* (London: Metheun & Co., 1919), 2–3.
7. Dionysius Longinus, *On the Sublime,* trans., William Smith (London: J. F. Dove, 1819), 92.
8. "In the poems words depend for their meaning on the actions they perform and the effects they produce," and thus may be regarded as speech acts similar to Austin and Searle. Speech acts display oratorical consciousness when the rules are brought into open and private play within and among interlocutors. David Roochink, "Homeric Speech Acts: Words and Deeds in the Epics," *Classical Journal* 85 (1990): 291.
9. Ernst Robert Curtius, *European Literature and the Latin Middle Ages* (Princeton, NJ: Princeton University Press, 1991), 64.
10. George Kennedy, *The Art of Persuasion in Greece* (Princeton, NJ: Princeton University Press, 1963), 5.
11. Brian Vickers, *In Defense of Rhetoric* (Oxford: Clarendon Press, 1998), 5.
12. Dobson, *The Greek Orators,* 2.
13. Charles Rowan Beye, *Ancient Literature and Society* (New York: Anchor Books, 1975), 85.
14. C. M. H. Millar and J. W. S. Carmichael, "The Growth of Telemachus," *Greece and Rome,* ser. 2 (1954): 58–64.
15. James M. Redfield, "The Economic Man," in *Approaches to Homer,* ed. Carl A. Rubino and Cynthia W. Shelmerdine (Austin: University of Texas Press, 1983), 218–219.
16. Jacqueline de Romily, *A Short History of Greek Literature,* trans. Lilian Doherty (Chicago: University of Chicago Press, 1985), 20.
17. Howard W. Clarke, "Telemachus and the 'Telemacheia,'" *American Journal of Philology* 84 (1963): 141; Charles W. Eckert, "Initiatory Motifs in the Story of Telemachus," *Classical Journal* 59 (1963): 51–57.
18. F. Ahl and H. M. Roisman, *The Odyssey Re-Formed* (New York: Cornell University Press, 1996).
19. R. B. Rutherford, *Homer (Greece and Rome: New Surveys in the Classics, No. 26)* (Oxford: Oxford University Press, 1996); D. S. Margoliouth, *The Homer of Aristotle* (Oxford: Basil Blackwell, 1923).
20. Werner Jaeger, *Paideia: The Ideals of Greek Culture,* trans. Gilbert Highet (Oxford: Oxford University Press, 1974), 1:30–31.

21. J. L. Myres, "The Pattern of the Odyssey," *Journal of Helenic Studies* 72 (1952): 1–19; A. B. Lord, *The Singer of Tales* (Cambridge, MA: Harvard University Press, 1969); A. B. Lord, "Composition by Theme in Epos," *TAPA* 82 (1951): 71–80; Rhys Carpenter, *Folk Tale, Fiction and Saga in the Homeric Epics* (Berkeley: University of California Press, 1946).
22. Takis Poulakos, *Rethinking the History of Rhetoric* (Boulder, CO: Westview Press, 1993), 56; H. I. Marrou, *A History of Education in Antiquity,* trans. George Lamb (London: Sheed & Ward, 1956), 9.
23. Gilbert P. Rose, "The Quest of Telemachus," *Transactions and Proceedings of the American Philological* Society 98 (1967): 391–398.
24. W. J. Woodhouse, *The Composition of Homer's Odyssey* (Oxford: Clarendon Press, 1930), 247.
25. Ibid., 248; Robert Flaceliere, *A Literary History of Greece,* trans. Douglas Garman (Chicago: Aldine, 1964), 28–29. Books 1 and 2 focus on Athena/Mêntes's advice, a public assembly, and encounters with suitors. Books 3 and 4 tell the tale of the visit to Pylos and Spart, where he meets Nestor. The so-called dead time is parallel to Odysseus's pause on Circe's island before postwar culture restarts.
26. M. I. Finley, *Democracy: Ancient and Modern* (New Brunswick, NJ: Rutgers University Press, 1973), 17.
27. Richard P. Martin, "Telemachus and the Last Hero Song," *Colby Quarterly* 29 (1993): 227.
28. Norman Austin, "Telemachos Polymechanos," *California Studies in Classical Antiquity* 2 (1969): 46.
29. Austin, "Telemachos Polymechanos," 51.
30. Homer, *The Odyssey,* trans. Robert Fitzgerald (New York: Doubleday & Co., 1961), 1.144–1.148. (Passage numbers are quoted in the body of the essay throughout.)
31. David E. Belmont, "Athena and Telemachus," *Classical Journal* 65 (1969): 112.
32. Many of the suitors appear to model bad argument, although each argument has its own distinctive qualities. See Walter Donlan, "The Politics of Generosity in Homer," *Helios* 9 (1982): 1–16; Donald Lateiner, "The Suitors' Take: Manners and Power in Ithaca," *Colby Quarterly* 29 (1993): 173–196.
33. George M. Calhoun, "The Homeric Picture," in *A Companion to Homer,* ed. Alan J. B. Wace and Frank H. Stubbings (London: Macmillan, 1962), 451.
34. Clarke, "Telemachus and the 'Telemacheia,'" 132.
35. Ibid, 129.
36. Richard Claverhouse Jebb, *An Introduction to the Iliad and the Odyssey* (Glasgow:

James MacLehose and Sons, 1887), 50.

37. Reputation and gossip were important in public culture. Virginia Hunter, "Gossip and the Politics of Reputation in Classical Athens," *Phoenix* 44 (1990): 299–325.
38. Kennedy, *The Art of Persuasion.*
39. Bruno Snell, *The Discovery of the Mind: The Greek Origins of European Thought,* trans. T. G. Rosenmeyer (Cambridge, MA: Harvard University Press, 1953), 9. "Wit, sap, and prudence are filled out as the human qualities of *psyche, thymos,* and *noos.*"
40. Homer, *Odyssey* 2.327–2.328.
41. Donald Lemen Clark, *Rhetoric in Greco-Roman Education* (New York: Columbia University Press, 1957).
42. Thomas Cole, *Origins of Rhetoric* (Baltimore: Johns Hopkins University Press, 1991), 6.
43. Edward Schiappa, "*Rhetorike:* What's in a Name," *Quarterly Journal of Speech* 78 (1992): 78.
44. Carol G. Thomas and Edward Kent Webb, "From Orality to Rhetoric: An Intellectual Transformation," in *Persuasion: Greek Rhetoric in Action,* ed. Ian Worthington (London: Routledge, 1994), 5.
45. Andrew J. Karp, "Homeric Origins of Ancient Rhetoric," *Arethusa* 10 (1977): 237.
46. Peter Toohey, "Epic and Rhetoric," in Worthington, *Persuasion,* 154.
47. G. Thomas Goodnight, "The Wiles of Argument: Protodeliberation and Heroic Prudence in Homer's *Odyssey,*" in *Anyone Who Has a View: Theoretical Contributions to the Study of Argumentation,* ed. Frans H. van Eemeren, J. Anthony Blair, Charles A. Willard, and A. Francisca Sneck Henkemans (Netherlands: Kluwer, 2003), 283–296.
48. John H. Finley Jr., *Homer's Odyssey* (Cambridge, MA: Harvard University Press, 1978), 139.

Lysander Spooner's *The Unconstitutionality of Slavery*: A Case Study in Constitutional Hermeneutics, Ethical Argument, and Practical Reason

James Jasinski

> What is most needed in law and literature alike is not abstract theoretical argument but a more fully informed and argumentative critical practice, from which generalizations of a different sort might emerge. Practice—not theory—is the level at which comparison is likely to be most helpful, at which the work of one community can best illuminate that of another.
>
> —James Boyd White, *Justice as Translation*

Lysander Spooner's 1845 treatise *The Unconstitutionality of Slavery* presents rhetorical scholars interested in constitutional argument with an interesting evaluative problem.[1] Rhetoricians have long struggled with the problem of critical evaluation. Almost fifty years ago Edwin Black argued that the then-dominant disciplinary paradigm "limits [rhetorical] criticism to the evaluation of immediate effects." As numerous scholars acknowledge, Spooner and his fellow "radical constitutionalists" failed any instrumental test.[2] Black recognized that rhetoricians in the mid-twentieth century ventured alternative modes of evaluation, but he argued that even when they sought to elude instrumentalism's gravitational pull via an assessment of rhetorical "quality," their efforts to identify what is "rhetorically good" collapsed into what is effective. The problem Black diagnosed remains: can rhetorical scholars evaluate arguments on grounds other than instrumental success?[3]

Indirectly responding to Black's challenge, in 1995 Edward Schiappa and his collaborators sought to identify analytic strategies for argument evaluation. In her contribution to the Schiappa volume, Kathryn Olson observed that in order to evaluate arguments ethically, rhetoricians needed to identify ethical standards internal to rhetorical practice; in that way they might avoid ethical standards that subordinate rhetoric to something external to it. In her study, Olson embraced Henry Johnstone's "basic imperative" for ethical argument to help develop an "evaluative position" for assessing arguments.[4] Like Olson and others in the Schiappa volume,[5] I want both to sketch and illustrate a form of rhetorical criticism that engages in ethical argument evaluation. Like Olson, I turn to allied scholars who have, explicitly as well as implicitly, sought to identify internal ethical standards of rhetorical argument. But, unlike Henry Johnstone, the scholars to which I turn are not committed to, in Olson's terms, "deontological ethicality."[6] As James Boyd White explains, reading, writing, and arguing are ethical activities because through them people can "becom[e] someone in relation to another."[7] White suggests that argument evaluation, especially the evaluation of constitutional argument, focuses on identifying and assessing "the activities it invites or makes possible for judges, for lawyers, and for citizens . . . the way it seeks to constitute the citizen, the lawyer, and the judge, and the relations among them . . . [and] the kind of discoursing community it helps create."[8] Evaluating arguments by assessing identities and relationships requires attention to context or situational particularities.[9] Put differently, ethical analysis needs to proceed prudentially, thereby linking ethics and practical reason.[10]

Since Eugene Garver's 2004 book *For the Sake of Argument: Practical Reasoning, Character, and the Ethics of Belief* explicitly attempts to work through the connection between ethics and practical reason, it will serve as my analytic touchstone for the remainder of the essay. In the next section of the essay I'll draw on Garver's insights to identify key questions that need to be explored in order to evaluate Spooner's argument. But since exploring those questions requires an understanding of context, before I can engage them I'll need to take a detour into antebellum constitutional culture in the essay's third section. In the fourth section of the essay I analyze the way Spooner's text aims at the internal and the external ends of constitutional argument, and I discuss the way he argues legitimately, plurally, and constitutively. I conclude that Spooner's text offers a compelling case of ethical argument, but I offer a final qualification of that evaluation in the conclusion by comparing Spooner's constitutional argument with that fashioned by Abraham Lincoln and the Republicans.

Ethical Argument and Practical Reasoning in The Unconstitutionality of Slavery

For Garver, ethical arguments do not merely follow a prescriptive set of rules. They constitute as they attempt to reveal individual and collective *ethos,* the fundamental ethical commitments that make us who and what we are. The question Spooner engaged—what is slavery's constitutional status—is ultimately an ethical question: to what interpersonal relationships and forms of community does the Constitution commit "We the People"? Did our founding document commit the nation's inhabitants to relationships of bondage and property or equality and justice? In arguing that the Constitution pledged "We the People" to the pursuit of equality and justice, Spooner engaged in an ethical act; he sought to transform a "notional possibility" into a "real possibility,"[11] or put differently, he sought to transform an "easy" case (the Constitution sanctions slavery) into one that is complicated and difficult (a "hard" case). My central claim is that by challenging slavery's assumed constitutional status, Spooner sought to substitute controversy for (federal) consensus,[12] and in the process he created space for new arguments and disclosed new ways of talking and new modes of civic association that must be engaged and evaluated.[13]

In describing rhetoric generally and ethical argument more specifically,

Garver introduces Alasdair MacIntyre's Aristotelian distinction between a practice's internal and external ends.[14] If we can identify the internal and external ends of constitutional argument/hermeneutics, those ends can serve as *topoi* for assessing the quality of Spooner's reasoning. As argument, constitutional hermeneutics shares rhetoric's internal, guiding, or constitutive end of discovering legitimate arguments (uncovering the available means of persuasion in a given case), as well as its external or given end "of actually persuading some audience."[15] But when we engage in hermeneutical argument, when we purport to disclose the Constitution's meaning and ethical commitments, additional internal and external ends emerge. Garver writes: "Hermeneutics is the attitude we adopt toward texts when we put two distinct demands on them. We want our interpretations to be faithful to the text, and we want the result of the interpretation to achieve further values, such as justice. . . . Our Constitution is like scripture in placing both requirements on the reader." The internal or guiding end of constitutional hermeneutics requires advocates to find or invent legitimate arguments while remaining faithful, while practicing constitutional fidelity;[16] the external end of constitutional hermeneutics is successful persuasion as well as attainment of further (presumably constitutional) values such as justice.[17]

Garver elaborates on the internal ends of ethical constitutional argument in an extended discussion of Philip Bobbitt's typology of constitutional argument.[18] According to Garver, Bobbitt demonstrates that ethical argument is inherently plural. Garver explains: "If I read the Constitution ethically, then I am committed to recognizing the other forms of argument [in Bobbitt's typology]. . . . [T]o argue ethically," he concludes, "is necessarily to be a pluralist with regard to argument."[19] Garver elaborates on the external ends of ethical constitutional argument in his discussion of the *Brown* decision. Ethical constitutional arguments are successful when they are "ampliative," when they transmit an "ethical surplus" (incipient ethical commitments in a state of potential waiting to be actualized) to immediate and future audiences through argument. *Brown*'s ethical surplus was, Garver contends, an "antidiscrimination model" of race relations that the Court actualized in subsequent decisions such as *Loving v. Virginia,* the 1967 case in which the Court overturned state laws banning interracial marriage.[20]

Following Garver's lead, we can identify two internal and two external ends in constitutional argument that can serve as evaluative *topoi*. Given Spooner's limited success at actually persuading readers (one of the external ends), that topoi has little value. But the other external end and both internal ends possess probative value. The two internal ends suggest the following sets of questions: (1) Did Spooner argue legitimately? Did he employ practical reason rather than engage in rationalizations? Did he acknowledge and engage plural arguments? (2) Can Spooner plausibly claim constitutional fidelity? Was he a faithful constitutional actor? The remaining external end can be engaged if we consider whether Spooner's text produced an ethical surplus. What, if any, ethical commitment was he able to offer his readers? Exploring these questions provides a more prudential approach for assessing the ethicality of *The Unconstitutionality of Slavery*.

Antebellum America's Constitutional Culture and the Performative Tradition of Common-Law Textualism

In order to appraise the legitimacy of Spooner's arguments, we need to reconstruct the argumentative context, the constitutional culture of antebellum America. Legal historian Paul Kahn provides a point of departure. Extending on the work of George Forgie and others,[21] Kahn opines that the founding generation's demise altered the nation's political psychology as Americans accepted a new civic responsibility: maintaining and perpetuating the founders' accomplishments. The Constitution was, of course, one of the founders' most significant achievements, and antebellum Americans accepted the idea that "[m]aintenance of the constitutional edifice will simultaneously honor the fathers, provide for posterity, and accomplish justice among contemporaries." Since "maintenance requires a reaffirmation of origins," constitutional actors had to display their commitment to the nation's founders. In the realm of constitutional hermeneutics, advocates displayed that commitment through a new mode of inquiry and argument: the search for original intention. Constitutional "originalism is," Kahn argues, "the methodology of maintenance."

Kahn devotes little attention to the origins of originalism, although he does claim that Chief Justice Roger Taney's opinion in *Dred Scott* represents a paradigmatic example of the "fundamental shift" in constitutional hermeneutics that originalism entailed.[22] Other legal historians provide some guidance on originalism's emergence. Hans Baade and H. Jefferson Powell both detect originalism's first stirrings during the House of Representatives' debate in spring 1796 over Edward Livingston's resolution directing President George Washington to transmit executive branch materials regarding John Jay's treaty negotiations with Great Britain. While Federalists introduced some originalist arguments during the debate, both Baade and Powell concur that the general consensus at the debate's conclusion was that such appeals were inconsistent with current interpretive norms and therefore illegitimate.[23]

According to Powell, "the watershed in the history of constitutional interpretation was the crisis provoked by South Carolina's strident response to the passage of a protective tariff by Congress in May 1828." Powell notes that scholars typically emphasize the "conflicting approaches to constitutional interpretation [that] emerged as the intellectual product of the crisis": the nationalist approach favored by Justice Joseph Story, Daniel Webster and others versus the states' rights approach favored by most Southerners and traceable, to at least some degree, to Jefferson and Madison's Kentucky and Virginia Resolutions. But Powell is less interested in the traditional story of constitutional conflict and more interested in identifying a new, still emerging interpretive trend. With a few exceptions, Powell asserts that "adherents of both camps increasingly expressed their views as explications of the 'original intent' of the framers, and earlier scruples against the use of 'extrinsic evidence' in constitutional interpretation gradually lost their force."

Virginia jurist Abel Parker Upshur functions in Powell's account as Roger Taney did for Kahn. Upshur's 1840 study, *A Brief Enquiry into the True Nature and Character of Our Federal Government,* was a states' rights response to Joseph Story's nationalist arguments in *Commentaries on the Constitution.* For Powell, Upshur's true significance lies in the fact that he "was an intentionalist in the modern sense." Upshur maintained that "strict construction" should seek "the intentions of the framers of the Constitution," and, Powell argues, "Upshur thought that the determination of that intention was an essay in historical reconstruction, to be carried out by investigating the proceedings and opinions of the Philadelphia framers." Powell's conclusion parallels Kahn's: "By the outbreak of the Civil War, intentionalism in the modern sense reigned supreme in the rhetoric of constitutional interpretation."[24]

Given the nature of Kahn and Powell's argument, Taney and Upshur clearly were not the only sources on which they might have relied. In 1844 the American Anti-Slavery Society published a collection of materials under the title *The Constitution, a Pro-Slavery Compact: Or Selections from the Madison Papers*. As the subtitle indicated, the collection featured numerous extracts from Madison's Philadelphia convention notes that purportedly revealed how the framers treated the subject of slavery during their deliberations. Another text in the collection which drew on Madison's extracts was an "Address of the Executive Committee of the American Anti-Slavery Society to the Friends of Freedom and Emancipation in the U[nited] States," dated May 20, 1844. Both the "Address" and the document collection were largely the work of Wendell Phillips, and both reveal the degree to which the Garrisonian wing of American abolitionism embraced the emerging interpretive norm of original intent. According to the "Address," the Constitution "is not a form of words to be interpreted in any manner, or to any extent, or for the accomplishment of any purpose" inconsistent with "the plain intentions of its framers." Discussing the possible interpretive value of the Preamble,[25] the "Address" insisted: "Nothing is more certain than that the preamble alluded to never included, in the minds of those who framed it, those who were then pining in bondage. . . . It is absurd, it is false, it is an insult to the common sense of mankind," the "Address" continued, "to pretend that the Constitution was intended to embrace the entire population of the country under its sheltering wing." The "Address's" repeated invocation of original intent helped justify its two main claims: first, the Constitution was "a covenant with death, and an agreement with hell" and, second, given the intent of the framers, the only legitimate solution was "No Union with Slaveholders."[26]

It will be instructive to consider why Phillips and the leadership of the American Anti-Slavery Society thought it necessary or useful to compose the "Address" and join the swelling chorus venerating original intent. On September 20, 1837, Alvan Stewart delivered an address to the New York

State Antislavery Society that, according to William Wiecek, "shocked the entire [antislavery] movement by arguing that the due process clause of the Fifth Amendment empowered the federal government to abolish slavery in the states. This speech," Wiecek continues, "marked the dramatic debut of radical antislavery constitutionalism."[27] Phillips's response to the potential threat posed by Stewart and other subversive constitutional actors suggests that the problems posed by slavery's continual, and expanding, presence, perhaps as much as the founders' demise, contributed to the development of originalist hermeneutics as both the search for and subsequent commitment to the framers' intentions.

For the Sake of Argument: Reading Spooner's The Unconstitutionality of Slavery

One year after *The Constitution, a Pro-Slavery Compact* first appeared, Lysander Spooner published the first edition of *The Unconstitutionality of Slavery.* Legal historian Robert Cover dismissed Spooner's case as a facile appeal to natural law, and if that's all there was to Spooner's argument, Garver would also dismiss it since such appeals "continue the philosophical project of judging reasoning in terms of how well it represents some truth independent of that reasoning."[28] But Randy Barnett contends that natural law "was not the principal method of constitutional interpretation [that Spooner] brought to bear on [slavery's] constitutionality."[29] Barnett directs our attention to the second paragraph of chapter 2, where Spooner wrote: "I shall not insist upon the principle . . . that there can be no law contrary to natural right; but shall admit, for the sake of argument, that there may be such laws."[30] Spooner's commitment to natural law clearly influenced his choice of interpretive norms (such as his effort to appropriate the concept of "irresistible clearness" from John Marshall's decision in *United States v. Fisher*), but in this passage he also announced his commitment to produce arguments, and we should take him at his word. As we'll see, Spooner's decision at the start of chapter 2 to abandon natural law and engage in constitutional hermeneutics "for the sake of argument" was the first of four key moments when he opted to assume *arguendo,* opted to entertain opposing positions in order to engage them argumentatively.[31]

Given the growing prominence of appeals to original intent in late antebellum America, at first glance it does not seem strange that Spooner's first interpretive norm or rule was "that the intention of the instrument must prevail."[32] What makes the passage unusual was the prepositional modifier "of the instrument." This modifier might strike early twenty-first century ears as strange, but it was a commonplace in Anglo-American law.[33] So too was Spooner's second interpretive rule, which maintained that "the intention of the constitution must be collected from its words." Both rules paraphrased language that Chief Justice John Marshall employed when, dissenting from the majority's 1827 decision in *Ogden v. Saunders,* he argued that a New York state insolvency statute violated the Constitution's contracts clause.[34] As scholars have demonstrated, Marshall's statutory and constitutional hermeneutics consistently relied on traditional common-law interpretive maxims that repudiated extra-textual evidence and appeals to subjective intention while foregrounding a text's wording and structure.[35] At the moment in time that many American constitutional actors embraced *intentio auctoris,* or authorial intent, Spooner's hermeneutic strategy sought to reanimate a tradition of common-law textual intentionality that he could then deploy in an innovative attack on slavery's constitutional status.

With intentionality established as the objective of constitutional hermeneutics, Spooner's argument moved in two complementary directions. The first direction culminated in Spooner's decision to assume *arguendo* for a second time, albeit in this instance the *arguendo* argument strategy was unmarked and remained implicit. Because Spooner had committed himself to seeking the intention of the instrument, he was unable to concede explicitly the possibility that subjective, authorial intention had any hermeneutic relevance. Nevertheless, for the sake of argument, Spooner considered the possibility that the framers' intentions might be a guide to the Constitution's meaning.

Spooner deployed both common-law textualism and a second line of argument that focused on the performative status of the framers' action to conclude that the framers' intentions "have nothing to do with fixing the legal meaning of the Constitution." In developing this claim, he appropriated an aspect of the Federalist argument during the ratification debate as an interpretive weapon against the relevance of authorial intention.

The Constitution, Spooner reminded his readers, was initially a "mere proposal, having no legal force or authority," observing in a footnote that John Marshall employed the term "proposal" to describe the convention's action in *McCulloch v. Maryland*. The question of the framers' authority (or lack thereof) was raised in 1787–1788, first in the Philadelphia convention and then in the public debates. Some members of the convention challenged the plan advanced by the delegates from Virginia, arguing that the plan's manner of reconstructing the national government exceeded the charge issued to the convention by the individual states and the Confederation Congress. James Wilson, delegate from Pennsylvania, argued that the convention need not be bound by the charge issued to them by the Confederation Congress, maintaining that they were "at liberty to propose any thing." George Mason echoed Wilson's idea of considering the convention's work as a proposal when he remarked that any "fiat is not to be here, but in the people." During the public debate a few months later, Publius (in *Federalist #40*) reaffirmed this characterization of the convention's illocutionary performance as an act of proposing. "It is time now to recollect," Publius wrote, "that the powers [of the convention] were mere advisory and recommendatory." They "have accordingly planned and proposed a Constitution which is to be of no more consequence than the paper on which it is written, unless it be stamped with the approbation of those to whom it is addressed."

In the context of the convention and ratification debates, reliance on the "proposal" characterization served the purpose of legitimation; it helped Federalists evade charges that the convention had usurped the authority of the Congress and the state legislatures in forwarding the Constitution to the states for consideration. Spooner, however, appropriated the proposal characterization as a way to render the framers' intentions irrelevant. He declared: "The members of the convention . . . were the mere scriveners of the constitution; and their individual purposes, opinions or expressions, then uttered in secret cabal, though now revealed [a reference to the publication of Madison's notes on the convention], can no more be evidence of the intentions of the people who adopted the Constitution, than the secret opinions or expressions of the scriveners of any other contract can be offered to prove the intentions of the true parties to such a contract." By appropriating their description of their act as only one of proposing, Spooner reduced the framers to mere scriveners who, as such, could give the Constitution "no validity, meaning, or legal force."[36]

But even as he resisted the emerging hermeneutic trend that privileged authorial intention, Spooner's decision to consider the issue required that he identify the individual(s) or group(s) whose intentions *might* be relevant. If not the framers at Philadelphia, then whose intentions mattered? While Spooner focused initially on "the people who adopted the Constitution," he must have sensed the difficulty in adducing quantitative evidence that "the people" intended an anti-slavery Constitution. In the end, Spooner was forced to invoke the idea of "a single honest man . . . who assented, in good faith, to the honest and legal meaning of the Constitution." While Wendell Phillips and others worried that the radical constitutionalists "advocate[d] fraud and violence toward one of the contracting parties," Spooner maintained that "it would be unjust and unlawful towards [the single honest man] to change the meaning of the instrument so as to sanction slavery."[37]

Spooner also engaged the relevance of authorial intention by relying on a version of common-law textualism fused with a commitment to interpretive charity.[38] Spooner had to confront the fact that most Americans understood that certain constitutional provisions euphemistically acknowledged slavery, if not exactly endorsing it. He initially did so by rewriting Article I grants of power to reveal the illegitimacy of *intentio auctoris*:

> We do not say, for example, that the Constitution *intended* to authorize Congress "to coin money," but that it *did* authorize them to coin it. Nor do we say that it intended to authorize them "to declare war." . . . It would be silly . . . to say merely that it *intended* to authorize them "to coin money" and "to declare war" when the language authorizing them to do so is full, explicit, and positive. Why, then, in the case of slavery, do men say merely that the Constitution *intended* to sanction it[?] . . . The reason is obvious. If they were to say unequivocally that it *did* sanction it, they would lay themselves under the necessity of pointing to the *words* that sanction it; and they are aware that the *words alone* of the Constitution do not come up to that point.[39]

After this initial effort to problematize slavery's assumed constitutional status, Spooner proceeded to examine the Constitution's language that purportedly sanctioned slavery and, again, his argument moved in two directions and, as it did so, he assumed *arguendo* for the third time.

As Spooner engaged the key passages (Article I, Section 2—the three-fifths clause; Article I, Section 9—prohibiting Congress from regulating the "Migration or Importation of such Persons as any of the States . . . shall think proper"; and Article IV, Section 2—prohibiting states from discharging a person's obligation "to Service or Labour"), he read both presence as well as absence. By reading presence, Spooner committed himself to the specific, explicit words found in the Constitution, and he undertook to locate plausible, noneuphemistic referents for those words. In doing so he tried to uncover and expose inconsistencies in the founders' discursive practices. For example, the euphemistic reading of the three-fifths clause insisted that the "other persons" contrasted to "free persons" must have been an oblique reference to slavery. Spooner countered by arguing that "English law had for centuries used the word 'free' as describing persons possessing citizenship . . . as distinguished from aliens" or other people such as convicted felons who had lost citizenship rights. Spooner maintained that his reading of this passage was consonant with the language in Article I, Section 8, regarding establishing uniform rules for naturalization. By recognizing the process of naturalization, Spooner insisted that the Constitution "necessarily supposes the existence of aliens—and thus furnishes the correlative sought for. It furnishes a class both for the word 'free' and the words 'all other persons' to apply to."[40]

Like other scholars, Wiecek concludes that in trying "to construe slavery out of the Constitution," radical constitutionalists like Spooner "appeared . . . obtuse or dishonest."[41] Wiecek's assessment merits consideration, because if in fact Spooner's arguments were contrived, then perhaps he was merely rationalizing and not reasoning and should therefore be judged a sophist. While Spooner's reading of presence may be tenuous, it should be considered in conjunction with his decision to read absence and therefore take its hermeneutic challenges seriously. If the words "other persons" are present in the Constitution, then what is absent are those words' euphemistic referents: slaves and the system of chattel slavery. Spooner could not explicitly concede that the expressions *were* euphemisms for slavery, because doing so would have undermined his reading of presence, his effort to enact interpretive charity and locate innocent referents for the words in the text. But for the third time, Spooner would assume *arguendo* and engage the counter position that, when it came to the subject of slavery, the Constitution should be read euphemistically.

Southerners and those sympathetic to the region's peculiar institution read the words "other persons" and "persons held to service or labour" as signs of what was absent—slavery—and concluded that these words established slavery's constitutional legitimacy. Garrisonians read the words "other persons" and "persons held to service or labour" as signs of what was absent—slavery—and concluded that the founders acted in bad faith when they reached "an agreement with hell." While never explicitly admitting that the words "other persons" and "persons held to service or labour" were signs of what was absent—slavery—Spooner managed to both acknowledge that slavery's lexical absence from the text was a sign and suggest that the Constitution's reliance on euphemisms need not be a sign of the framers' bad faith or their desire to legitimate slavery. Spooner maintained:

> If the instrument had contained any tangible sanction of slavery, the people, in some parts of the country certainly, would sooner have had it burned by the hands of the common hangman, then they would have adopted it, and thus sold themselves as pimps to slavery, covered as they were with the scars they had received in fighting the battles of freedom. And the members of the convention knew that such was the feeling of a large portion of the people; and for that reason, if for no other, they dared insert in the instrument no legal sanction of slavery.[42]

Garrisonians might well have agreed with Spooner's claim that the framers decided to render slavery absent and invisible to avoid unnecessarily antagonizing segments of the North. But acknowledging that the framers chose their language strategically would not have altered their charge of bad faith. For Spooner the framers' choice of euphemisms was more than rhetorical strategy; it was itself a sign of something else absent from the text. "Other persons" and "persons held to service or labour" signified not only absent slaves, but also the absent antislavery sentiments that motivated at least some Americans, the very sentiments that precipitated the framers' language choices. Spooner's hermeneutic sign argument unearthed an antislavery impulse in the specific provisions that purportedly sanctioned slavery. Given Spooner's sign reasoning, he could legitimately maintain that the intentions of the "single honest man" were as much a part of the Constitution as the intentions of southern slave owners, and constitutional arguments that acknowledged those intentions were legitimate, plausible, and necessary. When it came to the Constitution's ambiguous language on the issue of slavery, the fundamental argumentative and hermeneutic task was reconciling the specific words present in the text with the inherently incommensurable absent practices and sentiments that those words potentially signified. Such efforts at reconciliation cannot be evaluated epistemologically (what is the "correct" or "true" interpretation); they need to be appraised ethically. Just because Spooner's effort to reconcile the Constitution's conflicting pro- and antislavery impulses failed to achieve the external end (persuasion) in any quantitatively significant way does not mean that he failed to achieve the other external end or the internal ends of legitimate argument and constitutional fidelity.[43] Spooner's commitment to assuming *arguendo* exemplified how the pursuit of internal ends can curb an advocate's quest for external persuasive success.

As Spooner may have recognized, our apparent deontological commitment to constitutional fidelity is beset by an ontological problem: to what precisely are we pledging our fidelity? Given the various possible objects to which advocates and citizens might commit themselves (text, original intentions, etc.), constitutional fidelity is a contested and contingent internal end. To satisfy this end, Spooner must present a plausible argument that explains how he might legitimately lay claim to constitutional fidelity.[44] Spooner broached the ontological problem by posing two rhetorical questions: "Did Mr. Madison, when he took his oath of office as President of the United States, swear to support these scraps of debate which he had filed away among his private papers? Or did he swear to support that written instrument which the people of the country had agreed to, and which was known to them . . . as the Constitution of the United States?"[45] Spooner's disjunctive argument juxtaposed fidelity to the text, the words and nothing but the words' innocent meaning, with fidelity to the "scraps of debate," which divulged the framers' hidden intentions. But Spooner did more than profess fidelity to textual presence (his potentially contrived innocent meanings). Garrisonians and defenders of slavery pledged fidelity to euphemisms (and what those euphemisms represented), while Spooner pledged fidelity to a different absence: the founders' *choice* to employ euphemisms (and the antislavery sentiments that informed that choice). If Spooner's reading of presence appears strained and illegitimate, his reading of absence cannot be so easily dismissed. Spooner assumed *arguendo* (the language is euphemistic) and employed sign reasoning (what do the euphemisms represent) in order to resolve the ontological problem posed by the demand of fidelity (to what do we pledge our faith). Spooner pledged his fidelity to an unappreciated element of the Constitution: to its very imperfect antislavery sentiments revealed through the framers' decision to employ euphemisms.

In a brief discussion of slavery and the Constitution in *For the Sake of Argument,* Garver suggests that the Constitution's status as a political compromise and constitutional fidelity are unrelated.[46] But this suggestion overlooks an important issue in antebellum constitutional discourse. When, on July 22, 1850, Henry Clay proclaimed that "the Constitution of the United States" was the "greatest of all compromises," he was recognizing a significant aspect of the nation's constitutional ethos. Clay continued: "In deliberating upon what was best for the country, and perceiving that there were great and conflicting interests pervading all its parts, they [the framers] compromised and settled them by ample concession, and in the spirit of true patriotic amity. They adjusted these conflicting opinions, and the Constitution . . . is the work of their hands—a great, memorable, magnificent compromise."[47] For Clay and other adherents to the tradition Peter Knupfer describes as "constitutional unionism," compromise was the Constitution's essence, the fundamental practice that the founders bequeathed to posterity. It was the ethical commitment on which the nation was established, and as such fidelity to the Constitution entailed at least some degree of fidelity to the process of political compromise as well as the specific compromises reached in 1787.[48]

Fidelity to the text and fidelity to compromise are not mutually exclusive. "Other persons" and "persons held to service or labour" are ambiguous, euphemistic signs that, among other things, reflected the founders' numerous compromises. Fidelity to the linguistic euphemisms is commensurate with fidelity to both the specific compromises from which the euphemisms emerged, as well as the broader principle of compromise. Given his politics, Spooner would have considerable difficulty professing fidelity to the politics of sectional compromise. But could he assume *arguendo* a fourth time and plausibly claim to have remained faithful to the compromises, the lexical as well as the practical, crafted in 1787?

Spooner recognized, if only implicitly, a point raised by contemporary constitutional scholars: fidelity, like the act of compromise, entails risk; both involve, in Jack Balkin's words, "a gamble on the future."[49] Spooner suggested that by agreeing to the Constitution, all Americans put their faith in the document and gambled that it would produce and promote justice; fidelity and risk were two sides of the same coin. Northerners opposed to slavery took a risk that, by providing a vehicle for abolishing the African slave trade, the Constitution sanctioned a (potential) political decision (end the African slave trade) that might eventually place slavery on the road to extinction. Turns out they were wrong. Through his insistent textualism, Spooner insinuated that Southern slaveholders also took a risk when they signed a Constitution that did not contain the words "slave" or "slavery" and that did not explicitly recognize a constitutional right to slave property. For Spooner, the absence of these terms meant that the Constitution did not "legally sanction" slavery. In apparently acquiescing to antislavery sentiment, Southerners gambled that euphemisms would be sufficient protection for their peculiar institution.[50] Both parties compromised, and in so doing both parties assumed risks on the subject of slavery. Historians have long assumed that, via threats of disunion, Southerners got the better deal. But that would only be true if the nation retained a risk-free fidelity to euphemisms. In perhaps an ironic way, Spooner demonstrated his fidelity to the founding compromises by recuperating their associated risks, and by reminding the South that both parties made commitments that they might later find difficult to honor.[51] Spooner asked Southerners to remain faithful to their original gamble. If we criticize Spooner for his lack of fidelity to the Constitution's euphemisms, we should also criticize those, North and South, who minimized the compromises, and risks, those expressions signified.

In his 1951 book *The Antislavery Origins of the Fourteenth Amendment,* Jacobus tenBroek was one of the first twentieth-century scholars to devote substantial attention to Spooner and the other radical constitutionalists. According to Robert Cover, both tenBroek and Howard Jay Graham claimed "that the Fourteenth Amendment and its language—'due process,' 'equal protection,' and 'privileges and immunities'—cannot be understood except in the context of three decades of abolitionist legal theory." Spooner and the other radical constitutionalists, Cover continues, glossing tenBroek, articulated "a grand vision of society that they found *in potentia* in many of the phrases of the Constitution." Graham, tenBroek, and eventually Thurgood Marshall embraced the ideas of national citizenship and an expansive sense of equal protection as ethical commitments that helped shape the Fourteenth Amendment.[52] TenBroek's scholarship and Marshall's legal advocacy help us grasp one of Spooner's most important contributions to subsequent constitutional discourse. Spooner achieved the external end of constitutional argument by producing an ethical surplus upon which twentieth-century constitutional actors would draw, as well as by creating arguments that invited readers to imagine themselves part of the ethical community that the Constitution constitutes.

Garver argues that we demonstrate our "rational fidelity to the document [the Constitution] by becoming parties to it."[53] In what is perhaps his most significant accomplishment, Lysander Spooner fashioned arguments that invited Americans to manifest ethical commitment, and constitute ethical community, by "becoming parties to" the U.S. Constitution. To appreciate Spooner's achievement, we need briefly to explore the nation's African American communities in the late 1840s and early 1850s. Decades of deprivation and hardship had taken its toll. African American frustration continued to rise, leading a number of prominent leaders such as Alexander Crummell, Martin Delany, and Henry Highland Garnet to encourage emigration. Many rejected Garrisonian nonresistance in favor of vigorous self-defense against racially motivated attacks. And as Peter Ripley notes, "the enactment of the Fugitive Slave Law of 1850 provoked a wide-spread, emotionally charged response" among northern African Americans.[54]

For many abolitionists, the Constitution facilitated the growth of the slave power during the first half of the nineteenth century. Therefore, some readers of the *North Star* might have been surprised to find in their May 15, 1851, issue a short piece by Frederick Douglass under the headline "Change of Opinion Announced." In the brief account Douglass concluded that he "had arrived at the firm conviction that the Constitution, construed in the light of well established rules of legal interpretation, might be made consistent in its details with the noble purposes avowed in its preamble." Abolitionists should, he continued, "insist upon the application of such rules to that instrument, and demand that it be wielded in behalf of emancipation." Douglass noted that his new opinion "has not been hastily arrived at" and was based on "careful study of the writings of Lysander Spooner, of Gerrit Smith, and of William Godell."[55] As Douglass acknowledged, Spooner invited him to imagine that he might become a member of the political community ordained by the Constitution, that he too might become a party to the Constitution's ethical commitments to secure liberty and establish justice. Douglass augmented Spooner's constitutional hermeneutics by infusing it with a jeremiadic, often prophetic ethos, thereby inaugurating a tradition of African American constitutionalism that continues today.[56] We should be able to recognize Spooner's contribution to the tradition of African American constitutionalism without diminishing the significance of Douglass, King, and the many others who by word and deed professed their faith in our founding document. Through ethical argument, Spooner helped Frederick Douglass and other African Americans discover that they, too, could have rational faith in the Constitution.

Conclusion

In a brief discussion of slavery in *For the Sake of Argument,* Garver maintains that "a Constitution that legitimated slavery could not be read ethically."[57] In this essay I have relied on Garver's discussion of practical reasoning and ethical argument to advance the claim that Lysander Spooner's *The Unconstitutionality of Slavery* did just that. According to Garver, "argument will be ethical simply by being argumentative and aiming at its internal end. . . . [T]o argue ethically is to argue trying to achieve the internal end of argument, making a legitimate case, while to argue unethically is to aim directly at the external end of winning the case. . . . Argument is for the most part ethical by being argumentative, that is, by aiming at its internal end of finding and presenting the best argument in the situation."[58] Establishing argumentative legitimacy is not always easy, since "any mode of [constitutional] interpretation can be used to constitute a legitimate argument. Any mode can equally be used instrumentally to rationalize a favored cause. There is no method of interpretation or argument that cannot be abused by being used instrumentally."[59]

In order to establish Spooner's argumentative legitimacy, I turned initially to historical context and the performative tradition of common-law textualism. Spooner's focus on "the intentions of the instrument" strikes contemporary readers as strange because we have thoroughly assimilated the position that intentions are psychological and exterior to texts; texts represent or signify psychological intentions. But Spooner's early nineteenth-century legal education introduced him to traditional common-law interpretive maxims that rejected extratextual evidence and appeals to subjective intention. In interpretation, the only thing significant or relevant were the words (and word patterns or structures) found in the text. As fellow abolitionists joined Southerners in embracing the emerging fixation with "original intent" and used it to justify disunion and the destruction of argumentative community, Spooner responded by attempting to reanimate common-law textualism. Appreciating Spooner's relationship to this performative tradition enables us to recognize the plausibility and legitimacy of his arguments.

Ethical constitutional arguments aim at a second internal end: fidelity. Garver writes, "Rational fidelity demands allegiance to the written Constitution, but it turns out that the identity, meaning, rationality, and justice of 'the Constitution' are located by these modes of argument [textualism, structuralism, etc.], rather than by the methods we use to denote an extra-argumentative object." Garver avoids fidelity's ontological conundrum (to what exactly will we be faithful) by positing the priority of plurality. According to Garver, "these modes of argument [are] ultimate, needing no such foundation. They aren't ultimate premises but modes of reasoning. This is the priority of politics to epistemology, of rhetoric to philosophy." He continues: "If I read the Constitution ethically, then I am committed to recognizing the other forms of argument as well. . . . The textualist who recognizes the legitimacy of other modes of interpretation is reasoning ethically."[60]

Common-law textualism supplemented by a proto-Dworkian principle of interpretive charity was Spooner's preferred mode of interpretive argument. And while Spooner refused to endorse explicitly other forms of argument (intentionalism, a commitment to the ethos of compromise), he continually assumed *arguendo* and, for the sake of argument, engaged these alternative ways of reading the Constitution as argument. Given his commitment to natural law, it is unlikely that Spooner would ever embrace the abstract concept of pluralism, but that ethical commitment did not prevent Spooner from the equally ethical act of arguing pluralistically.

Ethical constitutional arguments also aim at external goals. All forms of ethical argument aspire to be "ampliative." Garver notes that when we "mak[e] legitimate modes of argument central" to our discourse practices, we "expand the range of community." Spooner's most remarkable ethical accomplishment was to help Frederick Douglass read the Constitution in a new way, so that Douglass could conceive that he, and all African Americans, might be part of the political community constituted by the Constitution. Ethical constitutional arguments also aim at external goals such as justice. "To seek justice through constitutional hermeneutic argument is," Garver contends, "to reenact the ratification of the Constitution."[61] The refounding that Spooner and Douglass sought was not accomplished with the Thirteenth Amendment's ratification, nor with the Fourteenth or Fifteenth. As Danielle Allen argues, the constitutional refounding that allowed African Americans to participate fully in the national polity took place between 1954 and 1965.[62] But that refounding began when Lysander Spooner sought justice through constitutional hermeneutic argument and persuaded Frederick Douglass to place his faith in the nation's Constitution and culture of constitutional argument.

Extending on observations made by Philip Bobbitt, Garver notes that as the possibility of amending the Constitution, for various reasons, becomes more remote, "the more its meaning becomes disputed and changed. Laws allowing and requiring racial segregation were once constitutional, but we don't need to amend the Constitution to change the constitutionality of those laws. We can simply supply better arguments."[63] We should not reduce the quality of constitutional argument to a form of epistemological validity (the "correct" understanding of original intention or the "right" account of constitutional structure); along with Wayne Booth, James Boyd White, and others, Garver encourages rhetoricians and argument scholars to understand argument quality ethically. Given Garver's account of ethical argument, Spooner argued ethically: his textual arguments were historically legitimate (common-law textualism), his recurrent *arguendos* enabled argumentative plurality, and the depth of his argument persuaded Frederick Douglass to join the culture of constitutional argument, revealing the constitutive dimension of Spooner's reasoning.

Could Spooner's argument have been "better," as in ethically stronger? Undoubtedly. Through his fourth and final *arguendo,* Spooner sought to do justice to southern slaveholders by recuperating risk; North and South alike took risks when they reached the compromises regarding slavery, and now both had to accept the consequences of their action. Such a stance in relation to the South, however, cannot be judged as ethically satisfactory. Southerners deserved to be treated better than they were in Spooner's argument. By adopting a more long-term (and therefore gradualist) temporal framework that focused on halting slavery's expansion, Republicans could plausibly argue that they were trying to do justice by the South.[64] But as circumstances changed, Lincoln in particular altered his understanding of slavery's constitutional status. David Donald nicely captures Lincoln's prudentialism: "The ability to face reality means a willingness to change with events. Lincoln willingly admitted that his opinions and his actions were shaped by forces beyond his control. His shifting position on emancipation clearly illustrates his flexibility. . . . [He finally acted] when ends and means were fitted, and the Emancipation Proclamation was a masterpiece of political sagacity."[65] As circumstances changed, Lincoln discovered the constitutional power to issue the Emancipation Proclamation, power that Spooner insisted had been there all the time. At certain historical moments, circumstantial change (and the capacity to be responsive to such change) rather than more ethical argument enables movement toward justice.

NOTES

1. Lysander Spooner, *The Unconstitutionality of Slavery* (1845; reprint, Boston: Bela Marsh, 1860).
2. The "radical constitutionalist" movement sought to persuade Americans that the U.S. Constitution was fundamentally antislavery. For an introduction to the movement's principal arguments and an assessment of its limited impact, see William M. Wiecek, *The Source of Antislavery Constitutionalism in America, 1760–1848* (Ithaca: Cornell University Press, 1977), esp. 249–275.
3. Edwin Black, *Rhetorical Criticism: A Study in Method* (1965; reprint, Madison: University of Wisconsin Press, 1978), esp. 60–74; quote on 75.
4. Kathryn M. Olson, "Aligning Ethicality and Effectiveness in Arguments: Advocating Inclusiveness Percentages for the New Lutheran Church," in *Warranting Assent: Case Studies in Argument Evaluation,* ed. Edward Schiappa (Albany: State University of New York Press, 1995), see esp. 81–85.
5. For two additional examples of ethical analysis and evaluation, see Ralph E. Dowling and Gabrielle A. Ginder, "An Ethical Appraisal of Ronald Reagan's Justification for the Invasion of Granada," and Jeffrey L. Courtright, "'I Respectfully Dissent': The Ethics of Dissent in Justice O'Connor's *Metro Broadcasting, Inc. v. FCC* Opinion," in Schiappa, *Warranting Assent,* 103–124, 125–152. For an example of ethical assessment closer in spirit to my own, see Frederick J. Antczak, "When 'Silence Is Betrayal': An Ethical Criticism of the Revolution in Values in the Speech at Riverside Church," in *Martin Luther King, Jr. and the Sermonic Power of Public Discourse,* ed. Carolyn Calloway-Thomas and John L. Lucaites (Tuscaloosa: University of Alabama Press, 1993), 127–146.
6. Olson, "Aligning Ethicality and Effectiveness," 84–85.
7. James Boyd White, *Justice as Translation: An Essay in Cultural and Legal Criticism* (Chicago: University of Chicago Press, 1990), 101. As we'll see, when we focus attention on constitutional argument, relationships beyond speaker-listener or writer-reader demand attention.
8. White, *Justice as Translation,* 102.
9. Garver contends that "it is right to apply the same context-relative standards to practical arguments as we do to action, including purpose and context in their evaluation" (Eugene Garver, *For the Sake of Argument: Practical Reasoning, Character, and the Ethics of Belief* [Chicago: University of Chicago Press, 2004], 98).
10. Olson indirectly makes much the same point, given the way she uses Booth's work

on "rhetorical stance" to modulate Johnstone's deontological imperative. Her path might have been easier had she turned to Booth's explicit treatment of ethical evaluation in *The Company We Keep: An Ethics of Fiction* (Berkeley: University of California Press, 1988).

11. Garver draws on Bernard Williams's distinction between "notional" and "real" possibilities in "After *Virtù*: Rhetoric, Prudence and Moral Pluralism in Machiavelli," in *Prudence: Classical Virtue/Postmodern Practice,* ed. Robert Hariman (University Park: Pennsylvania State University Press, 2003), 71–72.
12. According to Wiecek, "Americans in the early years of national independence neither questioned its [slavery's] legitimacy in the states where it survived nor believed that the federal government could abolish it in those states. This assumption will be called the 'federal consensus'" (Wiecek, *Sources,* 15–16). It is worth noting that Spooner and his fellow radical constitutionalists were not the only Americans disturbing the consensus. As Wiecek notes, as part of a response to the gag rule controversy, South Carolina's John Calhoun introduced six resolutions in the Senate on December 27, 1837, that, Wiecek explains, "were a momentous restatement of the nature of the federal union; if taken seriously they would have changed the basis of American federalism" (188). Calhoun and other Southerners deserve as much if not more credit for destabilizing consensus in seeking constitutional (as opposed to political) protection for the peculiar institution.
13. In a basic sense, then, *The Unconstitutionality of Slavery* argues ethically. But given the quixotic nature of Spooner's project, Garver might respond that *The Unconstitutionality of Slavery* did not present a serious or legitimate argument; the book was, at best, a parody of constitutional hermeneutics. (On the problem of distinguishing serious constitutional argument from parody, see Jordan Steiker, Sanford Levinson, and J. M. Balkin, "Taking Text and Structure Seriously: Constitutional Interpretation and the Crisis of Presidential Eligibility," *Texas Law Review* 74 [1995]: 237–257).

    Spooner was, to use a distinction Garver employs regularly in *For the Sake of Argument,* rationalizing a favored cause rather than employing practical reason. On this reading, despite his argumentative cleverness and ingenuity, Spooner was essentially a sophist. His text manipulated his readers as well as the nation's culture of constitutional argument; he tried to deceive readers into embracing his vision of national freedom. While the rationalizing/reasoning distinction is crucial in Garver's attempt to differentiate sophistic rhetoric from its ethical cousin, he acknowledges that the "demarcation between legitimate and illegitimate modes of argument, like the boundary between the rational and the irrational, is always subject to rhetorical negotiation." Further, he admits that "only in some circumstances can we make a principled distinction between reasoning and rationalizing" (Garver, *For the Sake*, 163, 168). So the question of Spooner's status—sophistic rationalizer or ethical practical reasoner—and the status of his text remains open, subject to further analytic assessment.

14. See Eugene Garver, *Aristotle's Rhetoric: An Art of Character* (Chicago: University of Chicago Press, 1994). Garver explains: "In the language of speech act theory, all persuasion aims at a perlocutionary *effect*, while Aristotle makes rhetorical argument into an illocutionary *act*. Perlocutionary effects are the given [external] end of rhetoric; illocutionary acts are its guiding and constitutive [internal] end" (35).
15. "To argue ethically is to argue trying to achieve the internal end of argument, making a legitimate case" (Garver, *For the Sake*, 172).
16. According to Jack Balkin, constitutional "fidelity is not a virtue but a precondition. . . . [it is] the point of the practice of constitutional interpretation." Put differently, fidelity is the fundamental deontological commitment in constitutional argument. But it is a commitment that cannot be reduced to a simple rule that must be followed in all situations. Constitutional fidelity is a relationship established between constitutional arguers and something else (in addition to readers and listeners). But fidelity will remain contested, and consequently incapable of functioning as a simple deontological rule, as long as Americans remain divided regarding to what or to whom fidelity is owed (the text? the framers' intentions? etc.). See J. M. Balkin, "Agreements with Hell and Other Objects of Our Faith," *Fordham Law Review* 65 (1997): 1705.
17. Garver, *For the Sake*, 166, 156–157.
18. Bobbitt, *Constitutional Fate: Theory of the Constitution* (New York: Oxford University Press, 1982); Bobbitt, *Constitutional Interpretation* (Oxford: Basil Blackwell, 1991).
19. Garver, *For the Sake*, 173.
20. For Garver's discussion of *Brown v. Board of Education*, see Garver, *For the Sake*, 69–86. Unfortunately, Garver does not acknowledge that alternative readings of *Brown* might identify a different ethical surplus. In his 2007 plurality opinion in *Parents Involved in Community Schools v. Seattle School District* (combined with *Meredith v. Jefferson County Board of Ed.*), Chief Justice Roberts maintained that *Brown* committed the nation to the ethical principle of anticlassification, and for that reason (among others) the chief justice reasoned that racial classification, even when used to promote integration, was unconstitutional. On the distinction

between anticlassification and antidiscrimination (or antisubordination), see Jack M. Balkin, "*Brown v. Board of Education*—A Critical Introduction," in *What* Brown v. Board of Education *Should Have Said,* ed. Jack M. Balkin (New York: New York University Press, 2001), 11.

21. George B. Forgie, *Patricide in the House Divided: A Psychological Interpretation of Lincoln and His Age* (New York: W. W. Norton, 1979).
22. Paul W. Kahn, *Legitimacy and History: Self-Government in American Constitutional Theory* (New Haven, CT: Yale University Press, 1992), 33, 46, 50, 57.
23. Hans W. Baade, "'Original Intent' in Historical Perspective: Some Critical Glosses," *Texas Law Review* 69 (1991): 1014–1022; H. Jefferson Powell, "The Original Understanding of Original Intent" (1985), in *Interpreting the Constitution: The Debate over Original Intent,* ed. Jack N. Rakove [Boston: Northeastern University Press, 1990]), esp. 71–74.
24. Powell, "Original Understanding," 86–87.
25. Powell quotes the sixteenth-century English jurist Sir James Dyer that the preamble of a statute is "a key to open the minds of the makers of the act" as evidence of this interpretive norm (Powell, "Original Understanding," 94). See also Blackstone: "If words happen to be still dubious, we may establish their meaning from the context. . . . Thus the proeme, or preamble, is often called on to help the construction of an act of parliament" (William Blackstone, *Commentaries on the Laws of England,* 4 vols. (1765; reprint, Chicago: University of Chicago Press, 1979), 1:60.
26. "Address of the Executive Committee of the American Anti-Slavery Society to the Friends of Freedom and Emancipation in the U[nited] States," in *The Constitution, a Pro-Slavery Compact: Or Selections from the Madison Papers* (New York: American Anti-Slavery Society, 1844), 93, 94, 96–97.
27. Wiecek, *Sources,* 254–255. Stewart's address appeared as "A Constitutional Argument on the Subject of Slavery," *Friend of Man* 2 (October 1837) and was reprinted in Jacobus tenBroek, *Equal under Law* (1951; reprint, New York: Collier Books, 1965), 281–295.
28. Robert M. Cover, *Justice Accused: Antislavery and the Judicial Process* (New Haven, CT: Yale University Press, 1975), 156–157; Garver, *For the Sake,* 155.
29. Randy E. Barnett, "Was Slavery Unconstitutional before the Thirteenth Amendment? Lysander Spooner's Theory of Interpretation," *Pacific Law Journal* 28 (1997): 988.
30. Spooner, *Unconstitutionality,* 15–16; cf. 155. Cover acknowledges that Spooner assumed *arguendo* but employs a dissociative argument to discount Spooner's

commitment; according to Cover, Spooner only assumed *arguendo* "in form," but not "in substance." Cover, *Justice,* 156–157.

31. As Garver notes, "Accepting something 'for the sake of argument' is a free act without commitments in scientific reasoning; not so for practical reasoning" (Garver, *For the Sake*, 99). Assuming *arguendo* reflects choice, and choices reveal (ethical) character.
32. Spooner, *Unconstitutionality*, 157.
33. H. Jefferson Powell summarizes an eighteenth-century English treatise on contract law by John Joseph Powell as follows: "At common law . . . the 'intent' of the maker of a legal document and the 'intent' of the document itself were one and the same; 'intent' did not depend upon the subjective purposes of the author" (Powell, "Original Understanding," 59). See also Umberto Eco's discussion of *intentio operis*, or the intention of the text, as part of his "trichotomy of intentions" in *The Limits of Interpretation* (Bloomington: Indiana University Press, 1990), 44–63.
34. Baade, "Original Intent," 1047, notes that Spooner "selectively quoted" Marshall's opinion.
35. On Marshall's textual approach to legal interpretation, see Baade, "Original Intent," 1025–1035; Powell, "Original Understanding," 84–85; John Choon Yoo, "Marshall's Plan: The Early Supreme Court and Statutory Interpretation," *Yale Law Journal* 101 (1992): 1607–1630.
36. Spooner, *Unconstitutionality,* 114–119. For Wilson and Mason's comments, see *The Records of the Federal Convention,* 4 vols., ed. Max Farrand (1911; reprint, New Haven, CT: Yale University Press, 1966), 1:253, 338. For Madison's comments in #40, see *The Federalist Papers,* ed. Clinton Rossiter (New York: New American Library, 1961), 252.
37. Spooner, *Unconstitutionality,* 123; "Address of the Executive Committee," 96.
38. Spooner argued that if you assume that justice is the *telos* of law, it is "imperative upon courts of justice to ascribe an innocent and honest meaning to all language that will possibly bear an innocent and honest meaning." A few pages later, he writes that any interpretive "*stretching . . . must always be towards the right.*" For Spooner, natural law operated as a hermeneutic frame when it was operationalized in the attitude of interpretive "innocence" that stretches the language of the law toward the "right." But natural law was not the only possible source of Spooner's interpretive charity. Spooner's stance of interpretive charity or innocence radicalized the "mood" of "candor" that Albert Furtwangler argues is central to the rhetorical authority of *The Federalist Papers.*

In order to understand candor as an interpretive frame and see its relationship to Spooner's text, we must begin by calling attention to the semantic shifts in the term. Furtwangler observes that "candor," or the related adjective "candid," "now denotes forthrightness, frankness, direct honesty. But in the eighteenth century it was more likely to mean almost the opposite: not bold, blunt truth but polite, deferential sweetness of temper." Furtwangler discerns two semantic threads interwoven in the term: first, the sense of honesty or forthrightness that has become its dominant modern meaning, which applies primarily to the production of discourse, and, second, the idea of a "generous impulse" that was reflected in Samuel Johnson's definition of candid as "free from malice; not desirous to find faults." This second sense of candor functioned as a principle of interpretation. Candor was, Furtwangler argues, the "attitude" (63) that Publius hoped to induce in his reader; "in the long run," Furtwangler asserts, "Publius directs his reader's candor not only toward himself and his arguments, but also toward the Constitution and the sources from which it sprang." In essence, Publius was trying to teach his readers *how* to read the Constitution: charitably, generously, without a desire to find fault. Furtwangler concludes: "Thus candor developed as a mood directed outward from Publius toward his opponents. But Publius stood as an ethical model, too, for the conduct and attitudes readers should adopt in return. He worked to elicit feelings of candor not only toward himself, or the *Federalist* papers, but also toward the work of the Convention, the new constitution, and the national government that would grow from its ratification."

Like Publius, Spooner was trying to counteract suspicion with candid generosity. And, like Publius, Spooner linked interpretive candor to political innovation. New possibilities could be uncovered through interpretive generosity that would stretch the language of the Constitution "toward the right." See Spooner, *Unconstitutionality,* 64–65, 70. Albert Furtwangler, *The Authority of Publius: A Reading of the Federalist Papers* (Ithaca: Cornell University Press, 1984), 62–63, 65, 69. As Randy Barnett notes, Spooner anticipated Ronald Dworkin's aspirational hermeneutics, in which "all interpretation strives to make an object the best it can be." See Dworkin, *Law's Empire* (Cambridge, MA: Harvard University Press, 1986), 53.

39. Spooner, *Unconstitutionality,* 57.
40. Ibid., 74–75. Barnett examines Spooner's reading of presence in detail. See Barnett, "Was Slavery Unconstitutional," 994–999.
41. Wiecek, *Sources,* 272. Barnett's assessment of Spooner's performance in "Was Slavery Unconstitutional" is much more sympathetic.

42. Spooner, *Unconstitutionality,* 119. In his 1788 pamphlet *The Genuine Information,* Philadelphia convention delegate Luther Martin confirmed Spooner's claim. Martin maintained that his fellow delegates "anxiously sought to avoid the admission of expressions [such as "the word slaves"] which might be odious in the ears of Americans." Spooner would have disagreed with Martin's claim that the delegates "were willing to admit into their system those *things* which the expressions *signified.*" In *The Complete Anti-Federalist,* 7 vols, ed. Herbert J. Storing (Chicago: University of Chicago Press, 1981), 2:60.
43. Given Spooner's audacious insistence that the Constitution is completely antislavery, I would argue that he is much less successful at reconciling the competing impulses (and consequently less prudential and ethical) than advocates such as Lincoln, who were much more willing to concede the text's proslavery dimension.
44. Garver notes the way advocates "subordinat[e] . . . the Constitution to a theory or favored object of belief" (Garver, *For the Sake,* 163; see also Jack Balkin's discussion of "Ideal Constitutionalism" in "Agreements with Hell," 1709ff). Had Spooner done so by framing his argument solely in terms of natural law (in effect, pledging fidelity to natural law and not the Constitution), he would have been guilty of this ethical failure.
45. Spooner, *Unconstitutionality,* 117.
46. See Garver, *For the Sake,* 159.
47. *Congressional Globe,* 19 (1849-50), 31st Cong., 1st sess., Appendix, 1408.
48. Peter B. Knupfer, *The Union As It Is: Constitutional Unionism and Sectional Compromise, 1787–1861* (Chapel Hill: University of North Carolina Press, 1991). In *Dred Scott and the Problem of Constitutional Evil* (Cambridge: Cambridge University Press, 2006), Mark Graber argues that constitutional fidelity entailed a commitment to the framers' vision of bisectional compromise on the issue of slavery.
49. Balkin, "Agreements with Hell," 1723.
50. I'm not suggesting that Southerners "put all their eggs in one basket" and rely exclusively on constitutional protections. As Mark Graber argues, Southerners (incorrectly) expected that sectional population growth (along with the three-fifths clause) would provide them ample political power to protect slavery. As the free state population increased, and with it antislavery agitation, Southerners led by Calhoun increasingly positioned the Constitution as slavery's ultimate safeguard. See Graber, *Dred Scott and the Problem of Constitutional Evil,* esp. 137–140.
51. On the possibility that Southerners might agree to a Constitution that was potentially hostile to slavery, see Spooner, *Unconstitutionality,* 185–186. See also page

126 ("The Constitution [w]as destined to destroy slavery, whenever its principles should be carried into full effect").

52. Jacobus tenBroek, *The Antislavery Origins of the Fourteenth Amendment* (Berkeley: University of California Press, 1951); Cover, *Justice Accused,* 154–155 (Cover was skeptical of tenBroek's claims). On Graham and tenBroek's contribution to Marshall's strategy in *Brown,* see Richard Kluger, *Simple Justice: The History of Brown v. Board of Education and Black America's Struggle for Equality* (1975; reprint, New York: Vintage Books, 2004), 628–638.

    Noticing the ethical thread that runs from Spooner to Thurgood Marshall helps rectify an aspect of Garver's reading of *Brown.* Garver writes that "because history did not yield a satisfactory result, the Justices declared that it was ambiguous" (Garver, *For the Sake,* 76). It is worth noting that the Justices were *persuaded* that "the historical record [was] ambiguous" (ibid.). Lawyers for the school boards observed repeatedly that the same Congress that adopted the Fourteenth Amendment authorized segregated schools for the nation's capital. As Mark Tushnet explains: "What they [LDF lawyers] had to do . . . was neutralize whatever the defenders of segregation came up with, and hope that, as Marshall put it, the justices would see that a 'nothin' to nothin' score means that we win the ball game." Marshall was able to "tie the score" and "win the game" by capitalizing on Spooner's ethical surplus as it was transmuted in and through the Fourteenth Amendment. See Tushnet, *Making Civil Rights Law: Thurgood Marshall and the Supreme Court, 1936–1961* (New York: Oxford University Press, 1994), 196.

53. Garver, *For the Sake,* 158. Cf. Sanford Levinson, *Constitutional Faith* (Princeton: Princeton University Press, 1988), 192–193.

54. C. Peter Ripley, "Introduction to the American Series: Black Abolitionists in the United States, 1830–1865," in *The Black Abolitionist Papers,* 5 vols., ed. C. Peter Ripley (Chapel Hill: University of North Carolina Press, 1991), 3:50.

55. In *The Life and Writings of Frederick Douglass,* 4 vols., ed. Philip S. Foner (New York: International Publishers, 1950), 2:155–156. On Douglass's conversion, see also James A. Colaiaco, *Frederick Douglass and the Fourth of July* (New York: Palgrave Macmillan, 2006).

56. Jack Balkin corroborates the jeremiadic aspect of Douglass's constitutionalism when he notes that Douglass is "part of a tradition of oppressed groups attempting to hold the Nation responsible for its failed promises," and he directly connects Douglass and King, as do Dorothy E. Roberts and Mark Brandon. See Balkin, "Agreements with Hell," 1710n18, 1716n28; Dorothy E. Roberts, "The Meaning of

Blacks' Fidelity to the Constitution," *Fordham Law Review* 65 (1997): 1761–1771; Mark Brandon, *Free in the World*, 218–220. Both Brandon and Roberts extend their discussions of African American constitutionalism beyond King.

57. Garver, *For the Sake*, 169.
58. Ibid., 172–173.
59. Ibid., 168.
60. Ibid., 162–163, 173.
61. Ibid., 158.
62. Danielle Allen, *Talking to Strangers: Anxieties of Citizenship since* Brown v. Board of Education (Chicago: University of Chicago Press, 2004), 7.
63. Garver, *For the Sake*, 166.
64. But see Graber's critique of republican constitutionalism in *Dred Scott and the Problem of Constitutional Evil*, especially the final section, "Voting for John Bell."
65. David Donald, *Lincoln Reconsidered: Essays on the Civil War Era*, 2nd enlarged ed. (1956; New York: A. A. Knopf, 1966), 137–138.

Kind Persuasion: Lincoln's Temperance Address and the Ethos of Civic Friendship

Michael Leff

Writing to his friend Joshua Speed in March 1842, Lincoln implored both Speed and his wife to read his "Temperance speech . . . as an act of charity to me; for I can not learn that any body else has read it, or is likely to."[1] The sincerity of Lincoln's plea is hardly certain—we are, after all, dealing with the man who said that the world would little note nor long remember what he said at Gettysburg. But whether genuine or feigned, Lincoln's anxiety about finding readers proved to be unfounded. Herndon, in his biography, reported that the speech was "so often published" that he had no need to quote it in full, and that during a congressional campaign four years after its delivery, it was remembered well enough to be turned against Lincoln when his political opponents claimed that the address revealed an irreverent attitude toward religion and provided evidence that Lincoln was not truly a Christian.[2]

More than 160 years later, the speech is still read and still remains controversial. Whole brigades within the army of Lincolnologists have marched into, through, and around the text, and they have scouted and attacked it from almost every imaginable angle—political, philosophical, sociological, biographical, psychoanalytical, and, of course, rhetorical. The rhetorical efforts in this adventure are so numerous, and some of them so learned and incisive, that further study of the text seems unlikely to do more than rediscover yesterday's intelligence.[3] Nevertheless, as David Zarefsky is fond of saying, there are occasions when equally well-informed and well-meaning people disagree with one another, and this is certainly one of them, since differing interpretations and assessments of the speech are almost as numerous as those who have done the interpreting and assessing. It seems appropriate to reconsider the Temperance Address, not in order to find something that has escaped the attention of others, but to reevaluate what has already been noticed and to reconsider the agreements and disagreements about its significance. Before turning to this task of interpreting the text and its readers, however, I need to say something about the context.

The Washington Temperance Society of Springfield, Illinois

The speech was delivered before Springfield's Washington Temperance Society on the 110th anniversary of Washington's birth. The Washington Society was a very recent and somewhat controversial addition to the temperance movement, which itself did not then have a long history. The first major national temperance organization, the American Temperance Society (ATS), was founded in 1826, and it represented what Robert Abzug has called a "sea change in attitudes about drink."[4] The Washington Society shared many of the goals of that older organization, and there was some overlap in membership, but it also differed in a number of crucial respects.

The primary leaders of the ATS were evangelical clergy, such as Lyman Beecher, Justin Edwards, and Timothy Dwight Weld; the ATS attracted wealthy patrons and drew its membership almost exclusively from respectable, churchgoing middle-class citizens. Its main goal was not to reform drunkards but to protect the temperate from the lure of drink. Intemperance was regarded as a sin that threatened the material and moral well-being of the nation, and alcoholics tended to be viewed as incurably corrupt. Thus, as Justin Edwards argued, salvation from this demonic force must come by keeping temperate folk temperate and letting the drunkards gradually die off. "Let temperate men give up the use of strong drink, and the evil will very soon be done away, for who are now intemperate will soon die, and there will be none to fill their places."[5]

Originally, the ATS relied on moral suasion to achieve its goals, but by the late 1830s the organization began to support coercive measures through various types of prohibition legislation. In part, this shift arose from a reaction to the growing numbers of Irish and German immigrants who shared neither the worldview nor the attitude about drink that characterized the adherents of the temperance movement, and legal restraint seemed necessary as a means to control the behavior of a class that, by the lights of some ATS leaders, was unwilling or unable to control itself.

The Washington Society was a different kind of temperance organization. Founded only two years before Lincoln's speech in Springfield, it represented the first temperance group formed by what Ira Tyrrell calls "humble artisans," and its chief mission was curative rather than preventive or coercive.[6] The Washingtonians focused attention on the drinkers themselves. Their chief tactic was to call on reformed drinkers to persuade those still under the influence of alcohol to accept, achieve, and maintain abstinence, and to that end their meetings featured "experience speeches," in which reformed members of the society shared tales about their former affliction, their successful efforts to overcome it, and the great benefits that followed from their reformation. Directed primarily toward the working class, dedicated to the belief that intemperance was corrigible, and firmly committed to the strategy of moral suasion, the Washingtonians proved an immediate and enormous success. Within a year they had attracted more than 200,000 members, and by 1842 their presence in Springfield was great enough to sponsor a major event on Washington's Birthday that included a parade, a series of entertainments, and a speech by a notable young orator who attracted a packed house at the Second Presbyterian Church.[7]

Academic Receptions of Lincoln's Address

The speech that Lincoln delivered that day is short (occupying less than ten pages in the Library of America edition), organized in a well-demarcated linear pattern, and, for the most part, argued in clear and logical terms. Yet, it is also generally considered as "perhaps his most puzzling speech."[8] While scholars disagree about most other aspects of the text, they almost all find it unconventional, complex if not convoluted, and oblique in its purpose and meaning. The rationale for such judgments and the precise points where they apply are often matters of dispute, but at the least, a consensus exists that the ostensible subject of the speech does not correspond to Lincoln's real concern. For Susan Zaeske, it is as much, if not more, about slavery as about temperance.[9] Harry V. Jaffa agrees, but he also locates a much more encompassing motive behind the text. Despite its "formal" or "apparent" subject concerning the drinking problem, Jaffa holds that the real subject "is the difference between the right and wrong way of effecting any moral reform in society. More specifically, it is the difference between a temperate and intemperate approach to moral reform."[10] Lucas Morel makes a similar but more rhetorically oriented point when he maintains that despite its apparent focus on intemperance with regard to liquor, the speech "at bottom . . . is about temperance or moderation in speech—how citizens go about persuading one another on a given social or political issue."[11] Both Douglas Wilson and David Herbert Donald connect the speech to Lincoln's private life and his concerns about sustaining reason against the force of uncontrolled emotions.[12]

These perspectives seem to scatter in different directions, but on close inspection, they align with one another and offer a coherent, general frame for interpreting the text. The issues of slavery and temperance fit together for Lincoln as part of a multifaceted anxiety about the danger to self-controlled reason posed by unconstrained emotions. Lincoln, like many of his contemporaries, speaks of intemperance as a form of slavery because drinkers give way to their appetites, lose rational self-control, and become slaves to a passion. Drunkards, then, are slaves, but their plight is worse than a chattel slave because they are in bondage to their own irrational passion rather than to external coercion. Slavery, however, also entails an internal disruption of rational self-control, and this is a problem that attaches not to the slave but to the slaveholder, who exercises an absolute control over another human being and thus succumbs to a tyrannical passion for power and dominance. Viewed from this angle, the institution of slavery produces a kind of intemperance, and just as drunkards are slaves to their passion for alcohol, so are slaveholders slaves to their passion for power.

For Lincoln, the problem does not end with the conjoined evils of slavery and alcoholism, for an equally great danger arises from a morally driven, single-minded effort to eliminate them. Abolitionists and temperance reformers may become so passionately committed to their own moral imperatives that they speak and act out of a passionate, unrestrained commitment to their cause. Hence, the reformer, much like the sinner, fails to exercise self-control, and the reform effort may strain the bonds of civic fellowship necessary for rational deliberation and the proper conduct of a self-governing polity.

As these themes coalesce within the Temperance Address, we can detect a unified theme that connects with but transcends the more immediate subject and occasion. Lincoln articulates a global concept of temperance—one that encompasses the specific issues of the day but that also makes a general, philosophical argument for personal and political moderation—an ethical and political standard that asks citizens to exercise self-control both in private and public. Putting this in the terms of Zaeske's gendered politics, Lincoln joins the personal and the political as he simultaneously constructs a conception of citizenship and a conception of masculinity based on the virtues of self-restraint. Moreover, this conception emerges in and through the medium of oratorical performance, and so Lincoln is doing what he is saying as he says it. Consequently, we should expect the speech to enact and embody the virtues that it preaches and avoid the pitfalls that it condemns.

The internal consistency of the text and its fidelity to Lincoln's own principles and purposes is a matter of considerable disagreement among scholars. Opinions range from Jaffa's effusive praise of the speech as an exemplary demonstration of political leadership and a work of "surpassing brilliance" to the more restrained commendation offered by John Briggs, to the critical comments about its abrasive passages, its inconsistencies, and its gaps and silences.[13] As I have indicated earlier, the literature is so comprehensive that I doubt that any genuinely new appraisal is likely—at least not from someone devoted to a close reading of the text. Nevertheless, in light of the synthetic account of the purpose of the speech that I have just sketched, I do think it possible to work some variations on the existing interpretations and assessments. Attention to Lincoln's commitment to reason and restraint helps to highlight an aspect of the speech that has been noted but insufficiently explicated and emphasized, and that is the dialectical structure of its body. By the term "dialectical," I am referring to both senses of its use in argumentation studies—dialectic as oppositional and as dialogical. Lincoln's text, I hope to demonstrate, proceeds systematically through antithetically opposed sequences and proleptically imagined dissenting voices.

Dialectical Form and Function in Lincoln's Temperance Address

The introduction of the speech sets out, in rather grandiloquent terms, a contrast between the recent triumphs of the Washington Society and the slow progress made by earlier temperance efforts. Then, in the first of the two main arguments developed in the body of the text, Lincoln inquires into the "rational causes" for this recent success, and he does so through a dichotomously organized set of arguments, each involving a critique of methods used by earlier temperance exponents followed by a dialectically opposed characterization of how the Washingtonians go about their business.[14]

The first move in this development is Lincoln's claim that earlier efforts failed either because they did not have the right "champions" or because their tactics were "not the most proper." As for the champions, the older reformers used preachers, lawyers, and hired agents as their spokesmen, and they proved ineffective because of the lack of "approachability" between them and the people they addressed. These speakers were unlike their audience, and so their motives seemed suspect; they failed to convey a "sympathy of feeling or interest with those very persons whom" they wished to persuade (81). On the other hand, the reformed drinkers who represented the Washingtonians could establish an immediate and firm rapport with the audience, and no one could doubt their sincerity or their sympathy for those they "would persuade to imitate" their examples (82).

As for the tactics used, the older reformers engaged in "too much denunciation of dram-sellers and dram-drinkers," and this strategy was, in Lincoln's judgment, both impolitic and unjust. It was impolitic because human nature resisted being driven to anything, and when people were chastised for their bad conduct, accused as the "authors of all vices," and told that their houses were "the workshops of the devil," it was little wonder that they "were slow, very slow, to acknowledge the truth of such denunciations, and to join the ranks of their denouncers in a hue and cry against themselves" (82–83).

These critical remarks prompt Lincoln to offer his own constructive views about persuasion. In the most famous and often-quoted passage of the speech, he asserts:

> When the conduct of men is designed to be influenced, persuasion, kind unassuming persuasion should ever be adopted. It is an old and true maxim, that a "drop of honey catches more flies than a gallon of gall." So with men. If you would win a man to your cause, first convince him that you are his sincere friend. Therein is the drop of honey that catches his heart, which, say what he will, is the greatest highroad to his reason, and which, one when once gained, you will find but little trouble in convincing his judgment of the justice of your cause. (83)

By contrast, efforts to dictate or command the judgment have no more chance of winning over an auditor than a rye straw has of penetrating "the hard shell of a tortoise" (83).

The dialectical movement of the speech manifests itself here as an antithetical contrast between the older reformers' strategy of denunciation and alienation and Lincoln's "kind, unassuming persuasion," and the pattern is completed when Lincoln ends the section by associating the Washingtonians with the better, more effective approach. The Washingtonians, he says, treat their audiences as friends and companions and address them in kind, generous, and brotherly terms (83–84).

Following the plan he had outlined earlier, Lincoln next advances to the claim that the methods of older reformers are unjust. But before turning attention to that section of the text, I want to consider both the rhetoric and the rhetorical implications of Lincoln's distinction between politic and impolitic modes of address. The key to understanding this distinction, I believe, occurs when Lincoln refers to "kind, unassuming persuasion." In modern English, the adjective "kind" means friendly, generous, benevolent, or considerate. But John Briggs, who is a student of Renaissance literature, as well as of Lincoln's speeches, notes that Lincoln would have known the Shakespearean sense of the word, which also connotes mutuality.[15] In this sense, "kind" as adjective shows its affinity with the noun "kind," whose primary meaning refers to a class or type, including kindred relationships among people. By kind persuasion, then, Lincoln means not only friendly or considerate discourse but also discourse that recognizes a mutual relationship linking speaker and audience and affirms friendship between members of the same community. This is a relationship of like to like, and it stands in stark, dialectical opposition to the social and moral distance that the older reformers express and enact in their discourse about the intemperate. Moreover, the point Lincoln makes about their tactics applies equally well to his remarks about the "champions" of the temperance cause. The older reformers are unpersuasive because they are "unapproachable," which is to say that they are unlike the people they seek to reform.

This concern for the relationship between speaker and auditor indicates an interest in what the classical rhetoricians call ethos, or proof drawn from the character of the speaker. The connection to the classical concept is strengthened when we recall the three dimensions of ethos that Aristotle lists in his *Rhetoric*—phronesis (prudence or practical wisdom), arête (virtue), and eunoia (goodwill).[16] It is the last of these that Lincoln stresses, because goodwill, whether in Aristotle or in modern usage, depends upon the demonstration of mutual interests and fellow-feeling. Goodwill is attributed to those who are like us, who share our commitments and see things from the same perspective. For Lincoln, such goodwill is connected with rational restraints on the tendency to alienate ourselves from others by yielding to self-interested preoccupations or pursuing exclusionary moral passions.

Nevertheless, Lincoln does not ignore or discount the force of passion. In his account of "kind persuasion," the first task is to persuade someone that you are a "sincere friend" and that becomes the "drop of honey that catches his heart" and provides the "highroad to his reason." The process, then, uses ethos to evoke an emotional response that opens the way to reason, and the exercise of friendship toward the intemperate becomes a vehicle to recall them from destructive passion to self-controlled reason through the force of constructive emotional appeals—a rhetorical choreography that steps from ethos to pathos to logos. Consequently, enfolded within the dialectical structure of Lincoln's text and running parallel to his search for rational causes of persuasive success, we find due consideration of character and emotion as effective instruments of persuasion and legitimate constituents of civic harmony.

One of the criticisms frequently made about the Temperance speech (as well as Lincoln's earlier Lyceum speech) is that, in effect, a performative contradiction exists between Lincoln's strong commitment to reason and his passionate outbursts in support of it. Thus, while the Temperance speech repeatedly extols the primacy of reason, the importance of rational inquiry, and the need for the exercise of rational self-control over the emotions, the peroration gushes with an unrestrained flow of hyperbolic and passionate sentiment about the coming reign of reason. Lincoln imagines the realization of temperance as the day "every son of earth shall drink, in full fruition, the sorrow quenching draughts of perfect liberty. Happy day, when all appetites controlled, all passions subdued, all matter subjected, mind, all consuming mind shall live and move the monarch of the world. Glorious consummation! Hail fall of Fury! Reign of Reason, all hail!" (89–90). This finale does seem strangely passionate in its celebration of the conquest of passion by reason, and Douglas Wilson judges it as a "telling disjunction between the medium and the message."[17]

Jaffa and Morel have attempted to explain the discrepancy by treating the peroration as ironic, as a parody of temperance rhetoric designed to reveal its flaws. This effort, however, entails a tortuously complex and optimistically benign reading of the text, and, like Wilson, I am skeptical about it.[18] Moreover, a better, though perhaps only partial, explanation follows from Brigg's understanding of "kind persuasion" and the role that mutual sentiment plays in establishing a highway to reason through the emotions. From this perspective, reason is not self-sufficient or self-standing, since its operation depends on and entails volitional and ethotic consideration, and so "not all passions are bad. Sympathy and friendship are good passions informed by reason, and they support reason in turn to help the drinker return to sobriety."[19] While this thesis still does not fully excuse the bathos of the peroration, it does indicate how Lincoln shifts from and improves upon the single-minded attention to reason displayed in the Lyceum speech, and it offers a basis for reconciling and rounding out important political and rhetorical dimensions of the Temperance speech. Reason and rational restraint develop within an atmosphere of mutuality and civic friendship, and "kind persuasion" provides both the medium and the means for sustaining this atmosphere and for correcting those who stray in an irrational direction. Stated abstractly in these terms, Lincoln's position seems balanced and coherent, but in both theory and rhetorical performance it encounters serious problems. To understand what they are, we need to return to the text and read on.

Lincoln's second objection to the older temperance movement is that its tactics are unjust, and he adduces three reasons to support this claim. First, he observes that the use of intoxicating liquor had been universally accepted through all human memory up to the previous twenty years, when, for the first time, serious objection to it had surfaced. It is no surprise, therefore, that some have been slow to join the temperance cause, and it is unjust, Lincoln believes, to denounce and assail those who are slow to reject a view that has enjoyed such universal favor for so long a time (84–85). Secondly, the older reformers wrongly take the position that "all habitual drunkards" are "utterly incorrigible" (85). Third and finally (in an argument that seems somewhat out of place) Lincoln criticizes these reformers because they look to benefits that are too remote in time to generate current support among the people (85–86). Against these older views, Lincoln, consistent with the dialectical scheme of the text, favorably contrasts the practices of the Washingtonians and concludes the section by reiterating their success in advancing the temperance cause (86–87).

For present purposes, the second of Lincoln's points is most important, and I want to call special attention to the tone of his remarks. He explains that by dismissing the drunkard as beyond redemption, the old reformers propose to set these people "adrift," and damn "them without remedy," and to rest content with the view that the benefits of temperance should accrue only to the already temperate. For Lincoln, these attitudes are "repugnant to humanity," "cold blooded and feelingless," and he who teaches such a doctrine cannot be loved or heard with patience. No generous man can adopt such a position, since it looks "fiendishly selfish, so like throwing fathers and brothers overboard, to lighten the boat for our security," and the noble-minded shrink "from the manifest meanness of the thing."

The language of this passage is unforgiving, harsh, and apparently incompatible with the "kind, unassuming persuasion" that Lincoln had just endorsed. There is no drop of honey, no sign of friendship or mutuality, and no effort to touch the hearts of the older reformers so as to open the highway to reason. In fact, Lincoln seems to denounce the older reformers with much the same kind of rhetoric that he had attacked them for using against the habitual drunkard, and in condemning these reformers for treating others as incorrigible, he treats the reformers themselves as incorrigible. This is a puzzling development.

Jaffa attempts to rescue Lincoln from inconsistency by suggesting that we can distinguish two different classes of incorrigibles. The first, which includes intemperate drinkers, are potential friends and thus open to friendly persuasion. The second, which includes the older reformers, are enemies of both the intemperate drinker and the genuinely temperate advocates of civic friendship and thus are potential friends to neither and not open to friendly persuasion.[20] This interpretative move has some merit, but even if we accept it as reason to deny that Lincoln is inconsistent, it raises other and perhaps even more difficult problems. To explain these problems adequately, however, we need to move forward in the text and follow the second major argument that Lincoln makes in the body of his speech.

This second argument attempts to prove that those who have never overindulged have a significant role to play in the temperance movement. Lincoln introduces the issue by raising and then responding to an objection: "But, if it is true, as I have insisted that those who have suffered personally, and have reformed, are the most powerful and efficient instrument to push the reformation to ultimate success, it does not follow, that those who have not suffered, have no part left them to perform" (87). Lincoln then moves through a series of objections, each introduced by the adversative "but" and attributed to some indefinite person or group and followed by a counterargument. The three objections are the following: (1) "But, says one, 'what good can I do by signing the pledge? I never drink even without signing.'" (2) "But it is said by some, that men will think and act for themselves; that none will disuse spirits or anything else, merely because his neighbors do." (3) But, some say, "'we are no drunkards; and we shall not acknowledge ourselves such by joining a reformed drunkard's society'" (87–88). The argument, then, is organized through the figure of prolepsis, and in the sequence of objections and responses, the text retains the dialectical orientation exhibited in the first main argument.

But there is a significant difference in the dialectical modality. In the first section, the argument is represented as a disagreement between two actually existing and well-known organizations, with Lincoln intervening to support of one of them. Of course, he has some liberty in how he represents the grounds and the content of the dispute, but the differences between the two sides existed before Lincoln's representation, are understood by many in his audience, and are malleable only within the limits of public knowledge. Hence, in this instance, Lincoln deals with ideas and policies and does not appear to engage in a direct exchange with another party. For this reason, the dialectical exercise emphasizes opposition rather than dialogue, and the text displays only a remote connection to a voiced exchange of differing positions. In the second argument, however, the use of prolepsis allows Lincoln to construct specific objections that punctuate and interrupt the flow of his own discourse, and even though these objections are attributed to no one in particular, they do assume some characteristics of another voice (indeed, in two of the three objections what "some say" is set off in quotation marks). Thus, the text creates the fiction of a back-and-forth dialogue between Lincoln and an interlocutor. Moreover, since the other party is not a person or group with known attitudes and beliefs, Lincoln is free to choose issues and express them in terms that suit his purposes. He can construct the "other" and guide the dialogue as he pleases.

The strategy of raising objections through an imagined interlocutor offers a useful instrument for setting the tone and parameters of a dispute.

Among other things, it can manage the interplay of arguments so as to intensify or relax the tension between opposing positions, and within the frame of the rhetoric of civic friendship we would expect speakers to construct objections in a way that encouraged discovery of common interests and an amicable resolution of differences. In many of his speeches, Lincoln displays great artistic skill in pursuing this possibility, not only by using prolepsis, but also by the related figure of *correctio,* where instead of attributing an objection to another person and then answering, Lincoln makes the case for one side of an issue and then reverses direction by correcting his original position.[21]

The Lyceum speech provides a striking example of this figurative strategy. One of Lincoln's main concerns is to show that the preservation of the nation's political institutions is at hazard because of what he calls a "mobocratic spirit." As instances of this problem, he cites lynchings that occurred in Mississippi and St. Louis and vividly describes their terrible consequences. But he then imagines that his audience asks what these events have to do with the preservation of our institutions, and he gives two answers based on the direct and remote consequences of these actions. In respect to direct consequences, the lynchings are not a great evil since they involved people who deserved punishment, but (as a correction for this first response) the long-term consequences are fearful since they endorse and encourage a spirit of lawless behavior and undermine respect for the law, which is the bedrock of the nation's political system. Each part of this sequence is developed at some length and in plausible or vivid terms, and the result is that the audience is led from revulsion against the acts, to a point where they might find them acceptable, and, finally, from a higher plane of understanding to condemnation of them through reasoned consideration of their significance. The unrestrained passions that would justify lynching or produce a hasty emotional reaction against it are encompassed within a unifying frame of reference.[22]

The Possibilities and Limits of Civic Friendship

In his two rhetorical masterpieces, the Gettysburg Address and the Second Inaugural, Lincoln uses the implied internal dialogue of *correctio* with great effectiveness. At Gettysburg, Lincoln observes that the dedication of the battlefield to those who have given their lives there is "altogether fitting and proper," and then in the next sentence he corrects himself: "But, in a larger sense we can not dedicate—we can not consecrate—we can not hallow this ground."[23] The shift here initiates a movement from the narrower, more conventional epideictic purpose of memorializing the dead to the broader, less conventional purpose of dedicating the living to fulfill the nation's ideals. Abstractly considered, the two purposes might appear distinct if not antithetical (i.e., as a contrast between the living and the dead), but Lincoln folds the first into the second as he voices his own hesitation and synthesizes both within the rising movement of his thought.

A more complex example of the same strategy appears in the middle of the Second Inaugural. Casting his thoughts back to the origin of the Civil War, Lincoln declares the following:

> Neither party expected for the war, the magnitude, or the duration, which it has already attained. Neither anticipated that the *cause* of the conflict might cease with, or even before, the conflict itself should cease. Each looked for an easier triumph and a result less fundamental and astounding. Both read the same Bible, and pray to the same God; and each invokes His aid against the other. It may seem strange that any men should dare to ask a just God's assistance in wringing their bread from the sweat of other men's faces; but let us judge not that we be not judged. The prayers of both could not be answered; that of neither has been answered fully. The Almighty has His own purposes.[24]

In this remarkable passage, Lincoln gathers, separates, and finally regathers the warring parties, and just as he verges toward placing blame on the Southern enemy, he pulls back from the curse of Genesis 3:19 with a correction from the Sermon on the Mount (Matt. 7:1). Amidst the stress of war, Lincoln identifies a common link between opponents and recognizes a higher purpose governing both of them. Within the parliament of his own rhetorical voice, the partisan dialectic of faction is countered and overcome by an irenic synthesis.

These three examples illustrate how dialogic figures can promote the objectives of civic friendship. But the prolepsis in the Temperance speech does not work toward the same end. As Lincoln comes to the third and final objection to his appeal to the temperate to join with the Washingtonians, he argues that those who refuse to sully themselves by associating with reformed drunkards are not acting consistently with their own values:

> Surely no Christian will adhere to this objection. If they believe, as they profess, that Omnipotence condescended to take on himself the form of sinful man, and as such, to die an ignominious death for their sakes, surely they will not refuse submission to the infinitely lesser condensation, for the temporal, and perhaps eternal salvation, of a large, erring, and unfortunate class of their own fellow creatures. (88)

This language, John Briggs comments, tests "the border between persuasion and sarcasm."[25] As in Lincoln's assessment of the justice of the old reformers' tactics, he once again does not speak as a friend but as a severe critic; he denounces rather than conciliates, and this response is more or less what Lincoln described as the reaction to older reformers' accusations and anathemas. As Herndon reported, the passage offended the church members in the audience and proved damaging to Lincoln's reputation for some time to come.[26]

All told, then, the dialogic and dialectical tactics of the Temperance speech engineered a significant element of hostility into the text and strained against Lincoln's professed commitment to "kind, unassuming persuasion." Yet, as just noted, the same tactics had often worked most effectively for him as instruments for surmounting oppositions and promoting rhetorical harmony. Why was this speech different?

The answer may rest in some incidental event in Lincoln's biography, or an accident connected with the occasion, or a simple lapse in his rhetorical judgment. But there might also be something more fundamental involved, something that reveals a limitation on the range and efficacy of the rhetoric of civic friendship. If friendship becomes the dominant metaphor for public deliberation, then its success depends on a commitment to the social resolution of differences. Where disagreement exists, matters are to be settled through the exercise of "kind persuasion" and require goodwill on the part of opposing rhetors and between rhetors and audiences. And it also entails a willingness to abide in friendship despite difference, to accept compromise to maintain solidarity, and to restrain the moral and emotional impulses of the individual for the sake of the public good. Among other things, this implicates conceptions of the good within notions of what is politically feasible—that is, the good is, to some extent, determined by the possibilities existing in the motile, pluralistic world of public deliberation.

This commitment to fellow-feeling, however, refers to only one constituent of character and opens only one way of conceiving the good. Another aspect of character is what Aristotle calls *arête*, virtue, and if we translate virtue from its classical Greek context into the environment of the Protestant evangelic world of modern America, then virtue may stand at cross-purposes with goodwill. Those who find truth solely by examining their conscience and who define virtue as believing and doing what conscience tells them is right will not settle for a social resolution to the things that really matter to them. If slavery is a sin, then contrary views are not just different but morally corrupt, and it is neither desirable nor possible to exercise goodwill toward those who hold these views. If strong drink and drunkenness are demons that undermine morality and decency, then liquor must be prohibited and drunks abandoned to their own depravity. What is at stake is righteousness and not solidarity; virtue is not and cannot be negotiated through deliberation, and the wavering sentimentality of fellow-feeling offers neither a path to nor a substitute for rectitude. Righteousness is not temperate.

It is in this sense that Jaffa can explain why Lincoln is not inconsistent when he resorts to denunciation rather than persuasion in dealing with the morally intemperate followers of the temperance movement. Appeals to fellow-feeling are not in order when a rhetoric confronts those who scorn the ethical value of social solidarity and insist upon achieving the absolute right without regard for what is ethically feasible. Within the terms of civic friendship, such people are incorrigible and thus not just opponents but enemies.

But if Lincoln is not inconsistent in defining and denouncing such people as enemies, he does become ensnared in a very uncomfortable dilemma. When he recognizes intemperate moralists as enemies to civic friendship, he can no longer engage them through the methods of his own choosing. To combat an enemy, he must speak like the enemy and transform himself rhetorically into the enemy he seeks to defeat. Little wonder, then, that the Temperance Address is such a puzzling text. Lincoln must resort to an idiom he dislikes and forces himself into rhetorical dilemmas he cannot surmount through his own ameliorative rhetoric of civic friendship. Thus despite the depth of its reflections about persuasion and the precision of its dialectical method, his speech angered much of his contemporary audience and confused later generations of readers. Yet, it is not fair to end on such a negative note. Something must be said in Lincoln's defense considering the difficulty of his problem. The dilemma Lincoln faced has a long and rather nasty history, and it has never yielded to a simple or permanent resolution. It still survives today and still evades disarmament by the friendly rhetoricians who hope to justify and practice an irenic version of their art.

NOTES

1. Abraham Lincoln, *Speeches and Writings 1832–1858,* ed. Don E. Fehrenbacher (New York: Library of America, 1989), 93.
2. William H. Herndon and Jesse W. Weik, *Herndon's Life of Lincoln* (New York: Da Capo Press, 1942), 206–207, 218.
3. The most detailed analysis of the speech is in Henry V. Jaffa, *Crisis in the House Divided: An Interpretation of the Issues in the Lincoln-Douglas Debates* (Chicago: University of Chicago Press, 1982), 236–274; Lucas E. Morel, "Lincoln among the Reformers: Tempering the Temperance Movement," *Journal of the Abraham Lincoln Association* 20 (1999): 1–34, generally follows Jaffa but adds useful information about the context; John Briggs, *Lincoln's Speeches Reconsidered* (Baltimore: Johns Hopkins University Press, 2005), 58–81, offers a detailed alternative reading; Susan Zaeske, "'The South Arose as One Man': Gender and Sectionalism in Antislavery Petition Debates, 1835–1845," *Rhetoric and Public Affairs* 12 (2009): 341–368, provides a fresh analysis of the text based on her interest in gender and race; Douglas L. Wilson, *Honor's Voice: The Transformation of Abraham Lincoln* (New York: Vintage Books, 1998), 259–262, provides a useful short summary and analysis of the speech.
4. Robert Abzug, *Cosmos Crumbling: American Reform and the Religious Imagination*

(New York: Oxford University Press, 1994), 81.

5. Ibid., 91.
6. Ian Tyrell, *Sobering Up: From Temperance to Prohibition in Antebellum America, 1800–1860* (Westport, CT: Greenwood Press, 1979), 159.
7. Abzug, *Cosmos Crumbling*, 103 (regarding the history of temperance movement in this period, see pp. 81–94); Tyrell, *Sobering Up*; John S. Blocker Jr., *The American Temperance Movement: Cycles of Reform* (Boston: Twayne Publishers, 1989), 1–60; and Bruce Dorsey, *Reforming Men and Women: Gender in the Antebellum City* (Ithaca: Cornell University Press, 2002), 90–135. Details about the circumstances surrounding the speech are found in Herndon and Weik, *Herndon's Life of Lincoln*, 206–207, and Albert J. Beveridge, *Abraham Lincoln, 1809–1858*, 2 vols. (Cambridge, MA: Riverside Press, 1928), 135.
8. Morel, "Lincoln among the Reformers," 2.
9. Zaeske, "The South Arose as One Man."
10. Jaffa, *Crisis in the House Divided*, 247.
11. Morel, "Lincoln among the Reformers," 4.
12. Wilson, *Honor's Voice*, 31; David Herbert Donald, *Lincoln* (New York: Simon & Schuster, 1995), 82–83.
13. Jaffa, *Crisis in the House Divided*, 249, 272; Briggs, *Lincoln's Speeches Reconsidered*, 81; Zaeske, "The South Arose as One Man"; Douglas L. Wilson, "Young Man Lincoln," in *The Lincoln Enigma: The Changing Faces of an American Icon*, ed. Gabor Boritt (New York: Oxford University Press, 2001), 30–31.
14. All references to the text of the Temperance speech are to the Library of America edition of his works, Lincoln, *Speeches and Writings, 1832–1858*.
15. Briggs, *Lincoln's Speeches Reconsidered*, 64.
16. Aristotle, *On Rhetoric*, trans. George A. Kennedy (New York: Oxford University Press, 1991), 2.1
17. Wilson, "Young Man Lincoln," 31.
18. I take it that when Wilson writes that the peroration has "no apparent sense of irony" that he is implicitly dissenting from Jaffa's interpretation (Wilson, "Young Man Lincoln," 31).
19. Briggs, *Lincoln's Speeches Reconsidered*, 76.
20. Jaffa, *Crisis in the House Divided*, 258–263.
21. Michael Leff and Jean Goodwin, "Dialogic Figures and Dialectical Argument in Lincoln's Rhetoric," *Rhetoric and Public Affairs* 3 (2000): 59–69.
22. Lincoln, *Speeches and Writings, 1832–1858*, 29–32.

23. Abraham Lincoln, *Speeches and Writings, 1859–1865*, ed. Don E. Fehernbacher (New York: Library of America, 1989), 537.
24. Ibid., 686–687.
25. Briggs, *Lincoln's Speeches Reconsidered*, 67.
26. Herndon and Weik, *Herndon's Life of Lincoln*, 206–207.

Andrew Johnson's Fight for States' Rights on the Battlements of the Constitution

Karlyn Kohrs Campbell

The extension of civil rights to minorities and women has always been closely linked to differing interpretations of the Constitution by the public, state governments, members of Congress, and the U.S. Supreme Court. That interpretive relationship is central to understanding the role that Andrew Johnson played, first in the Senate and then as president, and to differentiating his views from those of Abraham Lincoln. Johnson was a Southern Democrat who adhered strongly to a states' rights understanding of the Constitution and who based his opposition to all measures to ensure the equal treatment of former slaves on his understanding of the proper and limited role of the federal government. By contrast, in his July 4, 1861, message to a special session of Congress, Lincoln argued that the war was

> a people's contest. On the side of the Union, it is a struggle for maintaining in the world, that form and substance of government, whose leading

> object is to elevate the condition of men—to lift artificial weights from all shoulders—to clear the paths of laudable pursuit for all—to afford all an even start, and a fair chance, in the race of life.[1]

This understanding of the war would be central to his later address at Gettysburg. Because of Lincoln's assassination, Johnson used his understanding of the Constitution to forestall the efforts of Republicans in Congress to pursue policies consistent with Lincoln's views of the purpose of the war. The political conflict between Johnson and the Congress in the aftermath of the war persists in the present as a struggle over the extent to which the principles enunciated in the Declaration of Independence are to be understood as informing the provisions of the Constitution.

As I shall attempt to demonstrate, Andrew Johnson never deviated from the positions he first espoused in 1860 in the Senate, and his discourse as president consistently reflected his reading of the Constitution, a reading to which he adhered without regard to the altered conditions created by the war or efforts by the Congress to respond to the conditions facing newly freed slaves. Accordingly, Johnson's rhetoric is an early example of conservative views of federal power and states' rights, views that have reemerged in contemporary political discourse.

Contemporary historians and political scientists rank Andrew Johnson as among our most ineffective presidents. As biographer Hans L. Trefousse notes, however, assessments of him have varied greatly: "From early adulation to speedy castigation, from renewed rehabilitation to resurgent accusation, the reputation of the seventeenth president has fluctuated with the passing of time."[2] Johnson, a slave owner and Southern Democrat, became the vice presidential candidate on the Union Party ticket in 1864 under unusual circumstances, replacing the current vice president, Maine abolitionist and former Senator Hannibal Hamlin, chiefly because of speeches he made in the Senate opposing secession and because of his performance over three years (1862–1865) under extraordinarily difficult conditions as military governor of Tennessee.

Congressional and press reactions to Johnson's remarks during his 1866 "swing around the circle," including their use as an article of impeachment, have created a false impression of the president's rhetorical ability. Indeed, as Gregg Phifer has argued, Johnson's speeches during that campaign had much to commend them, despite some intemperate remarks responding to hecklers.[3] Here I focus on the address he made in the Senate on December 18 and 19, 1860, his veto messages, and his farewell address. The speeches that Johnson delivered in the Senate opposing secession made him the iconic Southern Unionist. There are many reasons for Johnson's problems as president, but his intransigence over reconstruction policies as enunciated in his veto messages helps to explain the deterioration of his relationship with the Congress. His fighting farewell address is important rhetorically as a clear and summative statement of his understanding of the Constitution and of his role in Reconstruction. Incidentally, Johnson stands alone in having a major speech—his farewell—omitted from the *Messages and Papers of the President*.[4]

Andrew Jackson Johnson, who ascended to the presidency on April 15, 1865, was born on December 29, 1808, in Raleigh, North Carolina. When Jackson was three, his father died; at age ten he was indentured to a tailor until he came of age, which included basic instruction in reading and writing. Public-spirited citizens read aloud to the young tailors. Johnson reportedly so cherished selections from the *Columbian Orator* that a copy was given to him as a gift. In 1824, to escape indenture, he ran away to Tennessee, settled in Greeneville, and married Eliza McCardle, daughter of a local shoemaker. His tailoring shop thrived, and his political career began with a public debate on President Jackson's Indian removal policy.

No man seemed better prepared for the presidency, suggesting that extensive political experience at many levels of government may not predict skillful presidential leadership. Starting in 1829, he began a thirty-year career in politics as an alderman, mayor, state assemblyman, presidential elector, state senator, U.S. representative and senator, Tennessee governor, military governor of Tennessee, and vice president and president. After his presidency, he returned to the U.S. Senate, where he served briefly until his death. His life is the story of the rise of a man of humble beginnings to political office at all levels of government, achievements directly related to his rhetorical skills. His conflict with the Congress while president, his impeachment, and his near removal from office, which failed by only one vote, provoke a question that biographer Trefousse poses this way:

> How was it that a statesman who experienced a spectacular rise from homeless newcomer to governor and senator, a political leader who succeeded in routing not only the powerful organizers of the opposing party but also the numerous antagonists in his own, a general who ruled with an iron hand as military governor of Tennessee, could be so seemingly inept in carrying out the functions of the president of the United States?[5]

Eric McKitrick lists a number of works on Andrew Johnson and Reconstruction that began appearing in the 1960s and comments: "In all these studies, despite the variation in focus, Andrew Johnson's refusal to cooperate with Congress is held fully responsible for the federal government's failure to work out an orderly program of Reconstruction."[6]

The Speeches that Made Him President

Andrew Johnson became a vice presidential candidate when the war was going badly, and Lincoln feared he might not be reelected. Accordingly, Republicans offered a Union Party ticket that included Southern Democrat and slave owner Andrew Johnson of Tennessee.[7] Johnson was an obvious choice because of his unswerving commitment to the Union and because he was the sole Southerner to remain in the Senate after eleven states, including his own, had passed ordinances of secession.[8] His opposition to secession and his commitment to the Union and the Constitution were developed at length in Senate speeches following Lincoln's election but prior to his inauguration.[9] When he spoke on December 18 and 19, no state had yet seceded, although South Carolina had withdrawn its representatives from Congress; a day later on December 20, South Carolina passed an ordinance of secession. Ostensibly, Johnson's speech was in support of three constitutional amendments: the first for presidential elections by districts rather than states, including a provision ensuring that presidents representing slave and free states would alternate every four years; the second for direct election of senators; the third setting terms for Supreme Court justices, with vacancies to be filled half from slave states and half from free states. Johnson claimed that if these had been in force, the difficulties the country now faced would have been averted. Obviously, these amendments would have protected the dominant position of the South in the federal government.[10] Johnson's speech, however, was a carefully developed brief against secession; indeed, the case was so well made that it is hard to imagine how those who urged disunion could have believed that their actions could avert war or preserve slavery.

Johnson's speech targeted fellow Southerners, and his thesis was that the sectional conflict should be fought "inside of the Union and on the battlements of the Constitution" (80). He attacked the North for committing acts of disunion; he pointed to Northern states that had passed personal-liberty laws forbidding state lawmen from participating in the return of fugitive slaves or refused to enforce the fugitive-slave law, both of which violated the Constitution, and, in so doing, he argued, those states effectively had seceded.[11] He offered his three amendments as the *constitutional* way to right wrongs. He argued that black Republicanism could be resisted more effectively within the Union than outside it.

Johnson began with familiar arguments, including those made by President Buchanan in his last annual message—to wit, that there was no legal basis for secession—but, unlike Buchanan, Johnson did not base his claims solely on the Articles of Confederation and the U.S. Constitution. Instead, in detailed refutation, he examined the Virginia resolutions of 1798 and 1799, which were being used by secessionists to justify their proposed actions, refuting their use by citing Madison's report in which Madison rejected the idea that "a State has the right to judge of an infraction of the Constitution or any grievance, and, upon its own volition, withdraw from the Confederacy" (87). He also quoted letters in which Madison reaffirmed that position. Specifically, when New York sought admission to the Union with certain reservations or conditions, Madison rejected that request emphatically, writing that "the Constitution requires an adoption *in toto* and *forever*" (92). Johnson concluded, "If the States have the right to secede at will and pleasure, for real or imaginary evils or oppressions, I repeat again, this Government is at an end" (94). He buttressed his interpretive claims with statements from such authorities as Thomas Jefferson (102–103), John Marshall (105–106), Daniel Webster (107), and President Andrew Jackson's 1833 Nullification Proclamation (108–112).

Johnson's second argument addressed the question of what action the federal government could take if a state passed an ordinance of secession. He conceded that, based on the Eleventh Amendment, the federal government did not have the power to coerce a *state*; however, he added, "this Government has the right to pass laws, and to enforce those laws upon individuals within the limits of each State" (95). He was evenhanded in his condemnations, but he held that unconstitutional acts by nonslaveholding states did not justify secession by slaveholding states. "Let us stand in the Union and upon the Constitution," he urged (96). Using a Northern example, he maintained that should Vermont

> resist or attempt to resist the execution of the laws of the United States, it would be a practical rebellion, an overt act; and this Government has the authority under the Constitution to enforce the laws of the United States, and it has the authority to call to its aid such means as are deemed necessary and proper for the execution of the laws, even if it were to lead to the calling out of the militia, or calling into service the Army and Navy of the US to execute the laws. (99)

In other words, acts of disunion warranted a military response by the federal government, a claim he illustrated with a powerful precedent, Washington's response to the Whiskey Rebellion in Pennsylvania, underscored by an extended quotation from Washington's annual message reaffirming federal power to enforce laws on individuals, by force if necessary (115–116). He also recalled President Jackson's 1833 response to South Carolina's efforts to nullify a federal law.

Turning to the present, Johnson asked, "Have we no authority or power to execute the law in the State of South Carolina as well as in Vermont and Pennsylvania?" (120). He responded by enumerating specifics:

> If South Carolina undertakes to drive the Federal courts out of the state, the Federal Government has the right to hold those courts there. She may attempt to exclude the mails, yet the Federal Government has the right to establish post-offices and post-roads and to carry the mails there. . . . She may undertake to take possession of the property belonging to the government which was originally ceded by the State, but the Federal Government has the right to provide means for retaining possession of that property. (120–121)

He cited the terms under which that state had joined the Union—to wit, that South Carolina had "granted all the right, title, and claim of the State to all lands reserved for Fort Moultrie, on Sullivan's Island" and the lands of Fort Johnson, Fort Pinckney, and much more, "a clear deed of cession" (121–122), an argument with direct application to later events at Fort Sumter. He asked whether by "attempting to dispossess the Federal Government from its own property, does she not. . . . put herself within the meaning of the Constitution, in the attitude of levying war against the United States?" (122) and "is not levying war upon the United States treason?" (123).

Johnson now imitated tactics used by Daniel Webster in his reply to Robert Y. Hayne during the nullification crisis of 1833, enumerating the implications of acts of disunion. If South Carolina seceded, it would become a foreign country, and the Monroe Doctrine, issued on December 2, 1823, which permitted no European power to plant colonies on this continent, would come into force. Suppose, then, that South Carolina allied itself with one or more of the principal powers of Europe, which then established a great naval station and an army rendezvous point whose intent appeared to threaten the rest of the states; would the Senate, would the country, permit it? (125). Indeed, a former governor of South Carolina already had proposed such an alliance (140).

Johnson extended this argument to states that joined the Union as a result of the federal government's power to acquire territory. He used the recent example of the Mexican War (1846–1848), noting the loss of life, the payment of $15 million for the territory acquired, and the $120 million cost of the war, money provided by taxes levied on the whole nation. Subsequently, California formed itself into an independent state and was admitted to the Union. After such costs in lives and money, he asked, "Is it not absurd to say, that, now that California is in, she, on her own volition,—without regard to the consideration paid for her, without regard to the policy which dictated her acquisition by the United States,—can walk out and bid you defiance?" (127). He applied this argument to the costs of acquiring Texas, Louisiana, and Florida. In the case of Louisiana, free navigation of the Mississippi River also was at issue, of special significance to his home state of Tennessee, whose 1796 Bill of Rights stated that "equal participation in the free navigation of the Mississippi is one of the inherent rights of the citizens of the State" (130). In the case of Florida, he pointed to the threatening possibility of its reattachment to Spain or the return of control to the Seminole Indians.

Next, Johnson turned to the issue of slavery, to whether secession was the best policy to protect it, and he made a rather startling but prescient claim:

> I believe the continuance of slavery depends upon the preservation of the Union, and a compliance with all the guaranties of the Constitution. . . . I believe that dissolution of the Union will, in the end, though it may be some time to come, overthrow the institution of slavery. Hence we find so many in the North who desire the dissolution of these States as the most certain and direct and effectual means of overthrowing the institution of slavery. (148)

He explained the logic of his position. Addressing Southerners as a Southerner, he asked, "Why should we go out of the Union? Have we anything to fear?" (164). He reminded them of the 1857 Supreme Court decision in the *Dred Scott* case, which protected property in slaves in the territories, and pointed out, "You were told that you had all the protection needed, that the courts had decided in your behalf under the Constitution; and that, under the decisions of the courts, the law must be executed" (165), a conclusion that had been affirmed by an overwhelming vote in the Senate that he now addressed (166).[12] In other words, the question of slavery in the territories had been settled. Given the Supreme Court decision, he asked, what are the true grievances of South Carolina or others? Although Southern States had "just cause of complaint," he said, "we are for remaining in the Union and fighting the battle like men." That such efforts might have been successful is attested by the compromise proposals offered in the House and Senate, including constitutional amendments guaranteeing slavery where it now existed in perpetuity.[13] Johnson posed questions to prompt reconsideration:

> Why should we retreat? Because Mr. Lincoln has been elected President of the United States? . . . Does not every Senator or otherwise know that if Mr. Breckinridge had been elected we should not be to-day

> for dissolving the Union? Then what is the issue? Is it because we have not got our man? (168)

He pressed those contemplating secession to admit that Lincoln's election was merely an excuse for disunion; preservation of slavery was the real issue.

Finally, Johnson made a shrewd assessment of what Lincoln's election actually meant, claiming that the newly elected president posed no threat to Southerners. Speaking as a Southerner, he said:

> [I] want to put down Mr. Lincoln and drive back his advances upon Southern institutions, if he designs to make any. Have we not got the power? We have. Let South Carolina send her Senators back; let all the Senators come; and on the fourth of March next we shall have a majority of six in this body against him. This successful sectional candidate, who is in a minority of a million, or nearly so, on the popular vote, cannot make his Cabinet on the fourth of March next, unless the Senate will permit him. (169)

He reminded them of the powers of the Senate and of wide political support in Northern states for the South:

> Can Mr. Lincoln send a foreign minister, or even a consul, abroad, unless he receives the sanction of the Senate? Can he appoint a postmaster whose salary is over a thousand dollars a year without the consent of the Senate? . . . Yes, we are defeated according to the forms of law and the Constitution; but the real victory is ours—the moral force is with us. . . . How many votes did we get in the North? We got more votes in the North against Lincoln than the entire Southern States cast. Are they not able and faithful allies? (170)[14]

He asked, "What, then, is necessary to be done?" and answered: "To stand to our posts like men, and act upon principle; stand for the country; and in four years from this day, Lincoln and his administration will be turned out, the worst-defeated and broken-down party that ever came to power" (171).[15]

In sum, there were no warrants for secession in the founding documents, in statements of the founders, or in the documents by which states joined the Union. Although the federal government could not coerce a state, it could enforce its laws on individuals; accordingly, acts of secession inevitably meant war. Given the costs and benefits to the Union of acquiring territory that became states and given the potential threat posed by alliances between these new entities and foreign powers, peaceful secession was impossible. Moreover, secession was irrational and unnecessary: Southern states had the constitutional power to forestall hostile actions by the federal government. Indeed, the best way to preserve slavery was to remain in the Union, enjoying its powerful constitutional protections, dramatically illustrated by the Supreme Court's *Dred Scott* decision.

These arguments were ably defended in rejoinders to opponents on February 5 and 6 (176–289). In the course of his refutation, Johnson cited from the treaty acquiring Louisiana from the French and reminded the Senate of the defense of New Orleans in the war of 1812 (187). Louisiana had grievances, he noted sarcastically: "Forts, arsenals, custom-houses, and property all belonging to all the people of the States have been ruthlessly seized, and their undisturbed possession is the sum total of the great wrongs that have been inflicted upon Louisiana by the United States!" (188). In fine debating fashion, Johnson quoted a speech that an opponent, Louisiana senator Judah P. Benjamin, delivered in California following Lincoln's election, in which Benjamin commented on the Lincoln-Douglas debates and Lincoln's candor in responding to questions, answers he acknowledged contradicted charges that he was a rank abolitionist (196).[16]

Johnson's speech to the Senate on December 18 and 19, 1860, illustrates the argumentative prowess that was the mainstay of his political career. It reveals a speaker who has mastered the historical evidence, who understands how to offer examples that are telling and authoritative, and who takes a stand and skillfully defends his position. Appropriately, it addressed his fellow Southerners who threatened secession; it was even-handed in recognizing their complaints and in acknowledging the provocative acts of Northerners. Like Lincoln's first inaugural, it attempted to persuade Southerners to pause and contemplate the implications of their actions, to assess more carefully and logically whether secession would achieve their goals. Johnson forcefully argued for the Constitution and the Union as bulwarks fully able to protect Southern interests.[17] As the record shows, he never deviated from these positions as president. Subsequently, Lincoln was inaugurated; secession and war followed.

Presidential Reconstruction: Defended by Veto Messages

On January 1, 1863, when President Lincoln issued the Emancipation Proclamation freeing slaves in the rebellious states, Johnson accepted it as a necessary war measure. On similar grounds, as president he accepted the Thirteenth Amendment abolishing slavery. Recall that the Eleventh Amendment, ratified in 1795, protected states from suits by individuals and the Twelfth Amendment, ratified in 1803, provided for the nomination of the president and vice president on one ticket. These had effected only minor modifications of the Constitution. The Thirteenth Amendment was the first significant expansion of federal power, and its ratification, as the result of war, was unusual.

When Johnson became president on April 15, 1865, Congress, as usual, was not in session. Accordingly, he began a program of presidential reconstruction that followed the 10-percent plan initiated by Lincoln. That plan decreed that a state could be reintegrated into the Union when 10 percent of voters (as counted in the 1860 presidential election) had taken an oath of allegiance to the United States and pledged to abide by emancipation. Next, states would formally elect a state government, and the state legislature would write a new constitution, which had to abolish slavery forever. At that point, the president would recognize the reconstructed government. This moderate policy was meant to shorten the war and to further Lincoln's emancipation policy by insisting that the new state governments abolish slavery.[18] By the end of the war it had been tried, not very successfully, in Louisiana, Arkansas, Tennessee, and Virginia. Congress, however, refused to seat the senators and representatives elected from those states, and at the time of Lincoln's assassination, the president and the Congress were at an impasse.

Congress had reacted sharply to Lincoln's December 1863 proclamation of amnesty, which incorporated this conciliatory policy. Republicans feared that the planter aristocracy would be restored, and freed slaves would be forced back into slavery. Lincoln feared that compelling enforcement of emancipation could lead to the defeat of the Republican Party in the 1864 election, with the result that Democrats would be able to overturn his proclamation.[19] In 1864 two Radical Republicans, Senator Benjamin Wade of Ohio and Representative Henry Winter Davis of Maryland, proposed a more severe program for Southern Reconstruction, which made readmittance to the Union contingent on a majority in each state taking the Ironclad Oath, which meant swearing that they had never supported the Confederacy.[20] The bill passed both houses of Congress on July 2, 1864, but was pocket-vetoed by Lincoln. Johnson had opposed it in the Senate. Both Lincoln and Johnson only required Southerners to swear an oath that *in the future* they would support the Union as part of the 10-percent plan.[21]

When Congress reconvened on December 4, 1865, President Johnson announced in his first annual message that Reconstruction had been completed.[22] Republicans demurred. Johnson had allowed ten of the eleven seceded states back into the Union. The only conditions he set were that states adopt a constitution that repudiated secession, acknowledged the end to slavery, and repudiated any debts they had incurred during the war. In 1866 the Congress passed the Civil Rights Bill, which granted African Americans equal protection under the law and renewed the Freedmen's Bureau, overriding President Johnson's vetoes of both laws. Space precludes a full recounting of the history of the conflicts that ensued. As a populist, Johnson held that the final arbiters of such disagreements were the people, and his past successes on the stump led him to seek public support in 1866 in a "swing around the circle." Hecklers provoked the president into what were perceived as untoward remarks. By April of 1866 Radical Republicans held a two-thirds majority in both houses of Congress and could override any presidential veto. Conflict escalated. Impeachment followed; Johnson's removal was averted by a single vote.[23] Nonetheless, the president succeeded in impeding efforts to ensure the rights of freedmen and freedwomen or to provide them with either the economic support or the protection they would need to make their way in the world.

What comes into sharp focus in Johnson's veto messages is the centrality of a reading of the Constitution that emphasized states' rights and limitations on the scope of federal action,[24] a stance that remained invariant despite postwar conditions or passage of the Fourteenth Amendment, ratified in 1868.[25] From Johnson's point of view, it was as if once slavery had been abolished and its abolition was recognized by the formerly rebellious states, conditions could return to the status quo of the antebellum period. No intrusion into legislation or administration by state governments or into states' rights generally was permissible. No intervention by the federal government in reestablishing state governments, including any effort to punish former rebels or exclude them from positions of leadership, was acceptable. No federal action to assist former slaves was allowed under the Constitution other than measures taken during wartime, which was now at an end. Moreover, no congressional action could be legitimate until representatives of the formerly rebellious states had been seated. Johnson's vetoes were ably defended primarily on a strict reading of the Constitution and secondarily on his firm conviction of the inferiority of African Americans—in particular, his belief that free blacks were incapable of voting intelligently.

During 1866, for example, the Congressional Joint Committee on Reconstruction held hearings on the condition of Unionists in the South, especially African Americans, and found that they were in dire straits, and, based on its findings, constructed a constitutional amendment designed to protect blacks' civil rights and to reduce representation whenever any of the formerly rebellious states denied the franchise to any of its male citizens over age twenty-one. This became the Fourteenth Amendment, which, as Trefousse notes, "offered a perfectly reasonable compromise to the administration. . . . black suffrage did not form part of the proposal."[26] Johnson, however, held firm; he rejected the legitimacy of any constitutional change as long as Southern states remained unrepresented in Congress.

Johnson's first veto, on February 19, 1866, was of "an act to establish a bureau for the relief of freemen and refugees," which he argued was not "consistent with the public welfare."[27] His objections were constitutional: military courts in the formerly rebellious states violated the jury system (399) and slavery, for which the bureau was originally created in 1865 under wartime conditions, was now eradicated. Similarly, he argued that "support to the destitute and suffering refugees and freedmen, their wives and children" was not a proper function of the federal government (401). In his veto message, he echoed Andrew Jackson's conception of the executive as super-legislator, stating that the president "stands toward the country in a different attitude from that of any member of Congress; . . . the President is chosen by the people of all the states" (404). Accordingly, it was his special duty to "present the just claims" of those who continued to be unrepresented in the Congress—that is, the formerly rebellious states (404), which, of course, presupposed that the reconstruction process was complete and that Congress was unjustly refusing to seat their representatives.[28]

Despite the best efforts of his friends and supporters, Johnson also vetoed the civil rights bill on March 27, 1866. His objections were primarily constitutional, limiting federal power and protecting states' rights. He objected to its definition of citizenship, subsequently incorporated into the Fourteenth Amendment, on grounds that it preempted a state's prerogative to confer state citizenship. However, he also asserted that former slaves did not possess the requisite qualifications to exercise "all the privileges and immunities of citizenship"; moreover, he strongly objected on the grounds that by this act "a perfect equality of the white and colored races is to be fixed by Federal law in every State of the Union," including rights previously "considered as exclusively belonging to the States" (407).[29] He questioned "whether it is sound policy to make our entire colored population and all other excepted classes citizens of the United States . . . when eleven of the thirty-six States are unrepresented in Congress" (406). Johnson also pointed to state marriage laws "that no white person shall intermarry with a negro or mulatto" in order "to inquire if Congress can abrogate all State laws of discrimination between the two races in the matter of real estate, of suits, and of contracts generally" (407). In other words, he objected that the bill's provisions would "assail the independence of the [state] judiciary" (409) in attempting to protect the rights of former slaves. His attitude toward those newly freed was clear in his description of the new postwar relationship between labor (former slaves) and capital: "Each has equal power in settling the terms, and if left to the laws that regulate capital and labor, it is confidently believed that they will satisfactorily work out the problem" (412), a readjustment he believed would be frustrated by this bill. In his view, federal enforcement power was limited to the provisions of the Thirteenth Amendment outlawing slavery, an extension of federal power legitimate only as a wartime necessity (411).

In a second veto of a bill to establish a freedmen's bureau on July 26, 1866, Johnson argued: "The only ground upon which this kind of legislation can be justified is that of the war-making power" (422), and he echoed his view that all protections of individual rights belonged to the powers of the States (423). In addition, he held that the civil rights bill, which had been enacted over his veto, made this legislation superfluous, although he hinted that that law might be found unconstitutional by the Supreme Court, a fate that would, in fact, befall the 1875 Civil Rights Act (424–25).[30] Finally, in an appeal to republicanism, he urged

> upon Congress the danger of class legislation, so well calculated to . . . encourage interested hopes and fears that the National Government will continue to furnish to classes of citizens in the several States means for support and maintenance regardless of whether they pursue a life of indolence or of labor, and regardless also of the constitutional limitations of the national authority in time of peace and tranquility. (425)

In 1867 Johnson vetoed a measure to extend the elective franchise to persons of color in the District of Columbia on the basis that an election by the qualified voters (all white) had made their will and opposition known (473–474). He also argued that this extension of the suffrage was not "necessary to enable persons of color to protect either their interests or their rights" (477), a stance that seemed to contradict his republican beliefs. In addition, he again asserted that newly freed slaves are not "as well informed as to the nature of our government as the intelligent foreigner who makes our land the home of his choice" and warned against potential fraud (478). The remainder of this message was a justification, using the authority of Justice Joseph Story, of the value and role of the executive veto (479–483).[31]

On March 2, 1867, Johnson vetoed a bill to place the ten rebellious states (Tennessee now had a state government and representatives in Congress) under military governorships until such time as "the selection of delegates to a state convention by an election at which negroes shall be allowed to vote," the formation of a constitution by that convention, including a provision to secure the franchise to freemen and nonrebels, its ratification by vote, and its submission to Congress for approval (499–500). He rejected such martial law, citing the opinion of the Supreme Court majority in *ex parte Milligan*: "The necessity must be active and present, the invasion real, such as effectually closes the courts and deposes the civil administration" (504), buttressed again by other legal authorities and historical examples. In an ironic reversal, he argued: "Those who advocated the right of secession alleged in their own justification that we had no regard for law and that their rights of property, life, and liberty would not be safe under the Constitution as administered by us. If we now verify their assertion, we prove that they were in truth and in fact fighting for their liberty" (509).[32]

In his third annual message of December 3, 1867, Johnson's commitment to executive reconstruction and to returning to the status quo antebellum was clear when he said that

> candor compels me to declare that at this time there is no Union as our fathers understood the term, and as they meant it to be understood by us. The Union which they established can exist only where all the States are represented in both Houses of Congress; where one State is as free as another to regulate its internal concerns according to its own will, and where the laws of the central Government, strictly confined to matters of national jurisdiction, apply with equal force to all the people of every section. (559)

Obviously, there would be no compromise on those issues. Moreover, he reminded Congress of his earlier warnings about "the great danger 'to be apprehended from an untimely extension of the elective franchise to any new class in our country, especially when the large majority of that class

. . . cannot be expected to comprehend the duties and responsibilities which pertain to suffrage'" (565). In all likelihood, Johnson's views were reinforced by the altered suffrage requirements in the new constitution that Tennessee ratified in 1835, which disenfranchised free blacks with property who had been able to vote there for some forty years while enfranchising all adult white males with or without property.[33]

In his fourth annual message of December 9, 1868, which followed his impeachment and trial in March, Johnson continued to assert the position he had taken from the outset: "States to which the Constitution guarantees a republican form of government have been reduced to military dependencies, in each of which the people have been made subject to the arbitrary will of the commanding general." He also reasserted his objections to enfranchising freed blacks. He contended that such efforts had been damaging: "The attempt to place the white population under the domination of persons of color in the South has impaired, if not destroyed, the kindly relations that had previously existed between them" (672).

In his veto messages Johnson showed that he was skilled in argument and adept at using constitutional principles to assert states' rights, to justify executive reconstruction, and to reject congressional legislation to enlarge the role of the federal government or intervene in states to protect the rights of African Americans. He was adamantly opposed to legislative initiatives that offered legal or political equality to former slaves. He rejected legislation that altered constitutional relationships between the federal government and the states, as he understood them, or that enlarged the purview of the federal government, until representatives of the formerly rebellious states had been seated in Congress, a move that would ratify Johnson's presidential reconstruction program. In effect, Johnson held firmly that the only change warranted by the war was the abolition of slavery.

The Last Defense: The Farewell Message

At the end of his troubled presidency, Johnson availed himself of one last opportunity to state his views. As General Ulysses S. Grant was taking the presidential oath of office, Johnson's farewell "was speeding over the telegraph wires."[34] In the spirit of the earlier farewells of Washington and Jackson, Johnson attempted to shape his legacy and to offer warnings based on his presidential experience. He said, "it is my privilege, I trust, to say to the people of the United States a few parting words . . . from the Presidential chair during the closing hours of a laborious term." Johnson wished his successor "the forbearance and cooperation of the American people, in all his efforts to administer the Government *within the pale of the Federal Constitution*" (italics added); however, he expressed an "earnest desire . . . to see the Constitution of the Republic again recognized and obeyed as the supreme law of the land." Johnson described his presidency as an effort to fully restore the Constitution and offered this speech "as a few parting words in vindication of an official course ceaselessly assailed and aspersed by political leaders to whose plans and wishes my policy to restore the Union has been obnoxious." That tone permeated the speech. He described presidential reconstruction as a policy "intended to reassure and conciliate the people of both sections of the country." As his legacy, he claimed his refusal of "the unlimited additional powers tendered to the Executive by the measures relating to Civil Rights and the Freedman's Bureau," declining them as "powers in violation of the Constitution, dangerous to the liberties of the people, and tending to aggravate rather than lessen the discords naturally resulting from our civil war."

His legacy was an unremitting commitment to preserving the Constitution as he understood it. He spoke of pressures to "pervert" the powers of the presidency, of his resistance to the proposals of "extremists," and of "obey[ing] at every personal hazard my oath to defend the Constitution." He said the recent war was waged "to vindicate the Constitution and save the Union" and added, "If I have erred in trying to bring about a more speedy and lasting peace to extinguish heartburning and enmities . . . I am content to rest my case with the more deliberate judgment of the people." Consistent with the views expressed in his 1860 speech in the Senate, he made this rather startling claim:

> The war, all must remember, was a stupendous and deplorable mistake. Neither side understood the other, and had this simple fact and its

> conclusions been kept in view, all that was needed was accomplished by the acknowledgment of the terrible wrong and the expression of better feeling and earnest endeavor at atonement shown and felt.

Those words are the clearest expression of his position that, apart from the abolition of slavery, all that was required was a return to the status quo antebellum.

Consistent with that position, the farewell also shifted attention from "the past and expiated sins of the South" to attack his congressional opponents, those "pretended patriots" who "crept . . . into place and power in the national councils" and "have since persistently sought to inflame the prejudices engendered between the sections, to retard the restoration of peace and harmony, and by every means to keep open and exposed to the poisonous breath of party passion the terrible wounds of a four years' war." Moreover, he declared, "By unconstitutional and oppressive enactments the people of ten States of the Union have been reduced to a condition more intolerable than that from which the patriots of the Revolution rebelled." Based on his experience, he warned against congressional government, concluding that, in the face of large majorities and extreme partisanship, the constitutional protections of the presidential veto power and of present forms of judicial review were inadequate: "It has been clearly demonstrated by recent occurrences that encroachments upon the Constitution cannot be prevented by the President, however devoted or determined he may be. That unless the people interpose, there is no power under the Constitution to check a dominant majority of two-thirds of the Congress of the United States."[35]

What had the war settled? That states may not secede. "The institution of slavery, also, found its destruction in a rebellion commenced in its interest," an outcome Johnson had predicted. Nothing more: "All the rights granted to the States or reserved to the people are therefore intact. Among those rights is that of the people of each State to declare the qualifications of their own State electors," words triumphantly reaffirming states' rights that would enable formerly rebellious states to enact black codes to reestablish slavery in all but name.[36] He claimed victory in his battle with the Congress: "I have nothing to regret. Events have proved the correctness of the policy set forth in my first and subsequent messages." He concluded by stating the principle that encapsulated his career: "The Constitution and the Union, one and inseparable," a significant variation of Webster's famous cry in his great speech in the midst of the Nullification Crisis, "Liberty and Union, Now and Forever, One and Inseparable."[37] *Liberty* had to be omitted; it too easily could refer to former slaves and be construed as positive liberty—that is, having the right and opportunity to pursue happiness or seek personal fulfillment.

Given its tone, the farewell aroused intense reactions. A sympathetic commentator described it as "vindicating the policy of his administration . . . and rehearsing 'the catalogue of crimes' of the majority in Congress in a style as direct and unsparing as that in which the writer of the Declaration of Independence denounces the usurpations of 'Great George, Our King.'"[38] The *New York Herald,* once a Johnson supporter, attacked his style and attitude in terms that echoed negative reactions to his 1866 speeches: "These parting words of the retiring President might have done very well at some political gathering in Tennessee. . . . But as they stand they smell of chagrin, distrust, ill nature, and bad blood."[39] Historian David Warren Bowen astutely characterizes the speech as Johnson's effort to frame the conflict between the president and the Congress. He notes that the president repeated the word "Constitution" forty-two times, but made "no reference to Negroes or freedmen or any equivalent term" and offered this telling comment: "It was as if four million people had simply ceased to exist and the only real problem between the president and his enemies concerned the Constitution. That perception was no accident; it was the way Johnson *consciously* defined the situation in his own mind as well as in public statements."[40]

In the final words of his farewell, "Constitution and Union, one and inseparable," Johnson summed up his political beliefs. Apart from wartime necessities, the Constitution was not to be altered; the Union was an entity designed to protect the rights of states not the rights of individuals.

In his interpretation of the Constitution, Johnson did not stand alone; the U.S. Supreme Court reaffirmed his views. True, bills that he had vetoed became the Fourteenth and Fifteenth Amendments to the Constitution (constitutional amendments passed by Congress cannot be vetoed by the president), but Supreme Court decisions gutted these amendments and declared unconstitutional the Enforcement Acts that were intended to protect the freedman's right to vote. In the *Slaughter-House Cases* (1873), by a bare majority, the Court ruled that the intent of the Thirteenth and Fourteenth Amendments was to ensure "the freedom of the slave race" but did not guarantee federal protection of individual rights against discrimination by state governments. In short, the Bill of Rights did not extend to actions by state governments.[41] In *Minor v. Happersett* (1875), the Supreme Court ruled unanimously that "the Constitution of the United States does not confer the right of suffrage upon any one." In *United States v. Cruikshank* (1875) and *United States v. Reese* (1876), freedmen brought suit under the 1870 Enforcement Act for protection of their political rights under the Fourteenth and Fifteenth Amendments.[42] The Court ruled against them, finding the Enforcement Act unconstitutional, and inasmuch as the Constitution did not bestow suffrage on anyone, it held that the federal courts were outside their jurisdiction in protecting the freedmen's political rights, an interpretation so narrow that the Fifteenth Amendment could not even ensure the freedmen's right to vote.

The Supreme Court also resisted applying the Fourteenth and Fifteenth Amendments to women. After ratification of the Fifteenth Amendment, Elizabeth Cady Stanton and Susan B. Anthony argued that women were enfranchised under its terms, which stated: "The right of citizens of the United States [now defined by the Fourteenth Amendment as "All persons born or naturalized in the United States"] shall not be denied or abridged by the United States or by any State on account of . . . previous condition of servitude." They claimed that the legal disabilities of married women under coverture, which rendered wives civilly dead—unable to own property, sue, testify, execute a contract, or exercise guardianship over their children—was the legal equivalent of servitude, although no one claimed that the actual conditions of married women and slaves were equivalent. What is significant, however, is that the "equal protection" and the "due process" clauses of the Fourteenth Amendment have been applied to issues of discrimination based on sex only recently, for the first time in 1971 in *Reed v. Reed* (404 U.S. 71). The most recent case, *U.S. v. Virginia* (518 US 515, 1996), regarding admission of women to the Virginia Military Institute, increased the level of scrutiny for sex-based classifications by demanding an "exceedingly persuasive justification."[43]

Obviously, we cannot know how differently Reconstruction would have proceeded under Lincoln, but there are important hints in Johnson and Lincoln's differing views of the Constitution. In *Lincoln at Gettysburg,*[44] Garry Wills ends his analysis of Lincoln's speech by commenting on the transformation Lincoln effected in that address:

> he not only put the Declaration in a new light as a matter of founding *law,* but put its central proposition, equality, in a newly favored position as a principle of the Constitution (which, as the *Chicago Times* noticed, never uses the word). What had been a mere theory of lawyers like James Wilson, Joseph Story, and Daniel Webster—that the nation preceded the states, in time and importance—now became a lived reality of the American tradition, . . . making *union* not a mystical hope but a constitutional reality. (145)

Wills notes, however, that states rights' advocates, such as former attorney general Edwin Meese and Judge Robert Bork, think that "equality as a *national* commitment has been sneaked into the Constitution" (146), and Wills quotes noted conservative Wilmoore Kendall, who holds that "Lincoln's use of the Declaration's phrase about all men being equal is an attempt 'to wrench from it a single proposition and make that our supreme commitment'" (146). In their constitutional views, these men stand with Andrew Johnson. Wills concludes, somewhat hopefully, that "for most people now, the Declaration means what Lincoln told us it means, as a way of correcting the Constitution itself without overthrowing it" (147).

The conflict between Andrew Johnson and members of Congress over the meaning and application of the U.S. Constitution is a reminder that advances in civil rights for minorities and women have always been and continue to be closely related to judicial interpretations of the U.S. Constitution and of the meaning and application of the post–Civil War amendments by which its fundamental character was altered.

Obviously, Andrew Johnson's views of federal-state relationships echo disputes that have become salient today, particularly arguments threatening secession or state nullification of federal acts. In my reading of his speeches, the evidence that he would have supported such claims is unclear. He was adamantly opposed to secession and to all efforts to make reintegration of the rebellious states more difficult. Moreover, he never cited the Kentucky Resolutions of 1798, authored by Thomas Jefferson in protest against the Alien and Sedition Acts, which included the statement that "where powers are assumed which have not been delegated, a nullification of the act is the rightful remedy: that every State has a natural right . . . to nullify of their own authority all assumptions of power by others within their limits,"[45] or the Virginia Resolution of 1798 authored by James Madison and Jefferson, which expressed similar views.[46] Never forget that his name was Andrew Jackson Johnson and that his hero, fellow Tennessean President Jackson, had rejected nullification as the prerogative of South Carolina in 1832.[47] Notably, Johnson's stands rested on the Tenth Amendment, that "the powers not delegated to the United States by the Constitution, not prohibited by it to the States, are reserved to the states respectively, or to the people," and on powers granted to the states in the Constitution. It is clear that what Johnson wanted, apart from the abolition of slavery, was to reestablish the status quo antebellum, with all of the rebellious states back in the Union able to exercise all of their former powers. In other words, President Johnson's attitude toward contemporary nullifiers and secessionists must remain conjecture.

NOTES

1. Abraham Lincoln, "Special Session Message, July 4, 1861," in *A Compilation of the Messages and Papers of the Presidents,* ed. James D. Richardson (New York: Bureau of National Literature and Art), 6:30.
2. Hans L. Trefousse, *Andrew Johnson: A Biography* (New York: W. W. Norton, 1989), 13. In the most recent C-SPAN poll of sixty-five presidential historians, the bottom five were Warren G. Harding, William Henry Harrison, Franklin Pierce, Andrew Johnson, and James Buchanan. The top five were Lincoln, Washington, FDR, TR, and HST. See the UPI poll at http://www.upi.com/Top_News/2009/02/15/Lincoln_tops_C-SPAN_presidents_ranking/UPI-32281234748562/.
3. The most detailed study of Andrew Johnson's speechmaking is Gregg Phifer's analysis of speeches delivered during the 1866 "swing around the circle," found in "Andrew Johnson Takes a Trip," "Andrew Johnson Argues a Case," "Andrew Johnson Delivers His Argument," and "Andrew Johnson Loses His Battle," *Tennessee*

Historical Quarterly 11 (1952): 3–22, 148–170, 212–234, 291–328. Phifer acknowledges historians' harsh verdicts of this rhetoric and challenges them: "The President's speeches were not crude and coarse unless the spectacle of a man fighting for what he believes in the only way he knows how deserves such adjectives. . . . Perhaps the fairest evaluation of the effects of the swing around the circle is that Johnson failed to achieve a political miracle" (318–319). Phifer's study is a very balanced assessment of Johnson's strengths as an oral persuader and his limitations as one who knew how to fight but not how to conciliate.

4. "The President's Address, Washington, March 3, 1869," *New York Times,* March 4, 1869, 8, cols. 3–6. It is not in volume 6 of Richardson. There is no explanation for its absence, but I surmise that its timing, going out over the telegraph wires as Grant was taking the oath of office, and its attitude toward the Congress probably explain why omitting it seemed appropriate.
5. Trefousse, *Andrew Johnson,* 13. All data about Johnson's life are drawn from this source.
6. Eric McKitrick, "Introduction," in *Andrew Johnson: A Profile,* ed. Eric McKitrick (New York: Hill & Wang, 1969), xx.
7. See *Life, Speeches, and Services of Andrew Johnson, Seventeenth President of the United States* (Philadelphia: T. R. Peterson & Brothers, 1865), 114–115, which reports that Marcus L. Ward, a member of the Republican National Committee, "solicited an expression of preference as to his preference as to the Vice-Presidential candidate to be nominated by that [1864] convention. The President, while declaring that he could not be expected to avow any distinct preference . . . referred frankly to the merits of each, . . and dwelt especially upon the claims of Andrew Johnson, whom he characterized as eminently a man for the times—capable, honest, and of inflexible loyalty and indomitable will, whose selection for Vice-President would afford him (Mr. Lincoln) supreme satisfaction."
8. On February 1, 1861, six states—Mississippi, Florida, Georgia, Louisiana, and Texas—followed South Carolina, and on February 7 they adopted a provisional constitution. On April 17, Virginia, North Carolina, Arkansas, and North Carolina joined them. Border states that remained loyal were Delaware, Maryland, Kentucky, and Missouri. However, as McPherson notes, "On December 13, before any state seceded or any compromise was voted on, thirty congressmen and senators from the lower South issued an address to their constituents: 'The argument is exhausted. All hope of relief in the Union, through the agency of committees, Congressional legislation, or constitutional amendments, is extinguished. .

. . The honor, safety, and independence of the Southern people are to be found only in a Southern Confederacy.'" See Edward McPherson, *The Political History of the United States of America during the Great Rebellion,* 2d ed. (Washington, DC: Philip & Solomons, 1865), 37.

9. Frank Moore, *Speeches of Andrew Johnson, President of the United States, with a Biographical Introduction* (Boston: Little, Brown, 1865), 77–175. He also delivered "On the State of the Union," in the Senate on February 5 and 6, 1861, 176–289, and "Reply to Senator Lane of Oregon," March 2, 1861, 290–315, all of which concern the same issues. Subsequent references are found in page numbers in the text. Eric L. McKitrick writes that "with a superb disdain for his own personal safety, Johnson—then a senator—defied the secessionists of Tennessee. True to the principles of the sainted Jackson (for whom he had been named), he defended the Constitution and the Union with bitter devotion until no drop of hope for his state was left." He also notes the important role that Johnson played as military governor of Tennessee for three years under the most difficult circumstances, commenting, "It was his finest hour; and it was for this that Lincoln in 1864 picked him for his Vice-President." See McKitrick, *Andrew Johnson,* 74.

10. "The selection of Supreme Court justices by geographical circuits gave the slave states, with their larger territory, a majority on the Supreme Court. . . . For two-thirds of the years from 1789 to 1861, the Presidents of the United States, the Speakers of the House and presidents pro tem of the Senate, and the chairmen of key congressional committees were Southerners" (2). "From 1789 to 1861, twenty-three of the thirty-six Speakers of the House and twenty-four of the thirty-six presidents pro tem of the Senate had been Southerners. Twenty of the thirty-five Supreme Court justices had come from slave states, and at all times since 1789 the South had had a majority on the Court. During forty-nine of these seventy-two years the president of the United States had been a Southerner—and a slaveholder. During twelve additional years, including most of the crucial 1850s, the presidents were Northern Democratic 'doughfaces'" (James M. McPherson, *Ordeal by Fire: The Coming of War,* 2nd ed. [New York: McGraw Hill, 1993], 1:136). Subsequently, the issue arose in *Ableman v. Booth,* 62 U.S. 504 (1859) in which a majority of the court ruled that the Fugitive Slave Law was constitutional and declared that any state interference with its enforcement was unconstitutional. See McPherson, *Ordeal by Fire,* 84.

11. The constitutionality of these laws came before the U.S. Supreme Court in *Prigg v. Pennsylvania,* 41 U.S. 539 (1842), which concerned a Maryland slave owner

convicted in Pennsylvania of kidnapping after he forcibly returned his runaway slave back to Maryland. The Court ruled that the Pennsylvania personal-liberty law was unconstitutional, but it also ruled that enforcement of the fugitive slave clause of the Constitution was entirely a federal responsibility; accordingly, Pennsylvania's law prohibiting state officers from participating in the recapture of fugitives was constitutional, a ruling that prompted passage of more personal-liberty laws, which in turn provoked Southern demands for a federal statute to strengthen enforcement of the fugitive slave clause. See McPherson, *Ordeal by Fire,* 80.

12. *Dred Scott v. Sandford,* 60 U.S. (19 How.) 393 (1857), was a decision by a 7–2 majority of the U.S. Supreme Court written by Chief Justice Roger Taney that ruled that people of African descent imported into the United States and held as slaves or their descendants—whether or not they were slaves—were not legal persons and could never be citizens of the United States, and that the U.S. Congress had no authority to prohibit slavery in federal territories. The Court also ruled that slaves could not sue in court, and that slaves—as chattel or private property—could not be taken away from their owners without due process. "The dissenting opinion of Justice Benjamin Curtis of Massachusetts was a powerful indictment of Taney's reasoning." See McPherson, *Ordeal by Fire,* 105. In his Cooper Union address, Lincoln noted the narrow margin of this decision and pointed to flaws in its reasoning.

13. During the second session of the Thirty-sixth Congress, which began on December 3, 1860, there were many proposals for reconciliation. "In its final report to the House, the compromise committee advocated the enforcement of the fugitive slave law, the repeal of the personal liberty laws, which prohibited state officials from returning fugitive slaves in some northern states, and the adoption of a constitutional amendment to protect the South against future interference with slavery in the states. The wording of this amendment was: 'No amendment shall be made to the Constitution which will authorize or give to Congress the power to abolition or interfere, within any State, with the domestic institutions thereof, including that of persons held to labor or service by the laws of said state.' . . . [I]t was adopted, with 40 percent of the House Republicans voting in the affirmative. . . . In the Senate, the efforts toward compromise officially centered on a 'Committee of Thirteen.' . . . Their plan . . . the 'Crittenden Plan' was to prohibit slavery north of the line 36° 30', but to permit its establishment and protection by the federal government south of that line, to allow future states, north or south of the line, to enter the Union with or without slavery as they chose, to prevent Congress from abolishing slavery in places under national jurisdiction surrounded by slave states, to

compensate owners in communities where intimidation prevented federal officials from arresting a fugitive slave; to enforce the fugitive slave law; and to let Congress recommend the repeal of all personal liberty laws. . . . These compromise articles, when ratified, were to become irrevocable amendments to the Constitution, and no future amendment was ever to be made which would authorize Congress to touch slavery in any of the states." David Herbert Donald, Jean Harvey Baker, and Michael F. Holt, *The Civil War and Reconstruction* (New York: W. W. Norton, 2001), 137–138.

14. Lincoln won only 39 percent of the popular vote but a clear majority of 190 electoral votes carrying all eighteen free states. In the free states, Lincoln won 1,838,347 popular votes, but his opponents received 1,572,637 votes in those states. See McPherson, *Ordeal by Fire,* 129.
15. Using the filibuster—the right to unlimited debate—to delay or prevent a vote in the Senate became popular in the 1850s. In 1917 senators adopted Rule 22, which allowed the Senate to end a debate with a two-thirds majority vote, a device known as "cloture." The new Senate rule was first put to the test in 1919, when the Senate invoked cloture to end a filibuster against the Treaty of Versailles.
16. Johnson reiterated these arguments in subsequent speeches prior to inauguration and in Cincinnati on June 18, 1861, where he is reputed to have "delivered an able address" (*Life, Speeches and Services of Andrew Johnson,* 30; speech on 30–38).
17. Tennessee politician and Johnson contemporary Oliver V. Temple writes: "It is true that his eighteenth and nineteenth of December speech, in the Senate of 1860, produced perhaps the most profound impression of any speech ever made in the country, but that was not because of its eloquence but because of its startling unexpectedness, its daring positions, its noble patriotism, and the breathless anxiety with which the North was listening—waiting, indeed—for a word of hope from the South. It was the spirit of the speech, the golden opportunity seized and well used, and not the words, that gave permanence to that effort. It inspired the bewildered, despairing North with a new hope. It was a vivid light suddenly flashed upon the profoundest darkness." Oliver V. Temple, "Impressions of Andrew Johnson," in *Andrew Johnson: A Profile,* 49–50.
18. Shortly after he became president, Johnson "extended recognition to the Southern governments created under the Lincoln administration (Arkansas, Louisiana, Tennessee, and Virginia), none of which had enfranchised blacks." See Eric Foner, *Reconstruction: America's Unfinished Revolution, 1863–1877* (New York: Harper Collins/Perennial Classics, 1988), 182.

19. The election of a Democrat in 1864 would have meant that, in effect, the South had won the war!
20. The Ironclad Oath required every white male to swear he had never borne arms against the Union or supported the Confederacy—that is, he had "never voluntarily borne arms against the United States," had "voluntarily" given "no aid, countenance, counsel or encouragement" to persons in rebellion, and had exercised or attempted to exercise the functions of no office under the Confederacy. In 1867 the U.S. Supreme Court held that the federal ironclad oath for attorneys and the similar Missouri state oath for teachers and other professionals were unconstitutional because they violated the constitutional prohibitions against bills of attainder and ex post facto laws. *Cummings v. Missouri,* 4 Wall. 277 (1867); *Ex parte Garland,* 4 Wall. 333 (1867). However, it was still applied by the Radical Republicans wherever they held power. The oath was effectively ended in 1871 and finally repealed in 1884. See Harold M. Hyman, *To Try Men's Souls: Loyalty Tests in American History* (Berkeley: University of California Press, 1959), 264–265.
21. Howard K. Beale writes that Johnson made three demands of the Southern states: "repeal of the ordinances of secession, ratification of the 13th Amendment, and repudiation of the rebel debts, Confederate and state. But even these fundamental and unquestionably just conditions, Johnson was determined to secure by voluntary action." See Howard K. Beale, "Johnson and His Policy," in *Andrew Johnson: A Profile,* 106.
22. Richardson, *A Compilation of the Messages and Papers of the Presidents,* 6:353–371. See also Johnson's proclamation of April 2, 1866, Richardson, *Messages and Papers,* 6:429–432.
23. For a more detailed analysis of the effort to impeach Johnson, see Karlyn Kohrs Campbell and Kathleen Hall Jamieson, *Presidents Creating the Presidency: Deeds Done in Words* (Chicago: University of Chicago Press, 2008), 280–290.
24. Foner writes that "Johnson had always believed in limited government and a strict construction of the Constitution. In Congress, he had moved to reduce the salaries of government workers, voted against aid to famine-stricken Ireland, and even opposed appropriations to pave Washington's muddy streets" (see Foner, *Reconstruction,* 178). In 1865, Johnson announced his adherence to "limited government" and "the support of the State governments in all their rights" (see Richardson, *Messages and Papers,* 6:355).
25. The Fourteenth Amendment of the Constitution was passed by both houses on June 8 and 13, 1866. The amendment was designed to grant citizenship to and

protect the civil liberties of recently freed slaves. It did this by prohibiting states from denying or abridging the privileges or immunities of citizens of the United States, depriving any person of his life, liberty, or property without due process of law, or denying to any person within their jurisdiction the equal protection of the laws. Most Southern states refused to ratify the Fourteenth Amendment; therefore Radical Republicans such as Thaddeus Stevens, Charles Sumner, Benjamin Wade, Henry Winter Davis, and Benjamin Butler urged the passage of further legislation to impose these measures on the former Confederacy. The result was the 1867 Reconstruction Acts that divided the South into five military districts controlled by martial law, proclaimed universal manhood suffrage, and required new state constitutions to be drawn up.

Reasons for supporting the Fifteenth Amendment were more than an idealistic desire to spread the fruits of democracy to former slaves. In the Election of 1868, Grant achieved a narrow majority of the popular votes nationwide. His support from black voters in the South made the difference in the outcome. Without those votes, he would have lost. The largest state Grant lost was New York, home state of Horatio Seymour, his Democratic opponent, which was conceded by a narrow margin. Blacks could not vote in the North; if they had had that right, Grant would have taken New York. The main impetus behind the Fifteenth Amendment was the Republican desire to entrench its power in both the North and the South. Black votes would help accomplish that end. The measure was passed by Congress in 1869 and was quickly ratified by the requisite three-fourths of the states in 1870. Republicans still controlled the state governments in the South, so the expected opposition lacked the means to block the amendment. See Donald, Baker, and Holt, *The Civil War and Reconstruction,* 575–576, 609–610.

26. Trefousse, *Andrew Johnson,* 251.
27. Richardson, *Messages and Papers,* 6:398. Subsequent references are in parentheses in the text.
28. See also his second annual message, December 3, 1866, especially in Richardson, *Messages and Papers,* 6:449, where he attempts to draw on the authority of his illustrious predecessors, Washington, Jefferson, and Jackson.
29. Foner writes, "In his December 1867 annual message to Congress, Johnson insisted that blacks possessed less 'capacity for government than any other race of people. No independent government of any form has ever been successful in their hands. On the contrary, wherever they have been left to their own devices they have shown a constant tendency to lapse into barbarism.' This was probably the most blatantly

racist pronouncement ever to appear in an official state paper of an American President" (Foner, *Reconstruction,* 180). See annual message in Richardson, *Messages and Papers,* 6:565.

30. For an analysis of the debate over the 1875 Civil Rights bill, see Kirt H. Wilson, *The Reconstruction Desegregation Debate: The Politics of Equality and the Rhetoric of Place, 1870–1875* (East Lansing: Michigan State University Press, 2002).
31. Johnson's veto of a bill "to regulate the tenure of certain civil offices," the veto that became an article of impeachment, is also supported with citations from Madison, Justice Story, and Chancellor Kent (Richardson, *Messages and Papers,* 6:492–498).
32. He vetoed a similar bill on March 23, 1867, another effort at establishing military governorships over the ten remaining rebellious states, including the elective franchise for newly freed slaves, and repeated the objections he had raised earlier (see Richardson, *Messages and Papers,* 6:533–535). He vetoed a similar act on July 19, 1867, but although the arguments are similar, they are presented here in greater detail (see ibid., 6:537–545).
33. Johnson's views about free black suffrage reflect changes that had occurred in his home state of Tennessee. The suffrage clause in its new constitution, ratified in 1835, had these effects: "For white males, even minimal freeholds were no longer required for voting, and no free black males, not even those possessing a freehold or substantial other property, were given relief from racial exclusion. Merely by inserting the word *white,* the convention of 1834 ended nearly forty years of voting by free black property owners and established the principle of herrenvolk democracy as the rule of voting rights in Tennessee. . . . [A]t its 1834 constitutional convention, Tennessee took major steps toward defining itself as a white man's democracy." Lacy K. Ford, *Deliver Us from Evil: The Slavery Question in the Old South* (New York: Oxford University Press, 2009), 416–417. For a more detailed report of the convention, see the chapter "Tennessee Debates Slavery," 390–417.
34. George Fort Milton, *The Age of Hate: Andrew Johnson and the Radicals* (New York: Coward-McCann, 1930), 652.
35. On August 2, 1848, in a speech in the House, Johnson defended President James K. Polk upholding the presidential right of veto (10) after tracing the history of the veto power from 497 B.C. (2–5), which is of interest because of his later use of the veto power as president. See Moore, *Speeches of Andrew Johnson,* 1–11.
36. "The codes legalized Negro marriages, permitted Negroes to hold and dispose of property, to sue and be sued. They took steps toward the establishment of racial segregation in public places. They prohibited interracial marriages, prohibited

Negroes from serving on juries or testifying against white men, and re-enacted many of the criminal provisions of the previous slave codes. In the economic sphere, South Carolina prohibited Negroes from entering any employment except agricultural labor without a special license; Mississippi would not permit them to buy or rent farm land; these states and others provided that Negroes found without lawful employment were to be arrested as vagrants and auctioned off or hired to landholders who would pay their fines. Louisiana required all Negro agricultural laborers to make contracts with landholders during the first ten days of January; once made, the contracts were binding for the year" (Kenneth M. Stampp, "Andrew Johnson: The Last Jacksonian," *Andrew Johnson: A Profile,* 136–137).

37. In his reply to Robert Y. Hayne of South Carolina on January 26, 1830, during the nullification controversy, Webster said, "Liberty and Union, Now and Forever, One and Inseparable," http://www.usa-patriotism.com/speeches/dwebster1.htm.
38. David Miller Dewitt, *The Impeachment and Trial of Andrew Johnson: A History* (New York: Macmillan, 1903), 614.
39. *New York Herald,* March 4, 1869, cited by Trefousse, *Andrew Johnson,* 352.
40. David Warren Bowen, *Andrew Johnson and the Negro* (Knoxville: University of Tennessee Press, 1989), 140.
41. See Foner, *Reconstruction,* 529–530; Wilson, *The Reconstruction Desegregation Debate,* 166–172.
42. In this case, brought under the Enforcement Act of 1870, the Court "argued that the postwar amendments only empowered the federal government to prohibit violations of freedmen's rights by *states;* the responsibility for punishing crimes by individuals rested where it always had—with state and local authorities" and "rendered national prosecution of crimes committed against blacks virtually impossible." See Foner, *Reconstruction,* 531.
43. Justice Ruth Bader-Ginsburg announced the opinion in this case on June 26, 1996. Writing for a six-person majority, which included Justice O'Connor, Ginsburg ruled that the lower courts had erred in holding that VMI did not have to admit women. She did not squarely address the question of strict scrutiny, and she noted that the Court had not equated gender classifications, "for all purposes," to classifications based on race or national origin—the classifications for which strict scrutiny had "thus far" been reserved. But she applied the gender standard with the same rigor traditionally seen in strict scrutiny cases, as dissenting justice Antonin Scalia pointed out in great detail. Ginsburg relied on the Supreme Court's prior intermediate scrutiny cases, but the phrase that leapt to the forefront of her opinion

was "exceedingly persuasive justification." The "core instruction" of the Court's previous cases, she wrote in beginning her analysis, was that "parties who seek to defend gender-based government action must demonstrate an 'exceedingly persuasive justification' for that action." And the justification for the government action "must be genuine, not hypothesized or invented post hoc in response to litigation." See http://www.supremecourthistory.org/learning/supremecourthistory_learning_womens5.htm

44. Garry Wills, *Lincoln at Gettysburg: The Words that Remade America* (New York: Simon & Schuster, 1992).
45. The Kentucky Resolution, 1798. Available at http://americanhistory.about.com/library/docs/bldockyres.htm?p=1.
46. The Virginia Resolution, 1798. Available at http://www.constitution.org/cons/virg1798.htm.
47. After Jackson issued his proclamation, Congress passed the Force Act, which authorized the use of military force against any state that resisted the tariff acts.

No End Save Victory: FDR and the End of Isolationism, 1936–1941

John M. Murphy

Franklin D. Roosevelt loved stamps. He began collecting them as a boy and the hobby never left him. When he became president of the United States, he asked the State Department what they did with the foreign envelopes sent to them. He learned they threw most away. Shortly thereafter, a Saturday courier began delivering a packet to the White House. FDR spent that day and sometimes Sunday as well, organizing, researching, and cataloging his new acquisitions. Of course, he also purchased stamps, and once foreign dignitaries discovered his interest they often made gifts of stamps. Admiral Ross McIntire, FDR's physician, estimated "that he spent well over 2,000 hours on his stamp collection during his twelve years in the White House." In that era, one biographer notes, "postage stamps evoked exotic places." The president spent his weekends traveling to those faraway nations with "over one million stamps in 150 albums." One suspects this hobby made the world come alive in his ever-curious mind.[1]

In fact, Roosevelt was, apart from cousin Theodore, "the most cosmopolitan American to enter the White House since John Quincy Adams in 1825."[2] FDR's family habitually traveled abroad; he first went to Europe at the age of three and spent time there each year until fifteen. He learned the rudiments of German and French, attended those nurseries for turn-of-the-century Anglo-American manhood, Groton and Harvard, and became a member in good standing of a "cosmopolitan, Anglophilic social class that took for granted the organic unity of the Atlantic world, a cultural affinity that rasped against the grain of popular American attitudes."[3] As he entered public life, FDR, like TR, saw the navy as the finest instrument for the projection of American power, read Mahan's *The Influence of Seapower on History,* and served as assistant secretary of the Navy, from which post he traveled to the front during the Great War.[4] He then supported Wilson's League of Nations and campaigned on that platform for the vice presidency in 1920. FDR appreciated the world—and its stamps—in ways matched by few American presidential aspirants.

Ironically, that mattered little during his first years as president. The Great Depression absorbed his energies, and his administration developed a distinctly nationalistic response.[5] As he bluntly put it in his first inaugural address, "Our international trade relations, though vastly important, are in point of time and necessity secondary to the establishment of a sound national economy. I favor as a practical policy the putting of first things first." The only other reference to foreign policy was this: "In the field of world policy I would dedicate this Nation to the policy of the good neighbor—the neighbor who resolutely respects himself and, because he does so, respects the rights of others—the neighbor who respects his obligations and respects the sanctity of his agreements in and with a world of neighbors."[6] One day later, "the German Reichstag placed absolute power in the hands of Adolf Hitler. Little more than a week before, Yosuke Matsuoka had marched the Japanese delegation out of the League of Nations in Geneva."[7] With neighbors like these, the president would eventually face a world on fire.

The road from the rise of Hitler to world war was neither clear nor easy, not to Roosevelt then nor to historians since. The earliest studies of that effort began at the time, David Reynolds writes, and stigmatized isolationists. "Court" historians, such as Robert Sherwood, lauded the president's courage. The nation was isolationist, partisan Republicans led the way, and the president saved the day. Yet revisionists, like Charles A. Beard, argued before and after the war that the United States did not face a threat to its vital interests. In this view, Roosevelt deceived the country into going to war. Conspiracy theories soon suggested FDR allowed Pearl Harbor to happen. In time, however, the revisionist case faltered, mostly because "Pearl Harbor ended the political argument; Auschwitz settled the moral argument."[8] Despite the continuing efforts of revisionists such as columnist Patrick J. Buchanan, most Americans accept the "Good War" and laud the "greatest generation."[9]

Assuming a righteous cause, historians focus now on Roosevelt's choices during this period. Broadly speaking, two positions have emerged. Some scholars, such as Robert Divine and James MacGregor Burns, see FDR as a political animal, frozen in the headlights of public opinion and driven to do the right thing only by the force of events.[10] Others, including Robert Dallek, David Reynolds, and George Herring depict Roosevelt as an internationalist "obliged by the strength of public opinion to conform to the nationalist and isolationist mood of the 1930s."[11] That mood required presidential circumspection and persuasion. On the one hand, he could not outrun his audience. Herring notes, "He has been criticized for his timidity in responding to World War II and for underestimating his powers of persuasion. But he had vivid memories of Wilson's defeat and feared getting too far out in front of public opinion."[12] On the other hand, Dallek and Reynolds emphasize FDR's persuasive efforts and their successful conclusion. Dallek writes, "His appreciation that effective action abroad required a reliable consensus at home and his use of dramatic events overseas to win national backing from a divided country for a series of pro-Allied steps were among the greatest presidential achievements of this century."[13] Reynolds notes "an awareness of global crisis was not the same as a recognition of world war. Roosevelt's carefully crafted speeches joined up the dots of disparate events into an interconnected pattern," one that, he writes, "moved his [FDR's] country from 'neutrality' to 'world war.'"[14] Neither, however, analyzes the "carefully crafted speeches," although we should forgive them that, since rhetorical critics have also ignored these texts.

My sympathies with the position held by Dallek, Reynolds, and others should by now be clear. A careful reading of Franklin Roosevelt's key foreign policy addresses from 1936 to 1941 reveals an extraordinary persuasive achievement and the development of a repertoire of ideas and images that served as an inventional resource for later American foreign policy discourse.[15] To explore that accomplishment, I first examine the obstacles faced by President Roosevelt and then turn to his effort to make *present*, as Chaim Perelman and Lucie Olbrechts-Tyteca would have it, the fascist threat.[16] Through three argumentative and stylistic tactics, he wanted the American people to know in their hearts and minds the magnitude of the threat facing them. He wanted to move them from indifference to all measures short of war. At the close, I consider the implications of his rhetorical achievement.

Global Crisis

Military historian John Keegan begins his 1998 history of the Great War: "The First World War was a tragic and unnecessary conflict."[17] Elsewhere, he writes: "Had it been foretold that the consequent war was to last four years, entail the [combat] death of 10 million [people], and carry fire and sword to battlefields as far apart as Belgium, northern Italy, Macedonia, the Ukraine, Transcaucasia, Palestine, Mesopotamia, Africa, and China . . . every individual and collective impulse to aggression, it might be thought, would have been stilled in an instant."[18] A generation of young men disappeared; nearly two million Frenchmen died in the war, and the cohort of German men who were between nineteen and twenty-two when war broke out dropped by 35 percent.[19] Several countries named by Keegan disappeared at war's end, as did the German empire, the Ottoman empire, and the Austro-Hungarian empire. David Kennedy concludes: "Victors and vanquished agreed only that the conflict had been a dreadful catastrophe, a blood-spilling, man-killing, nation-eating nightmare of unprecedented horror."[20]

In the comparatively unaffected United States, war's end brought starkly different views of the future. President Woodrow Wilson wanted a League of Nations to assure peace through collective security. Senator Henry Cabot Lodge wanted to balance power with power, favoring instead a U.S. guarantee to secure France against Germany. He disdained Wilson's idealism. Others wanted a pox on all their houses.[21] By the early 1930s, as the world slid into depression and democracy became a memory for much of the globe, the American view of the World War came to favor the latter. Historians and politicians agreed that the United States had been tricked into war by corporate profiteers and British propaganda. By abandoning what critics claimed as traditional U.S. policy—no entangling alliances—Wilson compromised American interests and morality by involving us in the quarrels of a corrupt and incorrigibly bloody Europe.[22] This view of the Great War as an unnecessary and immoral tragedy led many to believe that a strong peace movement, an unbending commitment to isolation, and clear limits on executive power were necessary to prevent a recurrence of the nightmare.

Isolationist prose seems purple, but when a respected historian writing in 1998 regards the war as tragic and unnecessary, interwar critics look more reasonable. They were certainly ubiquitous. Writers from Dos Passos to Hemingway to Remarque indelibly established the war's immorality. A "spate of revisionist histories," Kennedy notes, "drove the isolationist moral home to a broad reading audience. Taken together, books like Harry Elmer Barnes's *Genesis of the World War* (1926), C. Hartley Grattan's *Why We Fought* (1929), Walter Millis's *Road to War* (1935), and Charles C. Tansill's *America Goes to War* (1938) composed a formidable brief" that indicted American participation. Some of these books, as well as a lurid March 1934 *Fortune* magazine exposé titled "Arms and the Men," inspired a Senate Special Committee to investigate the arms industry. H. C. Engelbrecht and F. C. Hanighen provided a ringing moniker with their Book-of-the-Month Club selection *Merchants of Death*. Since most Americans would believe anything of big business by 1935, it was not a stretch to think the worst of its involvement in the Great War.[23] Dallek summarizes: "The message in all these pronouncements was the same. The First World War had been a grotesque disaster; another conflict would be pointless, and worse. American participation in another such struggle would profit no one except bankers, industrialists, and munitions makers. The losers would be the mass of Americans who would pay with their lives, their money, and their democratic institutions."[24]

As a result, a peace movement grew across the nation. Dallek writes that the movement "at its height boasted twelve million adherents and an audience of between forty-five and sixty million people." In 1931, 12,000 clergy declared that they would not support any war; in 1932, a mile-long automobile procession presented President Hoover with a peace petition; and in 1933, 15,000 students from sixty-five colleges committed themselves to absolute pacifism or to service only in case of invasion.[25] That year, British students reinforced such sentiments when the Oxford Union "notoriously voted" that "this house will in no circumstance fight for its King and its Country."[26] On April 6, 1935, the eighteenth anniversary of U.S. entry into the war, "50,000 veterans paraded through Washington in a march for peace. On April 12, some 175,000 college students across the country staged a one-hour strike against war."[27] The National Council for the Prevention of War, the National Peace Conference, the Federal Council of Churches, the Women's International League for Peace and Freedom, and other groups fought any step toward war. Albert Einstein endorsed the movement, while future Christian realist Reinhold Niebuhr urged "his fellow ministers to refuse to serve as chaplains in the event of war's outbreak."[28]

As the threat of war grew, so did the determination of isolationists to reject involvement with the world. A symptom was the Senate's 1935 decision to kill U.S. participation in an innocuous body, the World Court. H. W. Brands notes, "Only the willfully obstinate, one would have thought, could oppose such a worthy goal."[29] Thirty-six senators met that definition. The rejection signified a change in the mid-1930s. Kennedy claims, "American isolationism hardened from mere indifference to the outside world into studied, active repudiation of anything that smacked of international political or military engagement—or even, under some circumstances, economic engagement." Ironically, Roosevelt increasingly moved to an internationalist posture as his nation did the opposite, but found his hands tied, mainly because war became less a theoretical abstraction and more a practical problem. In September 1931, the Japanese invaded Manchuria; in October 1935, Italy invaded Ethiopia; in March 1936, Germany occupied the Rhineland; in July 1936, the Spanish Civil War began; in April 1937, the Germans bombed Guernica; in July 1937, Japan attacked China proper; and in December 1937, the Japanese raped Nanking. They also bombed the USS *Panay* in broad daylight while ignoring two eighteen-by-fourteen-foot American flags displayed on its topside. Planes strafed the survivors as they swam from the sinking ship. Two Americans died and thirty were wounded.[30] Congress was dismayed not at the Japanese action, but at the presence of U.S. ships in the area. It developed legislation during this period designed to make America—and, in particular, the president—mind their own business.

The problem, peace advocates felt sure, rested with the American definition of neutrality. To their discomfort, this was a policy set not by FDR, but by George Washington, and followed by all subsequent presidents. When war erupted between France and Great Britain, Washington declared American neutrality but insisted the United States had the right to sell what it wanted, including war materials, to all belligerents. His determination made freedom of the seas (and now the air) a fundamental U.S. principle. Walter Russell Meade explains, "In its narrowest sense, this involves the freedom of American citizens, American goods, and American ships to travel wherever they wish in the world in the interests of peaceful trade. . . . foreign nations must abide by international law in their treatment of neutral shipping during war." They must allow U.S. trade, respect American sailors, and accept U.S. goods. If they do not, dire consequences will result. Meade concludes, "No other principle has played such a major role in our diplomatic history; infringing on our freedom to travel by sea and air remains the fastest way for foreign powers to start a war with the United States."[31]

That was the problem for peace activists. Belligerents bought American products. American ships and sailors transported the products to combat zones. Other belligerents shot, sunk, and killed said American ships and sailors. Presidents demanded American rights and persuaded the nation to use military force to secure those rights, often, to borrow a phrase, by waving the bloody shirt. U.S. soldiers soon found themselves slogging through the mud and blood of battlefields while munitions makers and bankers counted the profits earned by the dead. American exceptionalism, in the eyes of the Senate's "Peace Progressives" and others, grew from its moral superiority to Europe.[32] But isolationists knew they were helpless to prevent military action if this train of events began. They needed an end to traditional neutrality, so that there would be no trade and thus no bloody shirt to wave.[33]

There were divisions in the ranks of isolationists. Senators Borah and Johnson, for example, supported traditional neutral rights, but also wanted to restrict the president's ability to identify with one side or another and thereby get the United States into war.[34] They believed Wilson's executive freedom to side with the Allies had led to U.S. participation. They were sure President Roosevelt would do the same thing. They meant to deny him that chance. In 1934, Johnson pushed through a bill prohibiting the purchase of bonds from or the grant of loans to countries in default on war debts.[35] That meant nearly everyone. Given how fast modern war absorbed a nation's financial reserves, this was a serious restriction. In 1935, the first of several Neutrality Acts passed.[36] After a debate in which the administration sought the authority to discriminate between belligerents and deny arms to aggressors, Congress required the president to impose an embargo on the sale of arms, ammunition, and "implements of war" to all belligerents. The president could define "implements." It empowered him to declare that Americans traveled on belligerent ships at their risk; there would be no more *Lusitanias*. In 1936 and 1937 extensions, traveling on belligerent vessels became illegal, raw materials joined the embargo, with presidential discretion to define those items, and, for anything, belligerents could buy only on a cash-and-carry basis. That is, they needed to pay before shipping, and they needed to ship in non-American bottoms. In short, this Congress restricted executive foreign policy power more than any other in American history. The legislation effectively prohibited Roosevelt from treating aggressors, such as Nazi Germany, any differently than, say, Denmark. In a vigorous response, President Franklin Roosevelt defended his office by signing each and every one of these acts.

Why did he do so? On one level, isolationists held a strong political advantage. Given the dominant interpretation of the Great War, a large peace movement, and the resulting obsession with evil internationalism, FDR was in trouble. Isolationists built a national consensus for their position, one powerful enough that Roosevelt felt he could not sustain a veto. On a second level, the debates often fell at a bad time. As the first Neutrality Act moved through Congress in the summer of 1935, for instance, he was fighting for the second New Deal. When isolationist senators threatened to filibuster until the Neutrality Act was passed and signed into law, FDR caved.[37] He signed the Social Security Act on August 14, and the Neutrality Act on August 31. No Neutrality, no Social Security. Yet he did include the 1935 equivalent of a signing statement, writing "the inflexible provisions [of the embargo] might drag us into war instead of keeping us out."[38] As things got worse abroad, they also grew worse at home. In 1937, Roosevelt squandered his enormous 1936 victory on a scheme to pack the Supreme Court with sympathetic justices, lowered his popularity further with the "Roosevelt recession," made his name mud in his party through a failed 1938 purge of conservatives, and raised talk of dictatorship with these efforts as well as his plan to reorganize the government.[39] His political leverage dropped. Finally, the votes he needed for domestic reform, Republican progressives such as Hiram Johnson, William Borah, Gerald P. Nye, and others, were isolationists, while those who supported internationalism were often southern conservatives who defied him on reform. For example, he tried to purge Georgia's Walter George shortly before George took the chair of the Senate Foreign Relations Committee. This did not endear FDR to Georgia or George. Given the contradictory coalitions backing his domestic and foreign programs, President Roosevelt often had to choose between these priorities, which meant that the New Deal lost its prime sponsor on September 1, 1939.

World War

David Reynolds knows fascism is "a notoriously slippery concept." Scholars debate its definition, differences between the three fascist powers, and even whether they *were* fascist. He argues, however, that contemporary observers had no such issues: "Fascists preached the politics of national renewal, seeking to mobilize mass movements by an often mystical vision of national greatness rooted in historical myths and directed toward imperial expansion." The means by which to achieve these ends were violence and war; they not only gave these nations material resources, but also rejuvenated "national character." The holy trinity of "nationalism, militarism, and imperial expansion" became particularly powerful in light of liberalism's failures during the Great Depression. As purchasing collapsed, tariff barriers grew, and nations sorted into regional trading blocs based on common currencies, planned economies pouring money into public works and rearmament recovered more quickly. In 1938, German unemployment fell to 2 percent.[40] At its best, the U.S. rate reached 15 percent in 1937. Unfortunately, thanks to FDR's conservative budget that year, the United States fell into recession. By 1938, "many Americans once more neared starvation." Chicago's relief rolls, for instance, "jumped from fifty thousand to one hundred and twenty thousand in the first five months of 1938."[41]

Feeling the flow of events moving their way, the two strongest fascist powers, Germany and Japan, sought living room, in the case of the former, and the "Greater Asian Co-Prosperity Sphere," in the case of the latter. Both powers wished to dominate their spheres of influence, extract needed resources and labor from them, control the sea lanes that regulated access to them, and use the peoples trapped within them to implement grotesque racial theories. They also developed discriminatory trading practices and, in doing all of this, created policies detrimental to American principles and interests.

In turn, FDR sought to bolster nations in the paths of these voracious powers and restrain or end their growth. Yet his electorate regarded Europe, in particular, and much of the world, in general, as either corrupt or distant. Most Americans felt comfortable ignoring and/or giggling at Herr Hitler's uncanny imitation of Charlie Chaplin. More viscerally, Americans felt no desire to join another "blood-spilling, man-eating, nation-killing nightmare." In the middle 1930s, FDR wanted to persuade Americans that world events affected them. When war broke out in 1939, he sought an Allied victory through all methods short of war. Such means inevitably created the risk of war. Roosevelt wanted to build a national consensus in favor of his policy, despite that risk. Fortunately for him, events, awful though they were, helped his cause. The "Phony War" from September 1939 until April 1940 did him no good, but in April 1940, Denmark and Norway fell. In May 1940, Luxembourg, Holland, and Belgium fell; in June 1940, France fell and Italy entered the war; and in August 1940, the Battle of Britain began. Many isolationists clung to their creed, but FDR found an increasingly receptive public as time marched on. But to move them from isolation to all aid short of war, FDR needed to make the Axis threat present and real.

Chaim Perelman and Lucie Olbrechts-Tyteca perceive presence as a condensed analogy. It names a strategy for making items or ideas real, alive, and salient. The two scholars describe presence as language "directed to filling the whole field of consciousness." They begin with the idea that a speaker never says all that could be said. Not only do orators select what needs to be said, but they also choose that which they wish to highlight. Perelman and Olbrechts-Tyteca argue, "By the very fact of selecting certain elements and presenting them to the audience, their importance and pertinence to the discussion are implied." While there are rational elements here, the two authors emphasize its pathetic power. Presence operates by "verbal magic alone" and "acts directly on our sensibility." Presence fills "the foreground of the hearer's consciousness." In terms of reason, presence "aspires to give the mind a certain orientation, [and] to make certain schemes of interpretation prevail."[42] This was Roosevelt's goal. He wanted Americans to see the threat's magnitude. How might he do that? FDR compared this crisis to a previous one, hoping to transfer the *ethos* of that moment to this one. He also made us look the threat in the eyes by using visual language. We expect people to face their personal crises, and so, too, did FDR demand we face our public problems. Finally, he shrunk time and space, making the danger visible, arguing that the threat was closer than the oceans suggested. Analogy, visuality, and perspective made the Axis into an American problem.

Re-creating March 1933

If Roosevelt wished to make these events into a new crisis, he could do worse than to compare them to an old one. Elsewhere, I have written of the relationship between analogy and presence, arguing "an extended analogy" can create a dominant interpretive frame.[43] Much as the president compared the economic crisis to war in his first inaugural address, so, too, did he compare the threat of war to the economic crisis in these speeches. The analogy linked the unfamiliar to the familiar, making this threat as present as that one. In addition, the world in 1940 offered a choice between good and evil just as the nation did in 1933 between the people and the moneychangers. Finally, the analogy re-created his early relationship with the American people. Political disputes had since soured the mood. FDR wanted a new beginning. He developed the analogy most fully in the 1936 State of the Union and the 1940 Arsenal of Democracy addresses.

The president began the 1936 address with what seemed an allusion to Lincoln: "Having come so far, it is fitting that we should pause to survey the ground which we have covered and the path which lies ahead."[44] What ground? "On the fourth of March, 1933," the president said, "on the occasion of taking the oath of office as President of the United States, I addressed the people of our country." Seldom do orators explicitly remind audiences of previous speeches, but he wanted it foremost in their minds. Using a rhetorical question, he created participation: "Need I recall either the scene or the national circumstances attending the occasion?" Apparently, he did. He noted the crisis then "was almost exclusively a national one" and "on that fourth of March, 1933, the world picture was an image of substantial peace."[45]

He briefly swerved to support the administration's "good neighbor" policy, but then, with a Shakespearean sigh, the president cried, "The rest of the world—Ah! there is the rub." Given that the speech fell shortly after Christmas, FDR noted "the temper and purposes of the rulers of many of the great populations in Europe and in Asia have not pointed the way either to peace or to good-will among men." He mischievously said on this third day of an election year, "Were I today to deliver an Inaugural Address to the people of the United States, I could not limit my comments on world affairs to one paragraph. With much regret I should be compelled to devote the greater part to world affairs."[46] Yet those affairs intertwined with domestic concerns and, in particular, with his need to win reelection and give another of those inaugural addresses.

As the rest of the speech demonstrated, electoral concerns dominated FDR's mind, and this annual message resembled few in the nation's history. It was a powerfully partisan address. Yet even in his belligerence, he connected foreign troubles to domestic problems, to his adversaries, and to 1933. In the initial section, the president explained that some nations have "impatiently reverted to the old belief in the law of the sword, or to the fantastic conception that they, and they alone, are chosen to fulfill a mission and that all the others among the billion and a half human beings in the world must and shall learn from and be subject to them."[47] He concluded: "The evidence before us clearly proves that autocracy in world affairs endangers peace." Autocracy became the key term in the address. He traced its implications: "If this be true in world affairs, it should have the greatest weight in the determination of domestic policies. Within democratic nations the chief concern of the people is to prevent the continuance or the rise of autocratic institutions that beget slavery at home and aggression abroad."[48]

From here forward, the president turned to domestic affairs and launched a vicious attack on conservative opponents. His fight was "no new thing." From the "Constitutional Convention of 1787" until 1936, "the battle has been continued, under Thomas Jefferson, Andrew Jackson, Theodore Roosevelt, and Woodrow Wilson." FDR joined the fight in "March 1933." He said that then he "spoke of the practices of the unscrupulous money-changers who stood indicted in the court of public opinion." He spoke also of the "rulers of the exchanges" who had abdicated their thrones: "Abdicated? Yes, in 1933, but now . . . they seek restoration of their selfish power." FDR intoned, "The principle they would instill into government if they succeed in seizing power is well shown by the principles many of them have instilled into their own affairs: autocracy toward labor, toward stockholders, toward consumers, toward public sentiment. Autocrats in smaller things, they seek autocracy in bigger things. 'By their fruits ye shall know them.'"[49] The wrath of a biblically literate president is a terrible thing to behold.

A contemporary critic might think the president was comparing his opponents to Hitler. I suspect the relationship went the other way. In 1936, his audience was likely to know the evil of Henry Ford, Herbert Hoover, and Joseph Martin better than they knew the Fuhrer. Roosevelt wished to re-create 1933 in the public mind; he wanted people to recall that occasion and transfer that feeling to "world affairs." Autocracy formed a seamless whole. Americans must oppose it here *and* there, whatever isolationists said. In a less political moment, Roosevelt turned to the same strategy to begin his December 29, 1940, "Arsenal of Democracy" address.

After a brief opening, he said, "Tonight, in the presence of a world crisis, my mind goes back eight years to a night in the midst of a domestic crisis. It was a time when the wheels of industry were grinding to a full stop, when the whole banking system of our country had ceased to function." FDR recalled, "while I sat in my study in the White House, preparing to talk with the people of the United States, I had before my eyes the picture of all those Americans with whom I was talking." In a lovely bit of anaphora, he put before our eyes what had been before his: "I saw the workmen in the mills, the mines, the factories; the girl behind the counter; the small shopkeeper; the farmer doing his spring plowing; the widows and the old men wondering about their life's savings."[50] By filling our consciousness with these images, FDR recalled us to the relationship we shared at the time of the banking address—the concern, the confusion, and the tentative confidence that, finally, someone understood our desperate straits.

Judging by the news, the same people were there again. *Time* magazine wrote, "At 9:30 P.M. more than 500 radio stations in the U.S. were tuned to his desk. Short-wave stations stood by, set to throw his words over the world. Attendance at movies dropped sharply. In barrooms, farmhouses, trains, planes and ships, people waited, listening. His words might mark a turning point in history. . . . He was deliberately trying to lead the nation as he had led it in 1933."[51] *Time* amplified the anaphora, providing the places where FDR's Americans sat listening. *Newsweek* did much the same, such was the power of the president's strategy. If he described listening Americans, *Newsweek* turned to the world (with some words that make us cringe today): "The world wanted to know where America stood. Chinese coolies . . . Mild-mannered little Dutch colonial officials . . . Normandy peasants, hungry hostages to their Nazi conquerors, wondered what America might do to rescue them."[52] As these popular magazines recognized, FDR invoked the 1933 religion: "I tried to convey to the great mass of American people what the banking crisis meant to them in their daily lives. Tonight, I want to do the same thing, with the same people, in this new crisis which faces America."[53]

The "same thing" included the same sort of binary that had marked 1933 and 1936. If autocrats were adversaries then, now the enemy was worse. FDR charged the "history of recent years proves that shootings and chains and concentration camps are not simply the transient tools but the very altars of modern dictatorships." The religious imagery ironically reinforced the evil and recalled the sacred allusions in the first inaugural address. In their "new order," he said, "there is no liberty, no religion, no hope." There was also no government "based upon the consent of the governed. It is not a union of ordinary, self-respecting men and women to protect themselves and their freedom and dignity from oppression." Rather, he argued, the fascists were "an unholy alliance of power and pelf to dominate and enslave the human race." Nor did this binary ever fade from his discourse. In a May 27, 1941, national address, Roosevelt cried: "Today the whole world is divided between human slavery and human freedom—between pagan brutality and the Christian ideal. We choose human freedom—which is the Christian ideal." In the battle under way, he quoted that day, "'The only thing we have to fear is fear itself.'"[54]

The analogy to 1933 made those desperate times present, making sense of current experiences through comparison with that moment. FDR reconstituted his relationship with the American people by drawing on the well of trust he had previously established. As he did so, he recreated the clarity of a divided world. Americans must again choose between good and evil, with, perhaps, higher stakes than in 1933. In turn, if he was to lead the American people through these harrowing times, he required the same "courage and realism" they had displayed then.[55] They must see clearly.

Visualizing the Crisis

In 1933, Americans *faced* a crisis. The president wanted that to happen again. Cara Finnegan notes his first inaugural address relied on language "with a distinctly visual inflection." Words such as "facing" infused the text as he exhorted Americans "to confront their anxieties about the Depression head-on." During the "first few years of the Depression, many in government and business had buried their heads in the sand," she writes, but he would not countenance timidity: "Roosevelt's choice of visual language in this speech cannot have been accidental, for the twin notions of 'facing' and 'recognizing' so clearly embody his purposes." She concludes the New Deal "instituted a range of material practices in which visual remedies were often positioned as the cure for—or at least the mode of diagnosis of—what ailed the nation."[56] Visual language filled these speeches as well, partly out of habit, I suspect, and partly because FDR addressed a people determined too often to bury their heads in the sand. The president intended to make them face what ailed the world.

He made the illness—and some possible cures—a palpable presence in their lives.

The language cited thus far offers considerable evidence for this claim. Roosevelt asked his listeners to "survey" the ground traveled even as "rulers" have not "pointed the way" to peace. He spoke "in the presence of a world crisis," he "saw" the American people, he saw "that the world picture was an image of substantial peace," and he wanted to discuss "this new crisis that faces America. The nation had met the issue of 1933 with courage and realism. It would face this new crisis—this new threat to the security of the nation—with the same courage and realism."[57]

The visual language, however, runs through many of these foreign policy addresses. In the famed "Quarantine Speech" of October 5, 1937, Roosevelt warranted his claims with visual evidence, "as I have seen with my own eyes, the prosperous farms, the thriving factories and the busy railroads, as I have seen the happiness and security and peace which covers our wide land, almost inevitably I have been compelled to contrast our peace with very different scenes being enacted in other parts of the world." Seeing is believing, and learning as well, as he said on May 16, 1940: "On the other side of the picture we must visualize the outstanding fact that since the first day of September, 1939, every week that has passed has brought new lessons learned from actual combat on land and sea."[58] Americans should trust that which they see and, as the world picture steadily darkened, the visual evidence turned against the isolationists.

In a Fireside Chat on May 26, 1940, as German panzers rolled to the English Channel, FDR displayed the crisis: "Tonight, over the once peaceful roads of Belgium and France millions are now moving, running from their homes to escape bombs and shells and fire and machine gunning, without shelter and almost wholly without food. They stumble on, not knowing where the end of the road will be." Note the iconic power of this passage, as the phrases shorten and pick up speed. The repeated hammering of the conjunction imitates the machine guns harrying the refugees. But when he asked his audience to "sit down together, you and I, to consider our own pressing problems that confront us," he reversed the imagery. He faced his domestic adversaries: "There are many among us who in the past closed their eyes to events abroad." "Closed their eyes" emerged as the key phrase in a parallel structure. He used it to articulate the arguments of those who had ignored the crisis, in a loose form of *dialogismus.* Many "closed their eyes, from lack of interest or lack of knowledge." Others "were persuaded . . . we could maintain our physical safety by retiring within our continental boundaries." Finally, "there are a few among us who have deliberately and consciously closed their eyes because they were determined to be opposed to their government." He concluded, "To those who have closed their eyes for any of these many reasons, to those who would not admit the possibility of the approaching storm—to all of them the past two weeks have meant the shattering of many illusions." The rhetorical equation was clear. Closed eyes offered only "fears and illusions"; open eyes "let us calmly consider what we have done and what we must do."[59]

In the "Arsenal" speech, the visual sarcasm expanded: "One telegram, however, expressed the attitude of the small minority who want to see no evil and hear no evil, even though they know in their hearts that evil exists. . . . we well know that we cannot escape danger, or the fear of danger, by crawling into bed and pulling the covers over our heads." FDR used visual language to make his opponents into children, unable to face the hard realities of adult life. The allusion, rhythm, and rhyme (in the form of assonance) that appear when the words above are read aloud make it sound as if it was a children's tale; once the listener is caught in the momentum of his prose, it is hard to escape the certainty that too many wanted to see and hear no evil. By contrast, the "American people" were courageous adults, able to recognize difficult challenges. As he said in the "Four Freedoms" address: "The American people have unalterably set their faces against that tyranny."[60]

The character of that tyranny and the steps Americans needed to take to face it also emerged from this visual lexicon. Roosevelt described the perfidy and evil of the Nazis too often for me to account for all variations, but here are two examples. In an allusive visualization, FDR spent part of a June 10, 1940, commencement address at the University of Virginia describing the efforts he and others had taken to persuade Italy to refrain from war. As Germany attacked, Italy held back until victory was certain. Then, "the hand that held the dagger … struck it into the back of its neighbor."[61] The fascists were all honorable men. The picture and allusion beautifully combined to craft the dominant interpretation of Italy's action. This is what happens when your neighbor does not believe in "the sanctity of agreements." Roosevelt was nothing if not consistent when he posited a world of neighbors.

In that same speech, he depicted the world as it would be if the honorable men won while the isolationists dithered. "Some," he stated, "still hold to the somewhat obvious delusion that" the United States could become "a lone island in a world dominated" by force. This "may be the dream of those who still talk and vote as isolationists." But to him and to most Americans, this island was "a helpless nightmare of a people without freedom—the nightmare of a people lodged in prison, handcuffed, hungry, and fed through the bars from day to day by the contemptuous, unpitying masters of other continents." This was as dismal a picture as any president has ever painted. But he noted that it was "natural also that we should ask ourselves how now we can prevent the building of that prison."[62] Later that year, FDR used another famous visual image to answer his own question.

During a wonderfully entertaining December 17, 1940, press conference, a jaunty and rested president began by saying, "I don't think there is any particular news, except possibly one thing that I think is worth my talking about." Roosevelt had been giving thought to the need to aid Great Britain and to "a great deal of nonsense in the last few days by people who can only think in what we may call traditional terms about finances." After much rambling, FDR finally got to his point. He thought the United States could "lease or sell [war] materials, subject to mortgage, to the people on the other side." In such transactions, he wanted to "eliminate the dollar sign, . . . I think—get rid of the silly, foolish old dollar sign." In case his audience did not see his point, he clarified the thought with his most famous "illustration": "Suppose my neighbor's home catches fire, and I have a length of garden hose four or five hundred feet away." Now, does he charge for the hose? Of course not: "I don't want $15—I want my garden hose back after the fire is over. All right. If it goes through the fire all right, intact, without any damage to it, he gives it back to me and thanks me very much for the use of it." But what if it burns? It is replaced: "Now, if I get a nice garden hose back, I am in pretty good shape."[63] I suspect the moment "implements of war" became a garden hose in the American mind, the Neutrality Act began to die. The image of fire is also noteworthy. For months, Americans had been listening to the reports of Edward R. Murrow and others, to the boom of bombs and the crackle of flames. The hose and the fire made complete sense as persuasive images. It is also gratifying for rhetoricians to know that the first Lend-Lease shipment "included 900,000 feet of fire hose."[64]

The visual language created presence. Roosevelt painted pictures. He depicted the evil that lay ahead, the attitude with which Americans should confront it, and the tools they should send to the fight. Adults faced such problems, and made such plans, much as Americans had done in 1933. Children saw no evil. Yet childish things appeared possible through much of this period because the enemy seemed so far away and the oceans so very wide. Crawling under the covers seemingly works if the storm stays away. The president insisted that they put aside childish things. He shifted their perspective on the Nazi menace through a reconfiguration of time and space.

Shrinking Time and Space

In his fine discussion of presence, James Jasinski, drawing on Perelman and Olbrechts-Tyteca, identifies "five key loci of presence that may be used for making an exigence more present or more vivid for the audience."[65] In a sense, all five—urgency, duration, proximity, magnitude, and severity—matter, but I am concerned here with urgency and proximity. President Roosevelt knew Americans had traditionally relied on their two great oceans to protect them from foreign harm. In his speeches, oceans turned from moats to highways. In modernity, he argued, technology had shrunk time and space, creating an urgent and proximate problem. The enemy was at hand and, perhaps, already within the gates. The perspective of the nation needed to shift.

In doing so, Roosevelt capitalized on a powerful cultural current. Since before the First World War, fear of air power, of death from the skies, had gripped the Western world. The *War of the Worlds* (1938) phenomenon captured that, of course, but was not H. G. Wells's sole literary contribution. In 1908 he published *War in the Air* and "painted a lurid picture of 'German air fleets' destroying 'the whole fabric of civilisation.'"[66] Given the horrific consequences of trench warfare, many analysts saw air power as a way around the mud and blood. Keegan notes that the bomber was viewed "as the instrument of a campaign designed to break the enemy's will and capacity to resist without the intervention or support of armies and navies."[67] Experts believed that science "was now harnessed sufficiently closely to military life to produce a stream of new weapons; of secret devices from the air whose nature could only be guessed at."[68] Italian Giulio Douhet published *Command of the Air,* which argued the modern bomber and those "secret devices" could annihilate an enemy's industrial base before its army could mobilize. Keegan called Douhet a visionary because he discerned in 1921 the logic of a nuclear first strike and mutually assured destruction.[69] By 1931 the retired head of the Irish air corps told American readers that "a hideous shower of death and destruction" would drop from the sky in the next war and survivors, "now merely demoralized masses of demented humanity" would curse "the fate that did not destroy them hurriedly and without warning in the first awful explosions."[70] In a frequently quoted 1932 speech, British Prime Minister Stanley Baldwin claimed that nothing could save "the man in the street": "Whatever people may tell him, the bomber will always get through." The only defense was a first strike: "you will have to kill more civilians, more women and children first, if you want to save yours from the enemy." The British took the idea seriously. They evacuated 1.75 million women and children from urban areas by September 1939.[71]

When the war began, no one could use bombers this way, and the misplaced confidence that they could always get through killed thousands of young flyers. Yet most believed the prophets before the war and reacted accordingly. The Allies lived in fear of the reconstituted Luftwaffe. Herring claims, "The fear of German air power—put on such brutal display in Spain—paralyzed Europe during the Munich crisis."[72] In a November 14, 1938, meeting with his military advisers, FDR averred, "Had we had this summer 5,000 planes and the capacity immediately to produce 10,000 per year . . . Hitler would not have dared to take the stand he did."[73] From that point, FDR unceasingly advocated for more planes and his military chiefs unceasingly pushed back, arguing for a balanced military force. Yet in his eyes, modern air power mattered most, not least because it threatened the American homeland.

Building off of existing discourse, Roosevelt made the world smaller through air power. This argument appeared after the war's start and began with contrasts between past and present. On May 16, 1940, Roosevelt emphasized "the potential speed of modern attack." He continued, "The Atlantic and Pacific oceans were reasonably adequate defensive barriers when fleets under sail could move at an average of five miles an hour," or, he claimed, "when fleets and convoys propelled by steam could sail the oceans at fifteen or twenty miles an hour." But that was no longer true: a "new element—air navigation—step[ped] up the speed of a possible attack to two hundred, to three hundred miles an hour." On May 26, recall that he said there were many "who closed their eyes, from lack of interest or lack of knowledge; honestly and sincerely thinking that the many hundreds of miles of salt water" protected them. He noted in the "Arsenal of Democracy" that "the width of oceans is not what it was in the days of clipper ships," a nicely condensed image that expressed more succinctly the earlier argument. In the "Four Freedoms," he "pointed out how quickly the tempo of modern warfare could bring into our very midst the physical attack we must eventually expect if the dictator nations win this war."[74]

Why was this true? Roosevelt emphasized the shrinkage in time/space created by bomber development. On May 16 he worried about "nearer bases" the enemy could control if European nations surrendered. For instance, "from the fiords of Greenland [a Danish possession], it is four hours by air to Newfoundland; five hours to Nova Scotia, New Brunswick and the Province of Quebec; and only six hours to New England." The Azores, he said, "are only 2,000 miles from parts of our eastern seaboard and if Bermuda fell into hostile hands it would be a matter of less than three hours for modern bombers to reach our shores." A more succinct set of analogies appeared in the "Arsenal" address: "At one point between Africa and Brazil the distance is less than from Washington to Denver, Colorado—five hours for the latest type of bomber. . . . Even today we have planes that could fly from the British Isles to New England and back again without refueling. And remember that the range of the modern bomber is ever being increased."[75] There was no defense except forward defense of Great Britain against "the modern bomber."

Finally, FDR framed the general dangers of modernity, or what we call globalization, in two ways. In each he wove together the fate of Americans and others, highlighting what he often called the "interdependence" of peoples. In 1937 he famously quarantined the Axis. Disease, as a public familiar with the 1918 influenza pandemic knew, jumped borders. FDR claimed an "epidemic of world lawlessness is spreading." He argued that when "an epidemic of physical disease starts to spread, the community approves and joins in a quarantine of the patients in order to protect the health of the community against the spread of the disease." He noted, "War is a contagion." It "can engulf states and peoples remote from the original scene of hostilities," like a disease.[76] What he meant by "quarantine" was not clear, then or now. He said it was an "attitude" and not a "program," but that helped little. *Time* magazine amusingly called it his "Bad Neighbor Policy," while Arthur Krock wrote this lead: "Nobody at the State Department today professed to know what the President meant."[77] Nobody wants to see *that* in the *New York Times* the day after a major speech.

Although FDR did not receive the support he wanted after this address, he remembered the metaphor.[78] If lawlessness and evil were contagions, then those "foreign agents" could move across the oceans and into the body politic as easily as the influenza virus. Modern means of transportation and communication meant that discursive diseases knew no barriers of space or time. Such insidious metaphors, anchored by the disease image, came to characterize his account of *domestic* adversaries. On May 26, 1940, for instance, FDR declared, "Today's threat to our national security is not a matter of military weapons alone. We know of new methods of attack. The Trojan Horse." The "method," he said, "is simple." The enemy foments discord "through false slogans and emotional appeals," which create "public indecision, political paralysis and, eventually, a state of panic." His paralysis metaphor could not have been an accident. The physical emphasis continued, as he argued that these "deliberately planned propagandas . . . divide and weaken us in the face of danger as others have been weakened before." Through discourse, "the unity of the state can be so sapped that its strength is destroyed." He ended this argument with a classic image: "These dividing forces are undiluted poison. They must not be allowed to spread in the New World as they have in the Old." In the "Four Freedoms," FDR deployed the metaphor again, arguing every "realist knows that the democratic way of life is at this moment being directly assailed in every part of the world—assailed either by arms, or by secret spreading of poisonous propaganda by those who seek to destroy unity and promote discord in nations that are still at peace."[79] Relying on the work of Gordon Wood and others, Jasinski and I note that "since the revolutionary era Americans have deployed images of poison and disease to mark the presence of civic corruption."[80] Corruption is, of course, a disease metaphor signifying a rotting civic body. The danger to America was clear, a fear rooted in our earliest republican discursive traditions.

In the "Arsenal" address, FDR expanded this metaphor, calling his enemies "trouble-breeders" and "foreign agents." The "evil forces" who "crushed and undermined and corrupted so many others are now within our own gates." The disease metaphor articulated nicely with the "Trojan Horse" (city gates) metaphor; all cast isolationists, as he said in the "Four Freedoms" address, as "secret agents and their dupes." There, he offered a solution; he repeated thrice that the nation needed "an impressive expression of the public will and [no] . . . partisanship." A united people, like a healthy body, could fight off disease, which spread rapidly in a shrinking world. "Singleness of national purpose," he said, "was essential to victory."[81]

Roosevelt also evinced his understanding of the horrors of modern technology in his second warning. At Virginia's commencement, he said the following of fascist philosophy: "But in this new system of force the mastery of the machine is not in the hands of mankind. It is in the control of infinitely small groups of individuals. . . . The machine in the hands of irresponsible conquerors becomes the master; mankind is not only the servant; it is the victim, too." This was an odd, even Wellsian view, one echoing motion pictures like *Metropolis*. Modern machines reduced the world; oceans could no longer protect the nation. That, at any rate, was the view FDR forwarded. In either the case of a global pandemic or of machines run wild, the warning was clear. No nation was an island, entire of itself, any more than any American was an island in 1933. Americans had to face that fact, boldly and frankly, their president felt. Fortunately, he knew "this nation [had] placed its destiny in the hands and heads and hearts of its millions of free men and women." From that "high concept, there can be no end save victory."[82]

Speculative Conclusion

Difficult as it is to ascertain the effects of rhetoric, Dallek was not wrong when he lauded these speeches as one of the great presidential achievements of the twentieth century. Steven Casey, in his study of public opinion and the war against Nazi Germany, notes one additional peculiarity. Public opinion polling began around the same time as these speeches. He writes that FDR followed numerous opinion gauges, including the new "scientific" polls. He began his day with six newspapers, read a weekly summary of editorial opinion, sent Eleanor Roosevelt, Harry Hopkins, and others to scour the nation and world for him, brought hundreds more to the White House, and, beginning in 1939, started studying Elmo Roper and George Gallup's polls, with a preference for the former. Until 1940 Americans strongly disliked Hitler, but, given anger and embarrassment over their susceptibility to World War I propaganda, thought the German people were "peace loving and kindly," although "unfortunate in being misled" by their rulers. As late as the winter of 1940, Americans believed the oceans, the British navy, and French army would save them. They were so entrenched in this psychological redoubt that in January 1939 only 43 percent thought it necessary to defend Mexico should that country be invaded. In one of the earliest polls, in 1936, 95 percent of Americans wanted no part of any conflict. Casey concludes, "The 1930s were the high-water mark of American isolationism."[83]

Although it is impossible to make direct attributions, two events seemed to do the most to change the public mind. The first was the fall of France. Polling data "revealed a sharp increase in respondents who believed they would be personally affected by the war, up from 48 percent in March, to 67 percent in July, and 71 percent by the following January."[84] As Reynolds pointed out, FDR connected the dots in his May 1940 speeches, but the surrender of France shocked an American public expecting the same stubborn Gallic performance as World War I. The second event was the "Arsenal of Democracy" speech, followed shortly by the "Four Freedoms" annual message. After them, the percentage of Americans willing to risk war to aid Great Britain and the percentage who thought the United States would get into the fight rose to above 60.[85]

Reynolds notes that 75 percent of those polled had seen or heard of the "Arsenal" speech, the highest for a Rooseveltian chat for which there are polls, and "61 percent agreed with his position."[86] Kennedy calls it "one of his most memorable Fireside Chats," while Dallek says the "speech was one of the most successful he ever gave."[87] As Congress started to debate lend-lease, FDR's popularity grew to 71 percent, the highest Gallup had recorded for him. He was beginning his ninth year in office.

Of course, no other president served for so long, and that alone established his continuing influence. Historian William Leuchtenburg has famously traced Roosevelt's effect on subsequent presidents; George McJimsey claims all struggled with FDR's "dynamic personal legacy."[88] Yet they also had available to them his language and, whatever resentments they might have felt, his words mattered. From 1936 to 1941, FDR created an enduring interpretive frame for understanding and acting in the world. Although scholars such as George Herring, Walter Russell Mead, and David Hendrickson have dispelled the myth of American isolation prior to the twentieth century, even they note FDR's pivotal role. As Dallek notes, FDR knew "that effective action abroad required a reliable consensus at home." These speeches helped to develop that support. Herring writes, "Many anxious Americans . . . concluded that their values and interests were threatened by events abroad and that their security required them to assist nations combating the Axis menace even at the risk of war. Franklin Roosevelt took the lead in educating Americans to this new perspective on world affairs."[89]

The discourse that helped cause Americans to feel "threatened by events abroad" included key elements that percolated through the public sphere after Roosevelt's death. As I have argued, FDR cut the globe in twain, constituting a "whole world . . . divided between human slavery and human freedom—between pagan brutality and the Christian ideal." In that world, Americans must choose, and, in doing so, they should remember the "courage and realism" of past generations as they struggled against serious threats. This threat was visible and evil. It was also imminent; it spread in a shrunken world like a disease, and the nation must beware not only of the enemy at the gates, but also of the enemy within.

His words became a great linguistic arsenal. For instance, Harry Truman, in his most famous address, argued "nearly every nation must choose between alternative ways of life." One "way of life" echoed the four freedoms: It was "distinguished by free institutions, representative government, free elections, guarantees of individual liberty, freedom of speech and religion, and freedom from political oppression." The other echoed fascism: "terror and oppression, a controlled press and radio, fixed elections, and the suppression of personal freedoms." Denise Bostdorff notes in her study of the Truman Doctrine speech that a "rich rhetorical stockpile" was open to him, one that included "the polarizing rhetoric used only recently to attack fascism."[90] Robert Ivie argues of the same address: "Vehicles of disease deeply embedded in the design of the speech . . . prompted arguments for aiding afflicted nations before an epidemic of communism could spread to the United States." He notes the natural reaction: "The *New York Times* and at least six other newspapers editorialized that Truman's address was comparable to Franklin Roosevelt's "'quarantine' speech against aggressors, a speech made under analogous circumstances in 1937."[91] The strategies, Ivie claims, created a sense of "impending disaster." Truman's speech is but one example of this "rhetorical stockpile" at work. Of course, he, too, added to the stockpile and developed yet more rhetorical trajectories that, in turn, influenced subsequent orators. But as Herring concludes, "By articulating the notions that America could be truly secure only in a world in which its values prevailed and that its way of life could best be defended by acting abroad, [FDR] set forth the intellectual underpinnings for an American globalism that would take form in World War II and flourish in postwar years."[92]

In short, I have argued that Franklin Roosevelt made the world's dangers "present" in ways matched by few American presidents. These strategies—analogy, visuality, and perspective—joined to create a dominant interpretive framework. The analogy implicitly structured the globe; Americans should see it now much as they saw it in 1933. FDR's visual lexicon placed that structure directly before the eyes; no longer could Americans avert their gaze from Herr Hitler. Finally, perspective made of fascism an urgent and proximate problem. In reverse order, war was here, Americans must face it, much as they had faced the earlier economic crisis. This threat was not manufactured by arms dealers or banks. It was real.

In this essay, I generally emphasize the positive charge of this discourse, operating under the assumption, shared with most other students of this period, that Auschwitz settled the moral debate. Yet FDR's determination to bifurcate the world and cast political opponents into the darkness disturbs twenty-first-century Americans. I suspect some of the unease leaks from the concept of presence itself. In their key discussion of it, Perelman and Olbrechts-Tyteca contrast presence to "rationalistic conceptions of reasoning" and emphasize its strategic fullness. As I note, presence "acts directly on our sensibility." It works "at the level of perception." It shapes the world through "verbal magic alone." They even note, in a nod to the visual, some "masters of rhetoric, with a liking for quick results, advocate the use of concrete objects in order to move an audience: Caesar's bloody tunic which Antony waves in front of the Roman populace, or the children of the accused brought before his judges in order to arouse their pity." Presumably, these objects so fill the field of consciousness that judgments favorable to the orator result. Even when the two turn to the rationality of presence, the spatial metaphors persist; elements with presence "occupy the foreground of a speaker's consciousness . . . give the mind a certain orientation . . . make certain schemes of interpretation prevail."[93]

Their only concerns with the concept rest in the realm of instrumentality. Some concrete objects may arouse the wrong emotions, and the "deliberate suppression of presence" may be a problematic strategy. In general, they argue with some heat that they want nothing to do with presence as a "cornerstone" for a philosophy: "We are interested only in the technical aspect of this notion, which leads to the inevitable conclusion that all argumentation is selective." Yet the latter idea leads to one last intriguing observation. They deploy the claim that all argument is selective in order to discredit the notion that argumentation can ever or should ever provide "the totality of informational elements." They "think this is an illusion and that passage from the subjective to the objective can be accomplished only by successive enlargements, none of which can be regarded as final." An orator "who effects a new enlargement will necessarily emphasize that the previous statements had involved a choice of data, and he will probably be able to show quite easily that this was indeed the case."[94] They are so strongly committed to such a pluralistic concept of rhetoric that they do not explore the choices of those who are not so inclined. As I read these words, however, I hear the inimitable voice of Kenneth Burke whispering that many orators will insist their "enlargements" *are* final and that "certain schemes of interpretation," as Perelman and Olbrechts-Tyteca put it, will inevitably become "rotten with perfection."[95]

Borrowing from part of the Aristotelian corpus, Burke notes the principle of "'entelechy,' the notion that each being aims at the perfection natural to its kind." Although Aristotle confines this term to beings, Burke turns to symbols and states simply: "There is a principle of perfection implicit in the nature of symbol systems; and in keeping with his nature as symbol-using animal, man is moved by this principle." Add in the usual Burkean irony and a vocabulary becomes "rotten with perfection." This idea is "revealed most perfectly in our tendency to conceive of a 'perfect' enemy. . . . The Nazi version of the Jew, as developed in Hitler's *Mein Kampf,* is the most thoroughgoing instance of such ironic 'perfection' in recent times, though strongly similar trends keep manifesting themselves in current controversies between 'East' and 'West.'" Just so. The problem with presence rests in its ability to infuse vocabularies with unwonted fullness. They then fill a field so thoroughly as to deny their own finitude: "A given terminology contains various *implications,* and there is a corresponding 'perfectionist' tendency for men to attempt carrying out those implications. . . . Insofar as any of these terminologies happen also to contain the risks of destroying the world, that's just too bad."[96] Perhaps due to the dialogic nature of their philosophical/rhetorical project, Perelman and Olbrechts-Tyteca fail to recognize fully that some orators regard their enlargement as final, suppressing its limitations, even if the finality is, well, that final.

A rhetorician can, perhaps, offer comic correction, and what Aristotle taketh with one thought, he giveth with another. Near the end of his life, Thomas Farrell became intrigued with the Aristotelian notion of "magnitude," which "has to do with the gravity, the enormity, the weightiness of what is enacted, a sense of significance that may be glimpsed and recognized by others." The last phrase is a key to magnitude; rather than merely size, or even the classical strategy of amplification, Farrell's interpretation emphasizes proportion. What can engaged interlocutors glimpse or recognize during public deliberation? He notes, "While much has been parodied in Aristotle's obsession with proportionality, there is also something recognizably 'right' about this intuition." Aristotle possessed, Farrell continues, "a profound awareness of scale, proportion, distance."[97] A disproportionate response, as it were, violates an ethical sense of presence; to colonize another's field of consciousness is to carry out the implications of a vocabulary to their final, rotten end. Presence needs proportion.

In the final analysis, it is important to remember that Franklin Roosevelt, unlike many of his successors, confronted an evil as perfect as humans have ever achieved. His profound sense of scale, proportion, and distance made that threat real to Americans. His eloquence also made the cause he championed as simple and ideal as words permit: Freedom of speech and expression everywhere in the world. The freedom of every person to worship God in his or her own way everywhere in the world. Freedom from want everywhere in the world. And freedom from fear. Anywhere in the world.

NOTES

1. Conrad Black, *Franklin Delano Roosevelt: Champion of Freedom* (New York: Public Affairs, 2003), 20. FDR's collecting is described more generally by H. W. Brands, *Traitor to His Class: The Privileged Life and Radical Presidency of Franklin Delano Roosevelt* (New York: Doubleday, 2008), 236.
2. Robert Dallek, *Franklin D. Roosevelt and American Foreign Policy, 1932–1945* (New York: Oxford University Press, 1979), 3.
3. David M. Kennedy, *Freedom from Fear: The American People in Depression and War, 1929–1945* (New York: Oxford University Press, 1999), 389.
4. Brands, *Traitor to His Class,* 86–90; Dallek, *Franklin D. Roosevelt,* 6–11; Kennedy, *Freedom from Fear,* 389.
5. Dallek, *Franklin D. Roosevelt,* 35–38; William E. Leuchtenburg, *Franklin D. Roosevelt and the New Deal* (New York: Harper Torchbooks, 1963), 199–205.
6. Franklin D. Roosevelt, "First Inaugural Address, 1933," in *American Speeches: Political Oratory from Abraham Lincoln to Bill Clinton,* ed. Ted Widmer (New York: Library of America, 2006), 400–401.
7. Leuchtenburg, *Franklin D. Roosevelt and the New Deal,* 197.
8. David Reynolds, *From Munich to Pearl Harbor: Roosevelt's America and the Origins of the Second World War* (Chicago: Ivan R. Dee Publisher, 2001), 7. My narrative

draws heavily from this source, from a graduate course taken many years ago from professors Wil Linkugel and Lloyd Sponholz at the University of Kansas, and from my reading. For an interesting collection of divergent opinions, see Warren F. Kimball, ed., *Franklin D. Roosevelt and the World Crisis, 1937–1945* (Lexington, MA: D. C. Heath & Co., 1973).

9. Patrick J. Buchanan, *Churchill, History and "The Unnecessary War": How Britain Lost Its Empire and the West Lost the World* (New York: Crown, 2008). Studs Terkel coined the phrase the "Good War," and Tom Brokaw created the "greatest generation."
10. James MacGregor Burns, *Roosevelt: The Lion and the Fox, 1882–1940* (New York: Harcourt, Brace & World, 1956); Robert A. Divine, *The Illusion of Neutrality* (Chicago: University of Chicago Press, 1962). See also Stephen E. Ambrose and Douglas G. Brinkley, *Rise to Globalism: American Foreign Policy since 1938*, 9th rev. ed. (New York: Penguin Books, 2011).
11. Reynolds, *From Munich to Pearl Harbor*, 8.
12. George C. Herring, *From Colony to Superpower: U.S. Foreign Relations since 1776* (New York: Oxford University Press, 2008), 537.
13. Dalleck, *Franklin D. Roosevelt*, 530.
14. Reynolds, *From Munich to Pearl Harbor*, 10–11.
15. I begin with FDR's 1936 State of the Union address, his first major effort to define the Axis in the public mind, and conclude with a May 27, 1941, address that declared an "unlimited national emergency." I believe the time from the attacks on "autocracy" in 1936 to war footing defined this period. I do not examine every speech, but I look at most of his substantial foreign policy texts. Although I make no claims to the rigor (or status?) of social science, I believe this study addresses FDR's major rhetorical efforts.
16. Chaim Perelman and Lucie Olbrechts-Tyteca, *The New Rhetoric: A Treatise on Argumentation*, trans. John Wilkinson and Purcell Weaver (Notre Dame: University of Notre Dame Press, 1969), 115–120.
17. John Keegan, *The First World War* (New York: Vantage Books, 1998), 3.
18. John Keegan, *The Second World War* (New York: Penguin Books, 1989), 11.
19. Keegan, *First World War*, 6–7.
20. Kennedy, *Freedom from Fear*, 381.
21. Reynolds, *From Munich to Pearl Harbor*, 27–28.
22. See Herring, *From Colony to Superpower*, 502–503.
23. Kennedy, *Freedom from Fear*, 387, 388.

24. Dallek, *Franklin D. Roosevelt*, 104.
25. Ibid., 85.
26. Kennedy, *Freedom from Fear*, 382.
27. Dallek, *Franklin D. Roosevelt,* 101; see also Divine, *The Illusion of Neutrality*, 84.
28. Brands, *Traitor to His Class,* 332.
29. Ibid., 329. See also Dallek, *Franklin D. Roosevelt,* 94–97; Leuchtenburg, *Franklin D. Roosevelt and the New Deal,* 215–217; Divine, *The Illusion of Neutrality,* 83.
30. Kennedy, *Freedom from Fear,* 393, 402.
31. Walter Russell Meade, *Special Providence: American Foreign Policy and How It Changed the World* (New York: Routledge, 2002), 105–106, 107.
32. Robert David Johnson, *The Peace Progressives and American Foreign Relations* (Cambridge, MA: Harvard University Press, 1995).
33. See Divine, *The Illusion of Neutrality;* Dallek, *Franklin D. Roosevelt,* 101–108; Herring, *From Colony to Superpower*, 505–508.
34. Dallek, *Franklin D. Roosevelt,* 119; Divine, *The Illusion of Neutrality,* 74–80. During the Great War, Wilson agreed to Great Britain's effort to blockade Germany, thereby interrupting U.S./German trade, and objected strongly to German submarine attacks on Allied shipping. Strict neutrality would have required acquiescence to both or protest to both. Secretary of State William Jennings Bryan, in fact, resigned, so strong was his anger toward Wilson's discriminatory neutrality.
35. Dallek, *Franklin D. Roosevelt,* 74; Herring, *From Colony to Superpower,* 504.
36. Dallek, *Franklin D. Roosevelt,* 108; Divine, *The Illusion of Neutrality,* 81–121; Kennedy, *Freedom from Fear,* 394–395.
37. Dallek, *Franklin D. Roosevelt,* 101–108; Herring, *From Colony to Superpower,* 505.
38. On Social Security, see Brands, *Traitor to His Class,* 311. On the rest, see Divine, *The Illusion of Neutrality,* 117.
39. Brands, *Traitor to His Class,* 357–395.
40. Reynolds, *From Munich to Pearl Harbor,* 18–19, 22.
41. Leuchtenburg, *Franklin D. Roosevelt and the New Deal,* 249.
42. Perelman and Olbrechts-Tyteca, *The New Rhetoric,* 116–119, 142.
43. John M. Murphy, "Presence, Analogy, and *Earth in the Balance,*" *Argumentation and Advocacy* 31 (1994): 5.
44. Franklin D. Roosevelt, "Annual Message to the Congress. January 3, 1936," in *The Public Papers and Addresses of Franklin D. Roosevelt,* ed. Samuel I. Rosenman (New York: Russell & Russell, 1938), 5:8.
45. Roosevelt, *Public Papers,* 5:8.

46. Ibid., 5:9.
47. Ibid., 5:10. Given America's habitual assertion of its exceptionalism, its Puritan legacy, the irony here is breathtaking.
48. Roosevelt, *Public Papers,* 5:12.
49. Ibid., 5:12, 13, 14.
50. Ibid., 9:633.
51. "The President Speaks," *Time,* January 6, 1941, 9.
52. "U.S. as Democracy's Arsenal Dares Dictators to Do Worst," *Newsweek,* January 6, 1941, 13.
53. Roosevelt, *Public Papers,* 9:634.
54. Ibid., 9:639, 10:191, 192.
55. Ibid., 9:634.
56. Cara A. Finnegan, *Picturing Poverty: Print Culture and FSA Photographs* (Washington: Smithsonian Books, 2003), x, xi.
57. Roosevelt, *Public Papers,* 9:634.
58. Ibid., 6:406, 9:201.
59. Ibid, 9:230, 231, 232.
60. Ibid., 9:636, 664.
61. Ibid., 9:263.
62. Ibid., 9:261.
63. Ibid., 9:604, 607.
64. Reynolds, *From Munich to Pearl Harbor,* 114.
65. James Jasinski, *Sourcebook on Rhetoric: Key Concepts in Contemporary Rhetorical Studies* (Thousand Oaks: Sage, 2001), 457.
66. Quoted in Richard Overy, *Why the Allies Won* (New York: W. W. Norton, 1995), 105.
67. Keegan, *Second World War,* 88.
68. Richard Overy quoted in Keegan, *Second World War,* 89.
69. Keegan, *Second World War,* 89. See also Herring, *From Colony to Superpower,* 515; James J. Sheehan, *Where Have All the Soldiers Gone: The Transformation of Modern Europe* (Boston: Houghton Mifflin, 2008), 129–131.
70. Quoted in Overy, *Why the Allies Won,* 105.
71. Sheehan, *Where Have All the Soldiers Gone,* 130.
72. Herring, *From Colony to Superpower,* 515.
73. Quoted in Dallek, *Franklin D. Roosevelt,* 173. It was at this meeting that the president "chummily" said to then-deputy chair of the Joint Chiefs, General George Marshall, "Don't you think so, George?" Marshall coldly replied, "I am sorry, Mr.

President, but I don't agree at all." It was the first and last time that FDR ever addressed Marshall by his first name. Perhaps more revealing of FDR's leadership style is the fact that he made Marshall chair of the Joint Chiefs less than a year later. Kennedy, *Freedom from Fear,* 430.

74. Ibid, 9:199, 232, 636, 665.
75. Ibid., 9:199, 636.
76. Ibid., 6:410, 411.
77. Reynolds, *From Munich to Pearl Harbor,* 37; "Bad Neighbor Policy," *Time,* October 18, 1937, 17; Arthur Krock, "The 'Quarantine' Policy Must Await Definitions," *New York Times,* October 6, 1937, 14.
78. David Hendrickson notes, "The noninterventionist movement reached its highest influence in 1937. In that year, 70 percent of the American public believed that U.S. participation in the Great War had been a mistake. They reacted coldly to Roosevelt's proposal, made in response to the Japanese offensive against China, that the peace-loving nations attempt to 'quarantine' the aggressors." David Hendrickson, *Union, Nation, or Empire: The American Debate Over International Relations, 1789–1941* (Lawrence: University Press of Kansas, 2009), 355.
79. Ibid, 9:238–239, 664.
80. James Jasinski and John M. Murphy, "Time, Space, and Generic Reconstitution: Martin Luther King's 'A Time to Break Silence' as Radical Jeremiad," in *Public Address and Moral Judgment,* ed. Shawn J. Parry-Giles and Trevor Parry-Giles (East Lansing: Michigan State University Press, 2009), 103.
81. Ibid., 9:638, 666–667, 239.
82. Ibid., 9:260, 672.
83. Steven Casey, *Cautious Crusade: Franklin D. Roosevelt, American Public Opinion, and the War against Nazi Germany* (New York: Oxford University Press, 2001), 17–19, 22, 23.
84. Ibid, 24. Ambrose and Brinkley term the fall of France "a shattering blow." Ambrose and Brinkley, *Rise to Globalism,* 5.
85. Casey, *Cautious Crusade,* 27.
86. Reynolds, *From Munich to Pearl Harbor,* 108.
87. Dallek, *Franklin D. Roosevelt,* 257.
88. William E. Leuchtenburg, *In the Shadow of FDR: From Harry Truman to Ronald Reagan* (Ithaca: Cornell University Press, 1983); George McJimsey, *The Presidency of Franklin Delano Roosevelt* (Lawrence: University Press of Kansas, 2000), 288.
89. Herring, *From Colony to Superpower,* 537.

90. Harry S. Truman, "Special Message to the Congress on Greece and Turkey: Wednesday March 12, 1947, 1:00 pm," in *Proclaiming the Truman Doctrine: The Cold War Call to Arms,* by Denise M. Bostdorff (College Station: Texas A & M University Press, 2008), 5, 79.
91. Robert L. Ivie, "Fire, Flood, and Red Fever: Motivating Metaphors of Global Emergency in the Truman Doctrine Speech," *Presidential Studies Quarterly* 29 (1999): 571, 583.
92. Herring, *From Colony to Superpower,* 537.
93. Perelman and Olbrechts-Tyteca, *The New Rhetoric,* 116, 117, 142.
94. Ibid., 117, 120.
95. Kenneth Burke, "Chapter One—Definition of Man," in *Language as Symbolic Action: Essays on Life, Literature, and Method* (Berkeley: University of California Press, 1966), 16.
96. Ibid., 17, 18, 19.
97. Thomas B. Farrell, "Sizing Things Up: Colloquial Reflection as Practical Reason," *Argumentation* 12 (1998): 6, 7.

Iraq as a Representative Anecdote for Leadership: Barack Obama's Address on the Fifth Anniversary of the Iraq War

Denise M. Bostdorff

From the moment that Barack Obama announced he was running for president, his experience—or, rather, lack thereof—was an issue. Obama had worked as a community organizer on Chicago's South Side, served seven years in the Illinois State Senate, risen to national prominence with his 2004 address to the Democratic National Convention, and then been elected to the U.S. Senate, where he had served only two years by the time he became a presidential candidate. In short, Obama had limited experience with national politics and issues.[1]

The question of Obama's experience was even more salient when it came to foreign policy. As political scientist James Barber once observed, citizens look to their presidents for reassurance and a sense of security.[2] Not surprisingly, then, candidates for the nation's highest office often tout their foreign policy and/or military experience. Obama, however, had neither, especially in comparison to the two individuals who would become his chief Republican and Democratic rivals. A former Navy pilot who endured more than five years as a prisoner of war in North Vietnam, Republican John McCain had served in the U.S. House for two terms and in the U.S. Senate since 1986. He was the ranking member of the Senate Armed Services Committee in 2008. As for Democratic frontrunner Hillary Rodham Clinton, she had been first lady from 1993 to 2001 and, in that role, had traveled extensively overseas and met frequently with foreign dignitaries. She had given a fiery speech on behalf of women's rights at a United Nations conference in Beijing in 1995 and claimed she had worked behind the scenes on a number of important foreign policy issues as first lady. In 2000 and 2006, Clinton was elected to the U.S. Senate, where she served on the Senate Armed Services Committee.[3] Like Clinton, Obama had not served in the military, but he also lacked her greater experience in national politics, and, though he served on the Senate Foreign Relations Committee, he obviously had done so only briefly. Obama reflected in November 2007 that the fact that he had lived in Indonesia as a child likely was "the strongest experience I have in foreign relations" because it had given him a greater sensitivity to other points of view. In response, Clinton had derisively observed, "Voters will judge whether living in a foreign country at the age of 10 prepares one to face the big, complex international challenges the next President will face."[4]

More often than citing his childhood years overseas, Obama defended himself from attacks on his experience by pointing to his judgment. Indeed, his 2002 opposition to the war in Iraq was the hook on which he hung his entire candidacy. His political adviser, David Axelrod, told reporters in January 2007 that Obama had proven his ability to make good decisions because "he managed to get it right on Iraq." In Obama's February 2007 speech announcing that he was running for president, the candidate featured Iraq prominently—how he had "opposed this war from the start" and how he had "a plan" that would bring combat troops home quickly.[5] Obama used this framework to define his leadership throughout the primary and general elections.[6]

In the essay that follows, I examine the speech that Barack Obama gave on March 19, 2008, the fifth anniversary of the Iraq War, as an exemplar for how the senator used Iraq as a representative anecdote for his leadership. Kenneth Burke explains that a representative anecdote is a drama or story line that provides a linguistic summation of human motivation. According to Burke, "A given calculus must be supple and complex enough to be representative of the subject-matter it is designed to calculate. It must have scope. Yet it must also possess simplicity, in that it is broadly a reduction of the subject matter."[7] In his Fayetteville, North Carolina, address, Obama used Iraq as just such a representative anecdote to establish his unique leadership and to counter questions about his national security experience, for he consistently relied on Iraq as the paradigm that best explained the superiority of his leadership.

Obama's March 19, 2008, address, albeit largely overlooked, is significant for several reasons. First, at the time of the speech, he was struggling in the nomination contest against his only remaining competitor—Hillary Clinton—and she appeared to be making significant inroads on the issues of national security and foreign policy experience. After winning eleven straight contests, Obama had lost the key states of Ohio and Texas on March 4, which raised questions about whether he could win in the general election. Clinton had emphasized her readiness to be commander-in-chief "on day one" prior to the March 4 contests and had also begun airing her infamous "3 A.M. phone call" ad that clearly called Obama's national security experience into question. On March 17, Clinton delivered an address on Iraq at George Washington University, where she emphasized her plan to end the war and underscored her national security experience as First Lady with a narrative about "landing under sniper fire" during a trip to Bosnia; in contrast, she described Obama as someone who "talks a great deal about a speech he gave in 2002" opposing the Iraq War.[8] With the March 4 Republican contests, McCain became the GOP nominee and quickly took advantage of the ongoing Democratic competition by setting out on a tour of the Middle East, including Iraq, with the goal of highlighting his foreign policy expertise.[9] The fifth anniversary of the Iraq War provided the opportunity for Obama to establish his readiness to be commander in chief, to refute his opponents' charges, and to counter with attacks on their leadership. Moreover, Obama had to address Iraq to avoid ceding the issue—*the* issue of his campaign—to his opponents.

Second, Obama's March 19 address is also significant because it followed two other problematic issues that had prompted doubts about what the senator claimed to be his strength: his judgment. On March 6, just two days after the Ohio and Texas defeats, Antoin "Tony" Rezko went to trial on federal corruption charges, and Obama once more had to explain his relationship with Rezko, who had raised money for previous Obama campaigns and had been part of a real estate deal that involved Barack and Michelle Obama.[10] Simultaneously, the senator had to contend with controversial excerpts of sermons from his pastor, the Reverend Jeremiah Wright of Trinity United Church of Christ on Chicago's South Side, that began to appear on YouTube and television. In these excerpts, Wright charged that "U.S. terrorism" in the world had led to the 9/11 attacks and condemned the United States for its treatment of black citizens, treatment that he said should lead blacks not to sing "God Bless America" but rather "God Damn America."[11] Obama responded with his address, "A More Perfect Union," in Philadelphia on March 18, in which he provided a context for the angry remarks of Wright and other blacks (while still maintaining that some of Wright's words "were not only wrong but divisive"), gave voice to the frustrations felt by many white Americans, and urged citizens to focus on what they have in common, rather than be distracted by differences.[12] Obama's address on Iraq the very next day, March 19, appears to have been an effort to "normalize" his campaign after a series of crises. That is, the senator's speech attempted to refocus public attention on the issue that had been the keystone to his candidacy: his judgment on Iraq.

Finally, Obama's address is important for what it reveals both about how he ultimately undercut the foreign policy experience and national security claims of his opponents and how Obama used Iraq and the criterion of judgment to adapt to the public's increasing sense of urgency about the economy. The senator's arguments in his March 19 speech were representative of those that he had begun to use and would continue to use in the months to come. More specifically, Obama argued that Clinton and McCain, despite their experience, had made judgments leading to an unwise war that had undermined the nation's security, whereas Obama had made the right judgment from the start. He also pointed to the economic impact of the war, which allowed him later to blame the poor judgment of his opponents for U.S. economic woes and to depict himself as the candidate best able to handle the economy. In the pages that follow, I first examine the rhetorical context that led to Obama's March 19 address on Iraq and then turn my attention to an analysis of the speech itself.

The Rhetorical Context of Obama's Address on Iraq

Obama's focus on Iraq was undoubtedly appealing early in his candidacy when the Bush administration's "surge" policy, which increased the number of U.S. troops in Iraq, appeared to be failing and U.S. casualties were rising. By the summer of 2007, McCain—who had both voted for the war and championed the escalation in troops—found public sentiments on Iraq so negative that they threatened the viability of his campaign.[13] On the Democratic side, Clinton's vote for the war and refusal to apologize for that vote had left her vulnerable on her left flank. Clinton's decision to support the war until November 2005 and her continued opposition to timetables for troops to leave appeared to some an obvious attempt to burnish her hawkish credentials. At a Take Back America rally in June 2006, Clinton again opposed a withdrawal timetable, prompting the antiwar Democratic activists in attendance to boo her.[14]

In fall 2007, violence in Iraq decreased, as did media coverage of the war, which led candidates from both parties to talk about Iraq less and citizens to focus on the economy more.[15] Nevertheless, Iraq endured as an issue to reckon with during the new year. Polls showed Americans almost evenly split on how well the surge was working and how soon U.S. troops should leave. In February 2008, Pew found that 54 percent of citizens thought going into Iraq had been the wrong decision, a number that remained unchanged from February 2007.[16] Exit polls also revealed that Iraq remained a key issue for Democrats in the early contests, with voters rating it as tied with or just slightly behind the economy in terms of importance. For their part, Republicans in Iowa evaluated immigration (33 percent), terrorism (21 percent), and the Iraq War (17 percent) as the top three issues, which together reflected an overarching concern with national security that maintained Iraq's cachet, especially when concerns over immigration began to fade.[17] The assassination of Benazir Bhutto in Pakistan in late December, the anniversary of President George W. Bush's announcement of the surge policy in January, and the impending fifth anniversary of the Iraq War in March all served to heighten the significance of U.S. policies in Iraq and in what had been dubbed the war on terror.[18]

In January 2008 Obama won a historic upset victory in Iowa over Clinton, who finished third, right behind former senator John Edwards of North Carolina. Exit polls indicated that Obama's theme of "change" had trumped Clinton's claims of "experience."[19] Clinton struck back by emphasizing the need for a steady hand in times of crisis and questioning whether Obama was ready to be commander in chief. When New Hampshire voters went to the polls, they defied projections showing Obama far ahead and gave the win decisively to Clinton. Surveys revealed that only 26 percent of voters there said that Obama would make the best commander in chief, as opposed to 38 percent who chose Clinton, and even New Hampshire voters who wanted to leave Iraq "as soon as possible" turned to Clinton rather than Obama.[20]

In the weeks that followed, the race between the two contenders remained neck and neck, with the candidates continuing to clash over Iraq. Clinton won in Nevada on January 19, while Obama took South Carolina. Super Tuesday on February 5 also provided no decisive victor. While Obama won the larger number of contests, including some in predominantly white states like Kansas and Connecticut, Clinton took two of the most significant prizes by winning both California and Massachusetts.[21] Voter concerns over the economy continued to grow, but the issues of national security generally and Iraq specifically retained a prominent role. Four days prior to the important contests in Ohio and Texas on March 4, Clinton rolled out a new ad that used the symbolism of the hotline between the Kremlin and the White House during the Cold War to question Obama's ability to respond to 3 A.M. phone calls about unexpected foreign crises. According to the ad's narrator, "Your vote will decide who answers that call. Whether it's someone who already knows the world's leaders, knows the military—someone tested and ready to lead in a dangerous world."[22] In response, Obama accused Clinton of engaging in fear tactics and countered, "The question is not about picking up the phone. The question is: What kind of judgment will you make when you answer." According to Obama, "We've had a red phone moment. It was the decision to invade Iraq. And Senator Clinton gave the wrong answer. George Bush gave the wrong answer. John McCain gave the wrong answer."[23] For his part, McCain was happy to capitalize on the Democratic squabble. The Republican senator observed that "my knowledge and experience and background clearly indicate that if the phone rang at 3 A.M. in the White House, and I was the one to answer it, I would be the one most qualified to exercise the kind of judgment necessary to address a national security crisis."[24]

When the Clinton campaign's internal polling showed her attacks on Obama's experience were having an impact, Clinton quickly aired a new ad in Texas and Ohio that criticized Obama for failing to hold oversight hearings as chair of a Senate Foreign Relations subcommittee that oversaw North Atlantic Treaty Organization (NATO) operations in Afghanistan. The ad intoned, "He was too busy running for president to hold even one hearing. Hillary Clinton will never be too busy to defend our national security."[25] Although Obama admitted that the charge was accurate, the ad conveniently overlooked the fact that the leading presidential candidates in both parties had been absent from their jobs for an extraordinary amount of time in order to campaign. Obama ranked number three in the Senate for missed votes in the 110th Congress by missing 41.8 percent of votes, according to the *Washington Post*. Clinton virtually tied with Senator Joseph Biden of Delaware for fourth place, with Clinton missing 31.7 percent of votes and Biden missing 31.8 percent. Although Clinton's record was certainly stronger than Obama's, it was hardly the degree of attendance one would expect from someone claiming she would "never be too busy" to protect the American people. McCain was the real standout, however, having missed more votes than anyone else in the Senate—60 percent of votes, in fact—which ranked him ahead of Senator Tim Johnson of South Dakota, who missed 53.9 percent of votes while recovering from a brain hemorrhage.[26] Taken as a whole, Clinton's attacks on Obama's experience and his failure to hold hearings on Afghanistan raised questions about his foreign policy leadership and his ability to compete against McCain in the general election. Clinton charged, "He [McCain] will put forth his lifetime of experience. I will put forth my lifetime of experience. Sen. Obama will put forth a speech he made in 2002."[27]

Although Obama also suffered from an election eve claim that his campaign had told Canadian officials not to take his criticisms of the North American Free Trade Agreement (NAFTA) too seriously, Texas and Ohio exit polls indicated that Clinton's attacks on Obama's foreign policy expertise had made an impact. A majority of voters in the two states made up their minds in the last three days of the campaign, when she hit this issue hard in her comments and ads, and the majority of voters there also told exit pollsters that they believed Clinton was more qualified to be commander in chief.[28] In the days that followed, the Clinton campaign declared Obama had not yet passed a commander in chief test, and both campaigns engaged in an escalating competition over how many retired admirals and generals endorsed their respective candidates.[29] Obama struggled to hold his own, but his campaign appeared to be in trouble, with the Rezko and Wright issues fueling further controversy.

At the same time, the efforts of Clinton and McCain to assert their national security experience had begun to show signs of weakness. FactCheck.org, a nonpartisan nonprofit project of the Annenberg Public Policy Center at the University of Pennsylvania, released an analysis on March 13 that drew media attention when it asserted that Clinton had more foreign policy experience than Obama due to her longer career, but also added that "many of Clinton's foreign policy claims are exaggerated." For example, the report noted that Clinton "has repeatedly referenced her 'dangerous' trip to Bosnia. She fails to mention, however, that the Bosnian war had officially ended three months before her visit—or that she made the trip with her 16-year-old daughter and two entertainers." Just a few days later, one of those entertainers, the comedian Sinbad, claimed her description of landing under sniper fire was inaccurate at best. He noted that "the only 'red-phone' moment was: 'Do we eat here or at the next place.'"[30] For his part, McCain fared little better. His March tour of Iraq, intended to underscore his national security credentials, was marred by acts of violence, including a suicide bombing in Karbala that killed forty people and injured sixty-five others. Blocks of Sunni and Shiite politicians also pulled out of a reconciliation conference in Baghdad, which prompted doubts about political progress in Iraq. In Jordan immediately following his Iraq visit, McCain mistakenly said to reporters, several times, that nearby Iran was training al-Qaeda, the terrorist group responsible for the 9/11 attacks, in Iraq. Actually, however, the U.S. government claimed Iran was supporting Shiite insurgents in Iraq, whereas al-Qaeda was a Sunni group. Only when Senator Joseph Lieberman of Connecticut, who accompanied McCain on his trip, quietly corrected the senator did McCain appear to notice and acknowledge his error.[31] In sum, events affecting the Clinton and McCain campaigns offered opportunities for Obama to strike back on the issues of national security and Iraq, opportunities that he could ill afford to let pass.

On March 19, 2008, only one day after his "A More Perfect Union" address, Obama delivered a speech at Fayetteville Technical Community College in Fayetteville, North Carolina. His campaign billed the event as a "major speech" on how ending the Iraq War would allow the United States to meet "national security challenges of the twenty-first century, and to advance American interests throughout the world." Because of limited space at the student center, the Fayetteville event was invitation-only, with a mere 150 people in attendance, which meant that Obama could better control audience responses to his message and potential news coverage.[32] The inclusion of military personnel from nearby Fort Bragg and Pope Air Force Base in the selected audience served to refocus attention on national security and, with their sixteen interruptions of applause, to imply that the military agreed with Obama's assessments. At an appearance later in the day, the senator avoided mention of the Wright controversy almost entirely, only talking of it in passing when an audience member at the event raised the question.[33] Obama clearly wanted to use the Fayetteville speech to change the topic from the volatile issue of race to the issue of Iraq, on which he had based his candidacy and which better served his interests.

Redefinition of Foreign Policy Leadership in Obama's Fayetteville Address

Obama delivered his speech in front of a blue curtain, flanked by American flags. Emblazoned on the podium was a blue sign—its message underlined by a row of white stars—that declared, "Judgment to Lead." Throughout his March 19, 2008, speech, the senator used Iraq as a representative anecdote for his leadership on foreign policy and national security and for the failed leadership of his opponents. More specifically, the senator (1) reframed the issue of national security by asserting the existence of a "security gap"; (2) attacked his opponents' foreign policy leadership and contrasted it with his own; (3) used Iraq as a bridging device to depict his overall leadership as substantive, mainstream, and presidential; and (4) offered a leadership of hope in keeping with American character. In the pages that follow, I support my arguments by relying on a transcript created by taking a copy of the speech text, available from the Council on Foreign Relations, and then comparing it to a video of the speech as Obama delivered it. Any quoted words in italics reflect Obama's own vocal inflections.[34]

Reframing National Security through the Assertion of a "Security Gap"

Several times throughout his speech, Obama echoed John F. Kennedy's claims of a "missile gap" from the 1960 campaign by arguing that a "security gap" currently existed. The senator from Illinois noted that Clinton had attacked his lack of foreign policy experience and then added, "But here is the stark reality: there is a security gap in this country—a gap between the rhetoric of those who claim to be tough on national security, and the reality of growing insecurity caused by their decisions." In essence, Obama dissociated the unitary concept of security by arguing that there was illusory security and real security, and he associated his chief rivals with the former and himself with the latter.[35] The senator then spent a great deal of his speech demonstrating how Iraq had not made the nation safer and how it had actually distracted the United States from the challenges that it faced.

In reflecting on the anniversary of the war, Obama somberly noted, "Nearly four thousand Americans have given their lives. Thousands more have been wounded." He also emphasized the economic costs when he said, "Even under the best case scenarios, this war will cost well over a *trillion* dollars. And where are we for all this sacrifice? We are less safe and less able to shape events abroad. We are divided at home, and our alliances around the world have been strained. . . . yet America remains anchored in Iraq." Obama stated that "fighting a war without end" would "not force the Iraqis to take responsibility for their future" and would "not make the American people safer." Indeed, he argued that the fact that the United States was tied down in Iraq had actually strengthened its enemies. He pointed to Iran's challenge to U.S. interests in the Middle East, its nuclear program, and its threats to Israel. Moreover, Obama said, "Instead of the new Middle East we were promised, Hamas runs Gaza, Hezbollah flags fly from the rooftops in Sadr City, and Iran is handing out money left and right in southern Lebanon." Nor were the problems limited to the Middle East. According to the senator, the Iraq War also "has emboldened North Korea, which built new nuclear weapons and even tested one."

Most troubling of all, Obama declared that the war had strengthened al-Qaeda. He asserted, "The central front in the war against terror is *not* Iraq, and it never was. What more could America's enemies ask for than an endless war where they recruit new followers, try out new tactics on a battlefield so far *away* from their base of operations?" In line with his dissociation of security into that which is false and that which is real, Obama argued, in effect, that the decision to go to war in Iraq was a decision to pursue an illusory enemy instead of the actual enemy who committed the 9/11 attacks. The senator emphatically stated, "Rather than fight a war that does not need to be fought, we need to start fighting the battles that need to be won on the central front of the war against al-Qaeda in Afghanistan and Pakistan. That is the area where the 9/11 attacks were planned. That is where Osama bin Laden and his top lieutenants still hide. That is where extremism poses its greatest threat." According to Obama, conditions in Afghanistan had deteriorated because the United States had not been able to devote its resources and attention to issues there. He warned that Americans "cannot prevail until we reduce our commitment in Iraq." Obama's pairing of Afghanistan and Iraq—both here and throughout his campaign—not only reflected his policy preferences but also served to reassure Americans that he was not a pacifist and, as president, that he would protect the American people.

Beyond Afghanistan and Pakistan, Obama depicted the decision to go to war in Iraq as a choice that had distracted the United States from other major challenges it faced, such as nuclear proliferation, global climate change, and a struggling economy. Iraq had, he argued, led to a state of lessened security for the United States as a whole. In a jab at an assertion that McCain had made on more than one occasion, Obama concluded, "We have a security gap when candidates say they will follow Osama bin Laden to the gates of hell, but refuse to follow him where he actually *is*."[36] Through dissociation, Obama reframed the national security arguments used against him such that he appeared to be the stronger candidate and his campaign's key issue—the war in Iraq—an exemplar of what can happen when politicians pursue false security.

Attacking Opponents' Leadership and Contrasting It with His Own

Throughout his candidacy, political pundits and journalists raised questions about whether Obama was tough enough in his responses to opponents or, in a favorite phrase, whether he could "throw a punch."[37] His Fayetteville address, however, was that of a candidate sure of his position and more than willing to attack his opponents and to contrast his leadership with theirs.

First, Obama blamed the decision to go to war in Iraq on leadership driven by ideology and politics, in contrast to his own leadership of pragmatism and principle. According to the senator, "History will catalog the reasons why we waged a war that didn't need to be fought, but two stand out. In 2002, when the fateful decisions about Iraq were made, there was a President for whom ideology overrode pragmatism, *and* there were too many politicians in Washington who spent too little time reading the intelligence reports, and too much time reading public opinion." Because Clinton and McCain had both voted for the war, Obama's words held them as accountable for Iraq as the unpopular George W. Bush. Obama's association of McCain and Clinton with Bush depicted them as part of the problem, part of the old politics that had led to the Iraq War and the reduced state of security that it had brought.

By contrast, Obama offered himself as the candidate of pragmatism and principle who would make wise decisions. He said, "I am running for President because it's time to turn the page on a failed ideology and a fundamentally flawed political strategy, so that we can make pragmatic judgments to keep our country safe. That's what I did when I stood up and opposed this war from the start. . . . And that's what I'll do as President of the United States." While Obama focused primarily on practicality, his allusion to opposing the Iraq War at a time when it was unpopular to do so conveyed idealism as well. He also did not mince words in comparing his leadership to that of his opponents. According to Obama, McCain's rhetoric, actions, and votes were impractical, for they would not keep the United States safe and would mean "we all lose." He likewise blasted Clinton when he observed that she "has tried to use my position to score political points" by implying "that because I want to withdraw prudently and would listen to our commanders on the ground that I am somehow less than fully committed to ending the war." Obama challenged, "So ask yourself: who do you trust to end a war—someone who opposed the war from the beginning, or someone who started opposing it when they started preparing a run for president?" The senator's words clearly portrayed him as the preferred leader of both pragmatism and principle.[38]

A second way in which Obama contrasted his opponents' leadership with his own was through the dichotomy of experience versus judgment. In the preceding weeks, Clinton and McCain had each promoted her/his respective experience in foreign relations and/or national security as greater than that of Obama. The senator from Illinois countered these charges by touting his superior judgment. To begin, Obama restated Clinton's claim, but in a way that equated experience with longevity, not expertise. He said, "Senator Clinton says that she and Senator McCain have passed a 'commander-in-chief test'—not because of the judgments they've made, but because of the years they've spent in Washington." However, Obama argued that a chasm existed "between Washington experience, and the wisdom of Washington's judgments." The senator likewise attacked both McCain and Clinton, who, he implied, was emulating McCain, when he said, "It is time to have a debate with John McCain about the future of our national security. And the way to win that debate is not to compete with John McCain over who has more experience in Washington, because that's a contest he will win." Interestingly, Obama's explanation not only diminished the significance of his opponents' brand of experience, but also depicted him as the practical choice for Democrats who wanted victory in November. The senator observed, "Since before this war in Iraq, I have made different judgments, I have a different vision, and I will offer a clean break from the policies and politics of the past. Nowhere is that break more badly needed than in Iraq."[39] After detailing the ways in which Iraq had led to diminished security and standing for the United States, Obama concluded, "This is why the judgment that matters most on Iraq—and on any decision to deploy military force—is the judgment made first." The senator offered judgment as a superior criterion for measuring leadership and his own judgment on Iraq as emblematic of his superior leadership.

A third way that Obama attacked his Republican opponent specifically was by associating McCain's leadership with tactics and his own leadership with strategy. By March 2008, violence in Iraq had decreased, and the number of Americans who thought the surge—a policy long advocated by McCain—had been successful had increased from 22 percent in July 2007 to 43 percent in February 2008.[40] For Obama, the challenge was to discredit the surge and McCain without appearing to discredit military personnel responsible for carrying out the policy.

The senator accomplished this task by praising the military, but also by depicting the surge as a tactical matter while arguing instead for the need to attend to strategy. For example, Obama said, "Our troops—including so many from Fort Bragg and Pope Air Force Base—have done a brilliant, magnificent job under the most difficult of circumstances. Yet while we have a General who has used improved tactics to reduce violence—and General [David] Petraeus deserves enormous credit for that—we still have the wrong strategy." To bring this point home, the senator charged that McCain had focused solely on tactics. Obama explained, "What he and the Administration have *failed* to present is an overarching strategy: how the war in Iraq enhances our long-term security or how it might enhance our long-term security in the future." The senator also prompted laughter by poking fun at how McCain's focus on tactics had led to what Obama depicted as circular reasoning: "And that is why Senator McCain can argue—as he did last year—that we couldn't leave Iraq because violence was up, and then argue this year that we can't leave Iraq because violence is down. When you have no overarching strategy, there is no clear definition of success." Obama likewise joked, "Just yesterday, we heard Senator McCain confuse Sunni and Shia, Iran and al-Qaeda. Maybe that is why he voted to go to war with a country that had no al-Qaeda ties.

Maybe that is why he completely fails to understand that the war in Iraq has done more to embolden America's enemies than any strategic choice that we have made in decades." Obama's words critiqued McCain's grasp of strategy versus tactics while simultaneously reinforcing Obama's questions about McCain's judgment. In contrast, the senator from Illinois said that he would set a "new goal" of ending the war or implementing a "shift in strategy away from Iraq" in order to meet the nation's security needs.

Throughout his speech, Obama used Iraq to attack his two adversaries, directly and indirectly, through skillful dissociation of the concept of leadership, opposing their ideology and political gamesmanship with his own pragmatism and principles, their longevity in the capital with his own wise judgment, and McCain's focus on tactics with his own concern for strategy.

Using Iraq as a Bridging Device to Depict His Leadership as Substantive, Mainstream, and Presidential

In his address, Obama also used Iraq as a bridging device that encouraged voters to align his leadership on Iraq with perceptions that his overall leadership was substantive, mainstream, and presidential.[41] He did this through three means: emphasizing policy talk, creating endorsements from Republicans, and making use of historical analogies.

First, Obama embraced policy talk that portrayed ending the Iraq War as the linchpin to a higher degree of security for the United States. In an address consisting of 4,658 words, as delivered, the senator devoted 2,065 words—or 44.3 percent of his speech—to policy exposition. Obama not only emphasized that he had made the right judgment on Iraq, but also demonstrated that he had policy proposals to bring the war to an end. He explained, for instance, that he would "end this war responsibly" by removing "1 to 2 combat brigades each month. If we start with the number of brigades we have in Iraq today, we can remove all of them in 16 months." In addition, Obama said that he would leave "enough troops in Iraq to guard our embassy and our diplomats, and a counter-terrorism force to strike al-Qaeda if it forms a base that Iraqis cannot destroy." The senator's proposal was fairly specific. Furthermore, he took pains to note that he had been proposing this same withdrawal policy "for many months," so it was not a new proposal of political convenience. While any policy would pose its dangers, Obama reassured his audience that he would be more than willing "to make tactical adjustments, listening to our commanders on the ground, to ensure that our interests in a stable Iraq are met, and to make sure that our troops are secure." The overall image that he constructed was that of a knowledgeable, flexible leader who had a "detailed and prudent plan," but who would continue to seek out information relevant to effective policymaking.

After discussing his withdrawal plans, the senator stressed how a reduced commitment in Iraq would allow the United States to focus on the more important strategic goal of security, and he explained exactly how he would implement policies that would better meet that goal. Obama observed, for instance, that decreased troops in Iraq would permit the United States to send "at least two additional combat brigades" to Afghanistan, a point that again underscored his commitment to protecting American citizens through military means when necessary. Additionally, the senator said, "This increased commitment . . . can be used to leverage greater assistance" from "our NATO allies." Obama also underscored that his was not a military policy alone, but rather that he would commit "an additional $1 billion of nonmilitary assistance" annually to reach the Afghan people.

Beyond Afghanistan, the senator discussed policy proposals for developing a "comprehensive counter-terrorism strategy," handling Pakistan, creating global "partnerships to take out terrorist networks," and tackling nuclear proliferation. He insisted that withdrawing from Iraq would allow the United States to deal with still other threats through new policies as well, such as "doubling our foreign assistance," instituting a "cap and trade system and investments in new sources of energy," and investing "in the education of our children." Through such references, Obama seemed determined to demonstrate that he was not a one-trick pony whose only claim to leadership was his opposition to the Iraq War. Nonetheless, Iraq served as a terminological bridge by which voters could reach Obama's intended destination: he was right on Iraq, had policies to end that war, and doing so would allow him to enact a whole array of other policies he had developed that would better meet the nation's security needs.

Obama also used Iraq as a bridging device to situate his leadership clearly within the mainstream through his creation of "endorsements" from Republican leaders. When criticizing the Bush administration's policy in Iraq and McCain's continued support for the war, for instance, Obama noted that neither could "answer the simple question posed by Republican senator John Warner in hearings last year: Are we safer because of this war?" The fact that a ranking Republican asked the same question as Obama imbued the query with a greater aura of legitimacy. Once he recounted this Republican endorsement of his views on Iraq—an issue on which many voters saw Obama as a wise leader—the senator then shifted to another national security issue by similarly recalling how he had "worked across the aisle with Richard Lugar and Chuck Hagel in the Senate" in order to "secure dangerous weapons and loose nuclear materials" around the globe. Surely if these two foreign policy veterans from the opposing party sanctioned his policies, Obama implied, then his proposals must be reasonable. By suggesting a Republican endorsement of his judgment on Iraq and then later moving to an implicit Republican endorsement of his work on another national security issue, Obama encouraged the audience to consider his overall national security leadership as eminently mainstream.

Lastly, the senator employed Iraq as a bridging device when he made use of historical analogies to depict his leadership as well within the norms of presidential greatness. According to Obama, President Woodrow Wilson's address to Congress shortly before World War I reflected the dual responsibilities of any commander in chief: "to never hesitate to defend America, but to never go to war unless you must. War is sometimes necessary, but it has grave consequences, and the judgment to go to war can never be undone." Obama then claimed that Bush, McCain, and Clinton "failed Wilson's test" by going to war in Iraq. His reference to Wilson lent credibility to his charge that he, rather than the other three, had acted appropriately by opposing the war, even though nothing in the quotation that Obama attributed to Wilson mentioned anything about a test of judgment. Just as the senator's reference to Wilson suggested that he was right on Iraq, Obama likewise refuted his opponents' criticisms of his proposals for renewed diplomatic efforts around the globe. He declared that "they are mistaken in standing up for a policy of not talking that is not working. What I've said is that we cannot seize opportunities to resolve our problems unless we create them. That's what Kennedy did with Khrushchev; that's what Nixon did with Mao; what Reagan did with Gorbachev. And that is what I will do as President of the United States of America." By starting with the Wilson analogy to show how Obama had been right on Iraq and his opponents wrong, the senator suggested that his judgment on that issue met the highest standards of presidential greatness. His subsequent comparisons of his proposed policies with past foreign policy triumphs achieved by presidents of both parties conveyed that Obama's overall foreign policy leadership was similarly reasonable and wise.

Offering a Leadership of Hope in Keeping with American Character

In his speech, Obama offered his listeners a choice between fear and hope, associating his leadership with hope and linking such hope with American character. Obama, of course, had long emphasized the theme of hope in his public communication, from his keynote address at the 2004 Democratic National Convention to his 2006 book, *The Audacity of Hope,* whose title was inspired by a Jeremiah Wright sermon, and from his 2007 announcement that he intended to run for president to his campaign rhetoric throughout the primary season.[42] In his address in Fayetteville, Obama used the word "hope" six times, primarily toward the end of his speech, where he once more discussed the two factors—ideology and politics—that contributed to the U.S. war in Iraq. The senator criticized the "rigid ideology" of the past eight years as out of step with the times and, hence, ineffective. Moreover, he claimed, "A politics that is based on fear and division does not allow us to call on the world to hope, and keeps us from coming together as one people, as one nation, to write the next great chapter in the American story." In their analysis of his 2004 convention address, Robert Rowland and John Jones argued that Obama employed hope as a "metaphor for a balance between individualism and communal responsibilities" in the American Dream.[43] That is, hope only exists when citizens act on their own strong personal values *and* society as a whole provides opportunity. In a similar fashion, the senator used hope in his March 19 address to suggest that Americans must take a new approach to foreign policy by not only embracing American values and interests, but also engaging with the world and fulfilling their responsibilities to others. Indeed, Obama argued that Americans historically have faced their fears by offering hope.

In detailing the poor current state of U.S. relations with other countries, for instance, the senator noted that lack of U.S. support for democracy in Pakistan had turned many Pakistanis against Americans. He stated, "A child growing up in Pakistan, more often than not, is taught to see America as a source of hate—and not hope." As a result of the U.S. diversion of resources to Iraq, Obama asserted that the United States had ignored nonmilitary aspects of security, but warned, "What lies in the heart of a child in Pakistan or Afghanistan matters as much as the airplanes we sell those governments. What's in the head of a scientist from Russia can be as lethal as the plutonium reactors in Yongbyon. What's whispered in refugee camps in Chad can be as dangerous as a dictator's bluster." In sum, not all the dangers the United States faced could be resolved with the use of military force. After detailing these threats, Obama declared that they called for American leadership. He stressed that engaging with others was a way "to protect our common security and advance our common humanity—for it has always been the genius of American leadership to find opportunity embedded in adversity; to focus on a source of fear, and confront it with hope." Just as hope in Obama's earlier rhetoric thrived in the balance of fulfilling individual and communal responsibilities, hope in his Fayetteville address could be achieved only when Americans reached out to the world while also securing their own safety and acting on American values. For Obama, American foreign policy should endeavor to maintain a delicate balance between self-interests and selflessness. He made the choice quite clear:

> We are at a defining point in our history.
>
> We can choose the path of unending war and unilateral action, and sap our strength and our standing around the world. We can choose the path of disengagement, and cede our leadership. Or, we can meet fear and danger head-on with hope and strength; with common purpose as a united America; and with common cause with old allies and new partners.

From Obama's perspective, the need for renewed nonmilitary engagement with the world was crucial, as was a citizenry joined in dedication to such a task.

The senator concluded by urging Americans to unite behind his leadership of hope. Throughout his peroration, Obama linked both common purpose and hope with what it means to be an American. He referred to soldiers from Fort Bragg and their work in Iraq and Afghanistan, praising their "sense of common purpose" and asserting, "*They've* shown a sense of service and selflessness that represents the very best of the American character." Obama's epideictic tribute laid the groundwork for linking the common purpose of admired soldiers with the common purpose of the nation as a whole and, especially important, with his candidacy. He intoned, "This must be the election when America comes together behind a common purpose on behalf of our security and our values. That is what we do as Americans. That's how we founded a republic based on freedom, that's how we faced down fascism. That's how we defended democracy through a Cold War, and shined a light of hope bright enough to be seen in the darkest corners of the world." The senator offered a new approach that, nonetheless, was consistent with American character. Spelling out the characteristics of his leadership once again, he concluded, "When America leads with principles and pragmatism, hope can triumph over fear. It is time, once again, for America to lead." Or, as he encouraged voters to surmise, it was time to elect Barack Obama.

Final Thoughts

Through this analysis, we might glean several lessons. First, this case demonstrates that efforts at political persuasion tend to be incremental affairs, as Obama's Fayetteville address was but a single step in a rhetorical effort intended to change the topic from Rezko and Wright back to the key issue of Obama's campaign, Iraq, and to respond to his political rivals' attacks on his foreign policy leadership while simultaneously assailing theirs. Given the aftermath of the Wright controversy, it is hard to imagine what Obama could have said on March 19 that would have immediately shifted the preponderance of public attention to another issue—or at least to another issue that would benefit the senator. Yet, his desire to do exactly that was all the more apparent when he followed his Fayetteville address on March 19 with another major speech on Iraq on March 20 in Charleston, West Virginia, that used similar arguments to discuss the cost of the war—its impact on both lives and the U.S. economy—and to raise questions about the judgment of Clinton and McCain.[44] The number of variables that came into play in mid-March 2008 certainly make it impossible to attribute particular outcomes solely to the senator's Fayetteville speech. For example, President Bush defended the war at the Pentagon on March 19, the number of U.S. deaths in Iraq reached 4,000 on March 23, the administration received a much ballyhooed videoconference briefing with General Petraeus on March 25, and tens of thousands of Shiites marched in Baghdad to protest the Iraqi and U.S. governments' crackdown on Shiite militias on March 27.[45] All of these events contributed to news coverage of Iraq, increasing its salience, while other campaign occurrences also led to greater discussion of foreign policy leadership generally. Still, Obama appeared to play a small role in helping to initiate such a shift, as his opponents were quick to counterattack, which began a renewed focus on the issue that had launched his campaign.[46] Iraq and foreign policy became a major topic of conversation again, which suited Obama just fine, because it was an argument that he thought he could win.

Another lesson of this analysis is that Obama's choice of Iraq as a representative anecdote for his leadership provided him with a terminological framework that was—to quote Burke—both "supple and complex" while also retaining "simplicity."[47] Obama's use of Iraq in his Fayetteville address adumbrated the rhetoric that he would use throughout much of the 2008 campaign to deal both with foreign policy and the economy. Indeed, the March 19 speech, followed by the March 20 message on the cost of the war, served to reassert the senator's foreign policy leadership *and* to link Iraq with U.S. economic woes. At Fayetteville, he emphasized how the war had cost over a trillion dollars and diverted needed resources to Iraq. Obama's speech in Charleston consistently made connections between the cost of the war and its impact on the American economy. In that address, he also took aim at his rivals, noting, "Now, at that debate in Texas several weeks ago, Senator Clinton attacked John McCain for supporting the policies that have led to our enormous war costs. But her point would have been more compelling had she not joined Senator McCain in making the tragically ill-considered decision to vote for the Iraq war in the first place."[48] While Obama would go on to lose the Pennsylvania and West Virginia primaries, he ultimately would have the support of enough delegates in other contests and enough super-delegates to secure the Democratic nomination. He does not appear ever to have invoked the term "security gap" after his March 19 address, perhaps because its echo of Kennedy's "missile gap" could have proven problematic—the missile gap, after all, was later found to be nonexistent.[49] Nonetheless, his Fayetteville address foreshadowed the arguments he would use against McCain on the issue of foreign policy and, as the economy worsened, to extend his claims of leadership to a new arena. The senator declared in the October 7 debate, for instance, "I don't understand how we ended up invading a country that had nothing to do with 9/11, while Osama Bin Laden and al-Qaeda are setting up base camps and safe havens to train terrorists to attack us. That was Senator McCain's judgment, and it was the wrong judgment." Immediately after making this assessment, the senator asserted that the war had "been costly to us" in lives and had put "an enormous strain on our budget," since the United States was spending "$10 billion a month in Iraq" when "we need that $10 billion a month here in the United States to put people back to work."[50] Obama argued that his superior judgment was not limited just to Iraq but extended to the economy as well. By the closing days of the campaign, Obama often made such parallel arguments more telegraphically by simply situating his claims about the war in close proximity to his claims about economic issues.[51] Fayetteville clearly was not Obama's only effort to establish his leadership nor Iraq the sole representative anecdote to which he turned to demonstrate his judgment. Nevertheless, the argumentative framework, established in Fayetteville on March 19 and extended in Charleston on March 20, helped Obama make the transition from *the* initial issue of his campaign—his judgment on Iraq—to his leadership on the economy, which would prove to be significant in the fall campaign.

A final lesson of this case study is what it suggests about how political candidates who are largely unknown and/or who appear to lack requisite legitimacy for the office they seek might establish their leadership. From the study of Obama's Fayetteville address, we learn that representative anecdotes will work best for candidates attempting to establish their credentials as unique yet reasonable leaders when they meet three criteria. First, a representative anecdote should set up dissociations that can shatter current perceptions and offer new ones that will benefit the rhetor's candidacy, just as Iraq allowed Obama to dissociate the issue of security into illusory versus real security. The senator's choice of Iraq likewise dissociated leadership to set up a number of conflicting pairs—ideology and politics versus pragmatism and principle, experience versus judgment, and tactics versus strategy—and to associate him with the more positive term of each pairing. Second, wise political candidates will choose representative anecdotes that can serve as supple bridging devices to link their particular brand of leadership, established through a representative anecdote, to other issues. Obama's portrayal of his judgment on Iraq allowed him to emphasize his policies for ending the war and to link his plans for a resolution to the conflict with his needed leadership on a wide array of other matters. Similarly, the senator aligned his judgment on Iraq with that of Republican Senator John Warner and Democratic president Woodrow Wilson, which in turn led smoothly to his creation of Republican endorsements of his leadership on other aspects of foreign policy and to his comparison of his desire for a greater focus on diplomacy with the diplomatic efforts of presidential greats from both parties. Third, political rhetors in need of establishing the legitimacy of their candidacy should choose a representative anecdote that not only depicts their leadership as unique, but also as optimistic and well within the norms of American history and character. Obama was not the only Democratic contender to oppose the war in Iraq; both former senator from Alaska Mike Gravel and Congressman Dennis Kucinich of Ohio had been against the war from its start. Unlike these two candidates, Obama chose a representative anecdote on Iraq that offered hope, rather than pessimism and fear; he also reassured citizens that his brand of leadership was consistent with the historic character of the American people. Given the typically upbeat tenor of presidential rhetoric, Obama's ability to use Iraq both to attack his opponents and to associate his leadership with American optimism was especially advantageous.[52]

The representative anecdotes that candidates adopt are significant, for they must be not only compelling but also flexible enough to adapt to the changing circumstances and issues of a campaign. In the case of Obama, his decision to emphasize his judgment on the Iraq War ultimately served him well in getting his campaign underway, countering attacks from his opponents, and adjusting to the newly dominant issue of the economy. His Iraq anecdote allowed Obama to refute his rivals' criticisms forcefully while establishing his own leadership as a substantive, hopeful alternative that was quintessentially American.

NOTES

1. Judy Keen, "The Big Question about Barack Obama," *USA Today,* January 17, 2007, http://usatoday.com; Jay Newton-Small, "Obama's Foreign-Policy Problem," *Time,* December 18, 2007, http://www.nytimes.com; Adam Nagourney and Jeff Zeleny, "Obama Formally Enters Presidential Race," *New York Times,* February 11, 2007, http://www.nytimes.com.
2. James D. Barber, "The Presidency: What Americans Want," in *Perspectives on the Presidency,* ed. Stanley Bach and George T. Sulzner (Lexington, MA: D.C. Heath, 1974), 145.
3. "Biography of John McCain," United States Senate, http://mccain.senate.gov; Patrick Healy, "The Resume Factor: Those 2 Terms as First Lady," *New York Times,* December 26, 2007, http://www.nytimes.com; "Biography of Hillary Rodham Clinton," U.S. Department of State, http://www.state.gov.
4. "Clinton Hits Obama Over Foreign Policy Experience," *U.S. News & World Report,* November 21, 2007, http://www.usnews.com; Newton-Small, "Obama's Foreign-Policy Problem."
5. Keen, "The Big Question about Barack Obama"; Barack Obama, "Illinois Sen. Barack Obama's Announcement Speech," *Washington Post,* February 10, 2007, http://www.washingtonpost.com.
6. For more, see Denise M. Bostdorff, "Judgment, Experience, and Leadership: Candidate Debates on the Iraq War in the 2008 Presidential Primaries," *Rhetoric & Public Affairs* 12 (2009): 223–278.
7. Kenneth Burke, *A Grammar of Motives* (1945; reprint, Berkeley: University of California Press, 1969), 59, 60–61.
8. "Obama Calls Clinton Ad a Scare Tactic," *CBS News,* February 29, 2008, http://www.cbsnews.com; Rick Pearson and John McCormick, "Clinton Hits Obama on

Experience; He Fires Back," *Chicago Tribune,* March 2, 2008, http://www.chicagotribune.com; Johnanna Neuman, "Obama Says Clinton Using 'Gamesmanship' in Campaign," *Los Angeles Times,* March 10, 2008, http://infoweb.newsbank.com, Rec. no. 200803102310LATWP__LA_Times_X4163; Hillary Clinton, "Iraq: Hillary's Remarks at the George Washington University," March 17, 2008, http://www.hillaryclinton.com.

9. Liz Sly, "Iraq Violence Greets McCain, Cheney—Visiting Senator, VP Laud Progress," *Chicago Tribune,* March 18, 2008, http://infoweb.newsbank.com.
10. Bob Sector and Jeff Coen, "Blagojevich's Name Surfaces Early in Case," *Chicago Tribune,* March 7, 2008, http://www.chicagotribune.com; David Jackson, "Obama: I Trusted Rezko," *Chicago Tribune,* March 15, 2008, http://infoweb.newsbank.com, Rec. no. CTR0803140838.
11. Maddy Sauer and Rehab El-Buri, "More from Obama's Pastor: U.S. a Racist Superpower," *ABC News*, March 18, 2008, http://www.abcnews.go.com; Jeremiah Wright, "God Damn America," YouTube, http://www.youtube.com.
12. Barack Obama, "A More Perfect Union," *ABC News,* March 18, 2008, http://www.abcnews.go.com. Also see Thomas L. Dumm, "Barack Obama and the Souls of White Folk," *Communication and Critical/Cultural Studies* 5 (2008): 317–320; David A. Frank, "The Prophetic Voice and the Face of the Other in Barack Obama's 'A More Perfect Union' Address, Mar. 18, 2008," *Rhetoric & Public Affairs* 12 (2009): 167–194.
13. Ron Claiborne, "Iraq Now Central to McCain Campaign, But Not to Voters," *ABC News,* December 22, 2007, http://www.abcnews.go.com.
14. Patrick Healy, "Senator Clinton Calls for Withdrawal from Iraq to Begin in 2006," *New York Times,* November 30, 2005, http://ww.nytimes.com; Dan Balz, "Liberal Activists Boo Clinton," *Washington Post,* June 14, 2006, http://www.washingtonpost.com.
15. Fareed Zakaria, "This Won't Be the Iraq Election," editorial, *Newsweek,* November 12, 2007, 58; Ken Dilanian, "Progress in Iraq Reshapes Debate Over War," *USA Today,* February 18, 2008, sec. A, pp. 1–2; Jeff Mason, "War? What War? Economy Trumps Iraq in Election," *Reuters,* January 7, 2008, http://www.reuters.com; Tom Raum, "The Economy Nudges Iraq War Aside in Political Campaigns," *Wooster (OH) Daily Record,* December 30, 2007, sec. A, pp. 1, 5; David Brooks, "The Postwar Election," editorial, *New York Times,* December 11, 2007, sec. A, p. 33.
16. Associated Press-Ipso poll cited in Raum, "The Economy Nudges"; Pew Research Center, "Obama Has Lead, But Potential Problems Too," February 28, 2008, http://

pewresearch.org.

17. "Profile of Caucusgoers," *New York Times,* January 3, 2008, and Mathew Continetti, "Another War Election," *New York Times,* January 13, 2008, both at http://www.nytimes.com.
18. For more on the shifting of Iraq as an issue during the primaries, see Bostdorff, "Judgment, Experience, and Leadership."
19. "Obama Wins Iowa as Candidate for Change," *CNN*, January 3, 2008, http://www.cnn.com.
20. Marcella Bombardieri, "Clinton Highlights Terrorism Rhetoric," *Boston Globe,* January 7, 2008, http://www.boston.com; Mark Murray, "Hillary Plays the al Qaeda Card," *MSNBC*, January 8, 2008, http://firstread.msnbc.msn.com; Edward Luce, "Clinton Defies Conventional Wisdom," *Financial Times,* January 9, 2008, http://www.FT.com; Continetti, "Another War Election."
21. "Primary Season Election Results," *New York Times,* accessed March 19, 2009, http://politics.nytimes.com/election-guide/2008/results/votes; David Epso, "McCain Seizes GOP Command on Super Tuesday; Clinton, Obama Battle for Democrats," *Milwaukee Marquette Tribune,* February 5, 2008, http://www.marquettetribune.org.
22. Quoted in Katharine Q. Seelye and Jeff Zeleny, "Clinton Questions Role of Obama in Crisis," *New York Times,* March 1, 2008, http://www.nytimes.com.
23. Quoted in "Obama Calls Clinton Ad."
24. Quoted in Libby Quaid, "McCain Says He Can Best Handle Crises," *Newsday,* March 3, 2008, http://www.newsday.com.
25. Quoted in Steven Thomma, "Clinton's Victories Mean the Race Goes On—and May Get Ugly," *McClatchy Papers,* March 4, 2008, http://www.mcclatchydc.com.
26. "Democratic Debate Transcript," Cleveland, February 26, 2008, American Presidency Project, http://www.presidency.ucsb.edu; also see "The U.S. Congress Votes Database," *Washington Post,* accessed May 19, 2008, http://projects.washingtonpost.com/congress/110/senate/vote-missers.
27. Quoted in Pearson and McCormick, "Clinton Hits Obama on Experience."
28. Lynn Sweet, "Barack Suffered Stumble, But Holds Key Strength," *Chicago Sun-Times,* March 5, 2008, http://www.suntimes.com. Also see polls cited in Thomma, "Clinton's Victories Mean the Race Goes On"; Tim Jones and Mike Dorning, "Clinton Stays in Picture," *Chicago Tribune,* March 5, 2008, http://infoweb.newsbank.com, Rec. no. CTR0803041361.
29. Ariel Alexovich, "Obama Aides Tout His Credentials to Be Commander in Chief,"

New York Times, March 10, 2008, http://www.nytimes.com; Julian E. Barnes and Peter Spiegel, "Clinton and Obama Struggle to Marshal Military Backing," *Los Angeles Times,* March 10, 2008, http://infoweb.newsbank.com, Rec. no. 200803102311LATWP__LA_TIMES_X4166.

30. "Hillary's Adventures Abroad," *FactCheck.org*, March 13, 2008, http://www.factcheck.org/elections-2008; Sinbad quoted in Mark Benjamin, "Hillary Clinton, Sniper Fire, and Sinbad," *Salon.com,* March 17, 2008, http://www.salon.com.
31. Sly, "Iraq Violence Greets McCain, Cheney"; Mark Harrington, "Iraq Remains on the Campaign Stage," *Newsday,* March 17, 2008, http://infoweb.newsbank.com; Waleed Ibrahim and Mohammed Abbas, "Iraq Reconciliation Talks Hit by Walkouts," *Reuters*, March 18, 2008, http://www.reuters.com; Michael Cooper, "McCain Missteps on Iraq; Democrats Pounce," *New York Times,* March 19, 2008, http://www.nytimes.com.
32. Jeff Zeleny, "Obama Marks Fifth Anniversary of the Iraq War," *New York Times,* March 19, 2008, http://thecaucus.blogs.nytimes.com/2008/03/19; campaign press release quoted in John Ramsey, "Obama to Give Major Speech on Iraq, National Security in Fayetteville, NC, March 19," *Fayetteville Observer,* March 18, 2008, http://www.democraticunderground.com.
33. Ramsey, "Obama to Give Major Speech"; Zeleny, "Obama Marks Fifth Anniversary"; "Obama Tries to Turn Focus Away from Issues of Race," *Houston Chronicle,* March 20, 2008, http://www.lexisnexis.com.
34. Barack Obama, "Speech on Iraq," March 19, 2008, Council on Foreign Relations, March 19, 2008, http://www.cfr.org; "Barack Obama Speech on Iraq War in Fayetteville, NC," *Think on These Things,* March 20, 2008, http://thinkonthesethings.wordpress.com.
35. For more on dissociation, see Chaim Perelman and L. Olbrechts-Tyteca, *The New Rhetoric,* trans. John Wilkinson and Purcell Weaver (Notre Dame, IN: University of Notre Dame Press, 1969), 415–426; David Zarefsky, *President Johnson's War on Poverty: Rhetoric and History* (Tuscaloosa: University of Alabama Press, 1986), 9–10; David Zarefsky, "Presidential Rhetoric and the Power of Definition," *Presidential Studies Quarterly* 34 (2004): 612.
36. See, for example, "McCain Promises to Chase Bin Laden to 'Gates of Hell,'" *Gulf News*, January 20, 2008, http://archive.gulfnews.com.
37. See, for example, Terry Moran, Julia Hoppock, and Melinda Arons, "Obama in Iowa: Gloves Off!," *ABC News*, November 26, 2007, http://www.abcnews.go.com; Margaret Talev and Steven Thomma, "Sure, Obama's a Smart, Sweet Guy—But

Can He Fight?" *McClatchy Papers*, March 9, 2008, http://www.mcclatchydc.com; Lauren Appelbaum, "Obama: Not the First Punch, But the Last," *MSNBC*, October 6, 2008, http://firstread.msnbc.msn.com.

38. Ivie and Giner noted that Obama, unlike the other major candidates, spoke of practicality and working collaboratively with the international community. See Robert L. Ivie and Oscar Giner, "More Good, Less Evil: Contesting the Mythos of National Insecurity in the 2008 Presidential Primaries," *Rhetoric & Public Affairs* 12 (2009): 284–288.
39. Stuckey noted Obama frequently contrasted himself with Clinton and McCain by associating them with "old," ineffective ways of doing things, an approach that was highly appealing to voters, especially new voters. See Mary E. Stuckey, "The Politics of Realignment," *Communication and Critical/Cultural Studies* 5 (2008): 322.
40. Dilanian, "Progress in Iraq Reshapes Debate"; *USA Today*/Gallup poll cited in Michael Luo, "McCain Says Prospects May Hinge on Iraq," *New York Times*, February 26, 2008, http://www.nytimes.com.
41. Burke writes of conceptual bridging devices: "When objects are not in a line, and you would have them in a line without moving them, you may put them in a line by shifting your angle of vision." Kenneth Burke, *Attitudes Toward History*, 3rd ed. (1937; reprint, Berkeley: University of California Press, 1984), 224.
42. Robert C. Rowland and John M. Jones, "Recasting the American Dream and American Politics: Barack Obama's Keynote Address to the 2004 Democratic National Convention," *Quarterly Journal of Speech* 93 (2007): 425–448; Deborah F. Atwater, "Senator Barack Obama: The Rhetoric of Hope and the American Dream," *Journal of Black Studies* 38 (2007): 121–129; Barack Obama, *The Audacity of Hope: Thoughts on Reclaiming the American Dream* (New York: Crown, 2006); Obama, "Illinois Sen. Barack Obama's Announcement Speech." For an analysis of Obama's rhetoric on race in his 2004 keynote, see David A. Frank and Mark Lawrence McPhail, "Barack Obama's Address to the 2004 Democratic National Convention: Trauma, Compromise, Consilience, and the (Im)possibility of Racial Reconciliation," *Rhetoric & Public Affairs* 8 (2005): 571–594.
43. Rowland and Jones, "Recasting the American Dream," 442.
44. Barack Obama, "The Cost of War," March 20, 2008, *The Page*, March 21, 2008, http://thepage.time.com.
45. Ben Feller, "Bush Defiantly Defends War in Iraq," *Des Moines Register*, March 20, 2008, http://www.DesMoinesRegister.com; Robert H. Reid, "Iraq: U.S. Death Toll in War Hits 4,000," *San Francisco Chronicle*, March 23, 2008, http://www.SFgate.

com; Steven Lee Myers and Thom Shanker, "Bush Given Iraq War Plan with a Steady Troop Level," *New York Times,* March 25, 2008, http://www.nytimes.com; Tina Susman, "Iraq-Times," *Los Angeles Times,* March 27, 2008, http://infoweb.newsbank.com, Rec. no. 200803271952LATWP_LA_Times_X5604.

46. Mike Dorning, "Obama Says Iraq War Has Hurt U.S. Security," *Los Angeles Times,* March 20, 2008, http://www.latimes.com; Mike Wereschagin, David M. Brown, and Salena Zito, "Clinton Slams Obama's Minister," *Pittsburgh Tribune-Review,* March 26, 2008, http://www.pittsburghlive.com; Jay Solomon, "Obama's Foreign-Policy Pledge Sparks Criticism from Rivals," *Wall Street Journal,* March 26, 2008, http://online.wsj.com; John McCain, "Foreign Policy Speech before the Los Angeles World Affairs Council," *New York Times,* March 26, 2008, http://www.nytimes.com.
47. Burke, *Grammar,* 60.
48. Obama, "The Cost of War."
49. For more on Kennedy and the missile gap, see Christopher A. Preble, *John F. Kennedy and the Missile Gap* (DeKalb: Northern Illinois University Press, 2004).
50. Presidential Debate at Belmont University in Nashville, October 7, 2008, American Presidency Project, http://www.presidency.ucsb.edu.
51. See, for example, Barack Obama, "Closing Argument Speech," Canton, OH, October 27, 2008, *The Page*, http://thepage.time.com.
52. For more on the rhetorical optimism of presidents and incumbent candidates, see Roderick P. Hart, *Verbal Style and the Presidency* (Orlando, FL: Academic Press, 1984), 34–36; Roderick P. Hart, *Campaign Talk: Why Elections Are Good for Us* (Princeton, NJ: Princeton University Press, 2000), 83–85.

Barack Obama's 2009 Inaugural Address: Narrative Signature and Interpretation

Martin J. Medhurst

> Just the image of him—the first African American to ascend to the presidency, standing with his right hand held aloft, his left resting on Abraham Lincoln's Bible—will send a message beyond the powers of any speechwriter to put into words.
>
> —Russell L. Riley

Long after the words of Barack Obama's inaugural address have passed into memory—a word here, a phrase there, a theme recalled—those who witnessed the ceremony of January 20, 2009, whether in person, on television, or over the Internet, will never forget the sea of humanity that surrounded the platform and carried west almost as far as the eye could see.[1] Whether people were watching on the Jumbotron at the National Mall or in the comfort of their own living rooms, the pictures said it all—or so it seemed to the expert observers, many of whom could not themselves find the words to express their feelings on this historic and emotional day. A black man was taking the oath of office as the forty-fourth president of the United States.[2]

Historians will be writing about this inauguration for years to come, but the burden of the rhetorical critic is to make sense of the words, even when the message of the image speaks very loudly in the hearts and minds of the viewing audience. This is a burden that rhetoricians have assumed since 1937, when Robert D. King examined the "textual authenticity" of FDR's second inaugural address.[3] Since that time more than forty articles in professional communication journals have examined inaugural addresses, with studies of Lincoln's second, Kennedy's, Roosevelt's first, and Jefferson's first accounting for almost half of the total.[4]

Yet it was an article published in an interdisciplinary journal, *Presidential Studies Quarterly,* that changed the way many scholars viewed inaugural addresses. "Inaugurating the Presidency," by Karlyn Kohrs Campbell and Kathleen Hall Jamieson, became a canonical work even before being expanded into a chapter for their book *Deeds Done in Words: On the Rhetorical Genres of Governance.*[5] In that book-length work, Campbell and Jamieson set forth their theory of rhetorical genres and then applied it to recurring types of presidential discourse, including the inaugural address. Identifying the inaugural as falling within the Aristotelian genre of epideictic, Campbell and Jamieson held that the presidential inaugural does the following:

> (1) unifies the audience by reconstituting its members as the people, who can witness and ratify the ceremony; (2) rehearses communal values drawn from the past; (3) sets forth the political principles that will govern the new administration; and (4) demonstrates through enactment that the president appreciates the requirements and limitations of executive functions. Finally, (5) each of these ends must be achieved through means appropriate to epideictic address, that is, while urging contemplation, not action, focusing on the present while incorporating past and future, and praising the institution of the presidency and the values and forms of the government of which it is a part, a process through which the covenant between the president and the people is renewed.[6]

These generic requirements were illustrated by examples drawn from inaugural addresses throughout American history.

While few disputed the accuracy of Campbell and Jamieson's observations, some did question the utility of Aristotelian categories and the seeming avoidance of counterexamples that appeared to show distinctly deliberative elements in many inaugural addresses. Chief among these critics was Halford Ryan, whose 1993 collection, *The Inaugural Addresses of Twentieth-Century American Presidents,* challenged the Campbell-Jamieson paradigm. In his introductory essay, Ryan wrote:

> At least in the case of inaugural addresses, genre theory hinders more than it helps. It invites the critic to confirm, which is usually the case, or to confute, which is rarely the case, certain generic tenets at the expense of examining the inaugural speech *in situ.* It entices the commentator to make *a priori* assumptions about an inaugural before beginning to analyze it; therefore, one may miss other significant rhetorical features of the inaugural under investigation.[7]

Both the Campbell-Jamieson and the Ryan paradigms had their strengths. Campbell and Jamieson were interested in generic form and how that form could be used to predict rhetorical practice in the future as well as to analyze oratorical practices of the past. Their focus was on the constellation of formal and functional elements that the occasion of inauguration called forth, without regard to the individual being inaugurated or the specific exigencies of the moment. Ryan's paradigm, based on Lloyd Bitzer's idea of the rhetorical situation, looked to the specific exigencies and constraints of the historical situation for its validation, as well as the rhetorical inventions and adaptations that individual presidents made to address those exigencies and constraints. In so doing, Ryan and many of his contributors, of which I was one, claimed to find significant departures from the generic model set forth by Campbell and Jamieson, particularly with respect to deliberative ends versus epideictic ends and action versus contemplation.[8]

And that is where the state of the debate has rested for the past nineteen years, with a durable generic model on one hand and an idiosyncratic situational approach on the other. Both approaches are useful, though in different ways and toward different ends, and both will doubtless be helpful in reading and understanding Barack Obama's January 20, 2009, inaugural address. Yet as I studied Obama's inaugural, I came to the conclusion that neither the generic nor the situational models were sufficient in themselves—or even in combination—to account for all of the rhetorical significance to be found in Obama's address. I came to this conclusion after doing an exhaustive study of twenty-six of the most widely circulated Obama speeches—from his speech opposing going to war in Iraq on October 26, 2002, when he was still an Illinois state senator, through his victory speech in Grant Park on November 4, 2008.[9] From that preliminary study, I isolated what I am calling Obama's Narrative Signature. A Narrative Signature is the unique way in which a person—any person—tells his or her story.[10]

The Narrative Signature

The Narrative Signature is premised on the idea that everyone has a story to tell. It may be an autobiographical story based on life experiences, a conversion story of insight and enlightenment, a survival story of life from death, or any other kind of story whose telling is definitive of one's life or mission. A Narrative Signature emerges over time and across genres. Once established, however, it does not change. Like the signature of one's name, it is a unique form of identity that only the narrator can perform with complete fidelity. It is replete with its own vocabulary, which functions as a grammar; its own strategy, which functions as a rhetoric; and its own method, which functions as a dialectical procedure. To understand a rhetor's Narrative Signature is to understand the power or motivation that drives the narrator to employ the signature in all types of situations and across multiple genres of discourse.

In the world of contemporary public affairs, one can readily identify several rhetors who appear to have employed a distinctive Narrative Signature. In the area of social protest, both Malcolm X and Martin Luther King Jr. had unique Narrative Signatures.[11] In presidential rhetoric, Ronald Reagan displayed a unique signature predicated on a standard narrative.[12] In the area of punditry and political commentary, William

F. Buckley's Narrative Signature was often the object of discussion and analysis.[13] And in the world of African American religion, it was elements of the Reverend Jeremiah Wright's Narrative Signature that brought him into conflict with the Obama campaign.[14]

In each of these cases—and many others—the rhetor has displayed, over the course of a lifetime, a *distinct set of ideas* that have been expressed in a *symbolically rich but finite vocabulary* that is drawn upon repeatedly. Because this vocabulary is limited and *repeats itself across time and genres*—public speeches, radio addresses, newspaper columns, debates, sermons, and the like—the discerning critic can track the development and refinement of the vocabulary over the course of a rhetor's career. But it is not the ideas or vocabulary alone that constitute the Narrative Signature. There must also exist the ability to weave these ideas together into a *coherent and persuasive discourse*. Such a discourse is characterized by its strategic nature; that is, it has a purpose and that purpose determines how the ideas and vocabulary are combined to form a *complete story that has designs on an audience*. This strategic design is the rhetoric of the Narrative Signature. It is what gives form and purpose to the ideas as well as to the individual elements of the vocabulary. The design can take many different forms—myth, quest story, narrative of personal growth, pursuit of a mission, disclosure of a revelation, or description of a transformation, among other possibilities—but the rhetorical function is always the same: to advance the strategic goals of the rhetor by inviting the audience to identify with the ideas, participate in the form, and ultimately to cooperate in the actions required to reach the goal. To energize these rhetorical forms and functions, a rhetor's Narrative Signature will also feature distinctive dialectical procedures by which the ideas and the strategic design are made logically and emotionally compelling to an audience. These dialectical procedures, like the vocabulary and the strategic design, will be regularly and repeatedly deployed in the rhetor's discourse as *ways of justifying, defending, defining, and publicly testing* the rationality and/or desirability of the rhetor's goals.

A Narrative Signature is thus composed of the ideas, vocabulary, strategic design, forms of appeal, and modes of logical justification that are characteristically and repeatedly employed in his or her discourse. The ways in which these factors combine to form a coherent story constitutes the rhetor's unique rhetorical signature.

Obama's Narrative Signature

Obama's Narrative Signature begins with a specialized vocabulary that serves as a grammar. From this grammar a strategic rhetoric is assembled that takes the form of a journey toward a destination—one's destiny. The methods by which this strategy is executed constitute the dialectical procedures that justify the journey, reveal the logic, differentiate ideas, and create knowledge as the narrative moves forward.

Grammatical Elements in Obama's Signature

After a close reading of the twenty-six speeches surveyed, I constructed frequency counts of all terms that appeared repeatedly across multiple speeches. Through this procedure, I isolated twenty-four distinct grammatical units that comprise the vocabulary of Obama's Narrative Signature. These twenty-four units can be grouped according to the role they play in the strategic design of Obama's Narrative Signature from 2002 through 2008.

- ROAD OF LIFE: Journey, Path
- IMAGINED GOALS: Dreams, Destiny, Calling, Promise
- ATTITUDINAL HELPERS: Faith, Hope, Courage, Sacrifice, Belief, Truth
- SITUATIONAL OBSTACLES: Cynicism, Crisis
- AGENCIES OF CHANGE: Imagination, Innovation
- TIMES OF TRANSFORMATION: Miracles, Moments, Rise Up, Opportunity, Measure
- FINAL DESTINATION: Common Good, One People, Perfected [Dream]

The grammatical elements in the "Road of Life" list appear 41 times over 14 of the twenty-six speeches surveyed. The elements in the "Imagined Goals" set appear 170 times in twenty-five speeches. Terms for "Attitudinal Helpers" are the most numerous of all, with 326 appearances across all twenty-six speeches, while the terms for "Situational Obstacles" appear only 42 times in thirteen speeches. The "Agencies of Change" terms appear 34 times over sixteen speeches, while the "Times of Transformation" vocabulary appears 168 times over twenty-five speeches. Terms for the "Final Destination" appear 53 times over sixteen speeches and often cycle back to the "Imagined Goals" terms, as when Obama speaks of perfecting the dream.

Two statistical facts stand out: First, that the vocabulary of faith, hope, and courage appears more often than any other terms; such "Attitudinal Helpers" are the only category of terms to appear in all twenty-six speeches. On the other hand, the vocabulary of crisis and cynicism appears far less frequently, with mentions in only thirteen speeches—only half of the total. From such a statistical perspective, Obama's speeches are overwhelmingly positive in orientation at the grammatical level of analysis.

Rhetorical Elements in Obama's Signature

These twenty-four grammatical elements can be combined in various ways to tell a persuasive story. This design strategy is what I call the rhetoric of the Narrative Signature—the persuasive story that can be constructed by skillful manipulation of the parts. In this case, it is a narrative grounded largely in two biblical myths—the story of Moses's journey into the wilderness in search of the Promised Land and the Christian redemption cycle of birth, death, and rebirth, as represented in the Christ figure. In Obama's adaptation of the myths, the journey is both individual and collective—it is his journey toward his destiny as well as America's journey toward the fulfillment of the promises made in its founding documents.[15] It is the story of a young man born into the world in less than ideal circumstances, who wanders through life with little purpose or direction, but who is transformed by a realization of who he is and what he is called to do. Simultaneously, it is the story of a nation that is born amidst high idealism, fails to realize those ideals even after a spasm of blood sacrifice, yet continues to work toward a rebirth that will restore to the nation that which it had lost through its "original sin."[16]

Thus, the strategy of Obama's speeches, considered as one grand text articulated through a mythic vocabulary and directed toward a nationwide audience, is something like this:

> We are all on a *journey,* a specific *path* that, if followed, will lead us to our *destiny.* We know what that destiny is because of our *dreams,* and if we but follow our dreams, they will help us to reach our destination. The path is neither easy nor straight. Many obstacles must be overcome through *imagination* and *innovation* if *opportunities* for advancement along the path are to be realized. *Faith* and *hope* are required to keep us on the path, even when the dream dims, *crisis* threatens, and the way seems unclear. If we maintain the faith there will be *moments,* aporias in time, when we hear a *call* and *rise up* as a people to fulfill our dreams and advance toward our destiny. Answering this call requires *courage, sacrifice,* and the will to believe in the dream even when the path is dimly lit and *cynics* tell us we should turn back or give up because we'll never make it. But with a commitment to the *common good* and with the *belief* that despite our differences we are all *one people,* together we can make real the *promise* of America and *perfect* the American Dream—yes, we can. Along the way, at those special moments when opportunity knocks and small *miracles* can be seen, we can *measure* our progress, renew our faith, and rededicate ourselves to the *truth* that out of many, we can become one.

This mythic rhetoric can be found throughout Obama's speaking from 2002 to 2008. In his speech to the American Library Association on June 27, 2005, he said: "And in that *moment,* there's nothing we want more than to nurture that *hope,* to make all those possibilities and all those *opportunities* real for our children, to have the ability to answer the question, 'What can I be when I grow up?' with 'Anything you want—anything you can *dream* of.'"[17] One month later, Obama told the AFL-CIO: "Our vision of America is not one where a big government runs our lives; it's one that gives every American the *opportunity* to make the most of their lives. It's not one that tells us we're on our own; it's one that realizes that we *rise* or fall together as *one people.*"[18]

On November 16, 2005, speaking about the legacy of Robert F. Kennedy, Obama noted:

> Rather, the idealism of Robert Kennedy—the unfinished legacy that *calls* us still—is a fundamental *belief* in the continuing *perfection* of American ideals.
>
> It is a *belief* that says if this nation was truly founded on the principles of freedom and equality, it could not sit idly by while millions were shackled because of the color of their skin. That if we are to shine as a beacon of *hope* to the rest of the world, we must be respected not just for the might of our military, but for the reach of our ideals. That if this is a land where *destiny* is not determined by birth or circumstance, we have a duty to ensure that the child of a millionaire and the child of a welfare mom have the same chance in life. That if, out of many, we are truly *one,* then we must not limit ourselves to the pursuit of selfish gain, but that which will help all Americans to *rise* together.
>
> We have not always lived up to these ideals and we may fail again in the future, but this legacy *calls* on us to try.[19]

Across the twenty-six speeches surveyed, this strategic design repeats itself in all but four of the speeches—suggesting that it is an intentional rhetorical strategy being deployed by means of Obama's Narrative Signature. This is the grand rhetorical strategy of the Obama candidacy—to use his Narrative Signature as a way of persuading the electorate to share the dream, hear the call, and join in the journey.

Dialectical Elements in Obama's Signature

For this grammar and rhetoric to be effective, there must also be an accompanying dialectic, a method of testing the competing pathways to make sure that the faithful stay on the right one. In Obama's Narrative Signature that dialectic is characterized by five procedures: elevation of reason and scientific truth over false belief and ideology, exposure of false choices and fallacious reasoning, praise for both empirical measures and the need for measuring, use of dissociation and differentiation, and employment of dialectical pairs as instruments of clarification and definition.

As early as 2002, Obama criticized the move toward war in Iraq as being based "not on reason but on passion."[20] Speaking to the American Library Association in 2005, he noted that we have "a deep faith in facts" and that jobs in the new economy are "about what you know" and "require innovative thinking, detailed comprehension, and superior communication." He spoke out against "a general culture that glorifies anti-intellectualism."[21] Addressing the Call to Renewal meeting in 2006, Obama held that "democracy demands that the religiously motivated translate their concerns into universal, rather than religion-specific, values. It requires that their proposals be subject to argument and amenable to reason."[22] And in December of that same year, Obama reminded his audience on World AIDS Day that "we should never forget that God granted us the power to reason so that we would do His work here on Earth—so that we would use science to cure disease, and heal the sick, and save lives."[23] Repeatedly, he calls upon his audience to apply reason as a test of worthiness.

In pursuit of this reason, Obama often exposes the logical weaknesses of his opponents by accusing them of using the black/white, either/or fallacy. "This is an issue that Washington always tries to make 'either-or,'" Obama said in reference to the Patriot Act. "Either we protect our people from terror or we protect our most cherished principles."[24] In reference to education policy, Obama noted that "like most ideological debates, this one assumes that there's an 'either-or' answer to our education problems. Either we need to pour more money into the system, or we need to reform it with more tests and standards."[25] In many instances, Obama's answer to such fallacious reasoning is a policy that transcends the extremes, often by incorporating the best features of each into a reconceptualized whole. Such was the case with AIDS prevention, when Obama observed: "Now, too often, the issue of prevention has been framed in 'either/or' terms. For some, the only way to prevent the disease is for men and women to change their sexual behavior—in particular, to abstain from sexual activity outside of marriage. For others, such a prescription is unrealistic; they argue that we need to provide people with the tools they need to protect themselves from the virus, regardless of their sexual practices—in particular by increasing the use of condoms."[26] He then went on to affirm the need both for moral norms *and* responsible behaviors and to argue for greater use of condoms and other means of stopping the spread of the disease. The use of this dialectical method often has the effect of making Obama appear to be the more reasonable of the contending parties, because he is seen as considering both sides before issuing a Solomonic decision that often splits the difference.

Closely related to his praise for reason and logical analysis is his penchant for empirical proofs and the need for measurement. At his keynote address to the 2004 Democratic National Convention, Obama said: "This year, in this election, we are called to reaffirm our values and commitments, to hold them against a hard reality and see how we are measuring up to the legacy of our forebearers and the promise of future generations."[27] There is, in Obama's rhetoric, a need to measure against a standard in order to make a reasonable judgment. Measuring is a dialectical form of investigation—a way of knowing. Speaking at the Center for American Progress, Obama argued, "We need new vision for education in America—one where we move past ideology to experiment with the latest reforms, measure the results, and make policy decisions based on what works and what doesn't."[28] Many commentators understand this to be pragmatism, but it is more accurately seen as a form of empiricism—an examination of evidence and an analysis of the results based on some kind of normative standard. As Obama told his audience at the University of Nairobi, "But elections are not enough. In a true democracy, it is what happens between elections that is the true measure of how a government treats its people."[29] Likewise, at the groundbreaking for the Martin Luther King Jr. Memorial, Obama recalled King's dream "of a land that measured itself by how it treats the least of these."[30] Throughout Obama's discourses measuring is used as a dialectical device of discernment.

The fourth dialectical method used by Obama is various combinations of differentiation, dissociation, and division. In differentiation, the speaker seeks to distinguish one thing from something closely related to it. In dissociation, the speaker seeks to divide a philosophical pair in such a way as to privilege one half of the pair over the other. And in division, the speaker takes a unified term and divides it into two or more terms of greater insight or import. Speaking at the Call to Renewal event, Obama employed differentiation when he said, "Whatever we once were, we are no longer just a Christian nation; we are also a Jewish nation, a Muslim nation, a Buddhist nation, a Hindu nation, and a nation of nonbelievers."[31] Obama differentiates the idea of a monolithic religious culture into the multireligious cultures that make up America—it's not this, it is that. In his famous speech on race, delivered in Philadelphia on March 18, 2008, Obama took the differentiation in the opposite direction, moving from multiplicity to singularity, when he referred to "problems that are neither black or white or Latino or Asian, but rather problems that confront us all."[32] In the same speech, Obama uses dissociation when he refers to "real change," thus drawing on the philosophical pair appearance/reality and dissociating the real from false or merely apparent change. The appearance/reality pairing is Obama's favorite target of dissociation. Speaking to the AFL-CIO National Convention on July 25, 2005, Obama noted that "unions can play a real role in finally creating a real system of lifelong learning so that workers who lose a job can retrain for other high-wage jobs."[33] The implication is that the earlier roles and systems were not real or legitimate or serious efforts. Closely related to dissociation is division, where one unitary concept is split into two parts. Central to Obama's vision is the idea of responsibility, which he often divides as a means of differentiating types or kinds of responsibilities. On June 14, 2006, at the "Take Back America" conference, Obama used division when he said, "We know that we've been called in churches and mosques, synagogues and Sunday Schools to love our neighbors as ourselves, to be our brother's keeper, to be our sister's keeper. That we have individual responsibility, but we also have collective responsibility to each other."[34] Here the unitary term "responsibility" is divided into individual and collective responsibility. Differentiation, dissociation, and division are all techniques used as methods for creating knowledge through analysis of terms.[35]

The final dialectical method used by Obama is dialectical opposites, with ordinary/extraordinary, easy/hard, seen/unseen, right/wrong, few/many, rise/fall, and past/future being chief among them. In a speech to the NAACP on May 2, 2005, Obama observed that "in America, ordinary citizens can somehow find in their hearts the courage to do extraordinary things."[36] Two months later, in Chicago, he noted, "For this has always been the way with us—at the edge of despair, in the shadow of hopelessness, ordinary people make the extraordinary decision that if we stand together, we rise together."[37] The ordinary/extraordinary binary was the one most used in the twenty-six speeches I examined. Presidential acceptance addresses always feature such dialectical opposites, and Obama's was no exception.[38] "It is that American spirit—that American promise," he proclaimed, "that pushes us forward, even when the path is uncertain, that binds us together in spite of our differences; that makes us fix our eye not on what is seen, but what is unseen, that better place around the bend."[39] Even as Obama uses these dialectical methods to test claims, define terms, and generate knowledge, he is simultaneously articulating the myths that lie at the heart of his Narrative Signature. The grammatical terms and the rhetorical strategy interface with the dialectical methods to produce the Narrative Signature that is Obama's alone. As he reminded the audience in his victory speech, "In this country, we rise or fall as one nation, as one people."[40]

Having set forth an outline of Obama's Narrative Signature as it manifests itself through the combination of his grammar, rhetoric, and dialectic, I now turn to the inaugural address of January 20, 2009. My argument is that knowledge of his Narrative Signature will materially aid us in our interpretive task, as we seek to discover the rhetorical dynamics of the text.

Obama's Inaugural Address

In the days leading up to the inauguration, many professors of rhetoric or political science were asked to predict what Obama was going to say. As one such professor, I dutifully played along, writing:

> President Obama's inaugural address will pivot between crisis and hope. He will set forth the dimensions of our challenges as a nation and call upon the people to enact the politics of hope. He will remind us that we have faced many challenges in the past and have met each of them with courage and determination. He will call on all Americans to unite behind his leadership and to live up to our national calling as "the last, best hope of earth." Like Lincoln, he will speak of "a more perfect Union," and like King, he will tell us that "now is the time" to act immediately and aggressively to meet the problems that confront us. Like FDR, he will remind us that "this great nation will endure as it has endured, will revive and will prosper." It will be an inspirational and

> uplifting speech that challenges us to rise to the occasion and serve the common good.[41]

My prediction was based on three sources—my knowledge of what inaugurals as a genre are supposed to be and do, my assessment of the current political and economic situation that Obama faced, and my growing familiarity with the key grammatical terms in Obama's lexicon. I could not, of course, know exactly what Obama would say, but I could be fairly certain that the speech would meet the criteria set forth by Campbell and Jamieson, would address elements of the current rhetorical situation, and would do so using the specialized language, what I am now calling his Narrative Signature, that Obama had developed over the course of his life in elective office. In general, the speech did not disappoint, but it did surprise in one regard. Rather than deal with the "crisis" in the front part of the speech and then "hope" in the remainder, as I had supposed he would do, Obama chose to use crisis as a central motif throughout the speech. This was surprising insofar as, out of the twenty-six speeches surveyed, crisis as an organizing or structuring term appeared only twice over a seven-year period—once in reference to corruption in Kenya and once in reference to the AIDS pandemic. But the financial and banking situation had deteriorated so much from the end of the campaign until Inauguration Day that Obama clearly felt compelled to respond to the situation by elevating "crisis" to a stature it seldom occupied in his earlier discourses.

The Generic Perspective

From a generic perspective, the only unusual aspect of the address is Obama's decision to use the crisis—a term he repeats four times—as the means of unification. Immediately after the formalities, Obama says,

> Yet, every so often the oath is taken amidst gathering clouds and raging storms. At these moments, America has carried on not simply because of the skill or vision of those in high office, but because we the people have remained faithful to the ideals of our forebears, and true to our founding documents.

> So it has been. So it must be with this generation of Americans.
> That we are in the midst of crisis is now well understood.[42]

Thus, the unification is as a people who have faced crises before and face them once again. Obama then follows with a paragraph in which the terms "we" and "our" appear eight times, a thought unit that ends, once more, with "these are the indicators of crisis." It is crisis that unifies us, both with the past and with one another in the present. This choice, though not unexpected, produced some responses that were probably not what Obama intended, particularly among those who were expecting an address for the ages.

Obama's other enactments of the generic form were more traditional. In his attempt to reconstitute the people through rehearsal of communal values, Obama soared.

> For us, they packed up their few worldly possessions and traveled across oceans in search of a new life.
>
> For us, they toiled in sweatshops and settled the West; endured the lash of the whip and plowed the hard earth.
>
> For us, they fought and died, in places like Concord and Gettysburg; Normandy and Khe Sahn.
>
> Time and again these men and women struggled and sacrificed and worked till their hands were raw so that we might live a better life. They saw America as bigger than the sum of our individual ambitions; greater than all the differences of birth or wealth or faction.
>
> This is the journey we continue today.

In his articulation of the principles that would guide his administration, Obama used specific policy areas and called for action, much as FDR did in 1933, but he remained well within the rhetorical parameters of the genre, especially as those parameters are construed by Campbell and Jamieson.

> Starting today, we must pick ourselves up, dust ourselves off, and begin again the work of remaking America.
>
> For everywhere we look, there is work to be done. The state of the

> economy calls for action, bold and swift, and we will act—not only to create new jobs, but to lay a new foundation for growth. We will build the roads and bridges, the electric grids and digital lines that feed our commerce and bind us together. We will restore science to its rightful place, and wield technology's wonders to raise health care's quality and lower its cost. We will harness the sun and the winds and the soil to fuel our cars and run our factories. And we will transform our schools and colleges and universities to meet the demands of a new age. All this we can do. And all this we will do.

Finally, Obama moved to enact the subordination of the office to the will of the people and of God. "For as much as government can do and must do," he said, "it is ultimately the faith and determination of the American people upon which this nation relies."

> Our challenges may be new. . . . But those values upon which our success depends—hard work and honesty, courage and fair play, tolerance and curiosity, loyalty and patriotism—these things are old. These things are true. They have been the quiet forces of progress throughout our history. What is demanded then is a return to these truths. What is required of us now is a new era of responsibility. . . .
>
> This is the price and the promise of citizenship.
>
> This is the source of our confidence: The knowledge that God calls on us to shape an uncertain destiny.

Clearly, Obama fulfilled the generic requirements of an inaugural address. Just as clearly, he drew upon his understanding of the exigencies and constraints of the moment, as well as a sophisticated understanding of the audiences he wanted to reach.

The Situational Perspective

The president identifies by name the exigencies faced by his listeners—war, a faltering economy, the home mortgage crisis, the loss of jobs, business failures, and the challenge of new energy resources. He also points to the intangible exigencies such as the "sapping of confidence" and a "nagging fear that America's decline is inevitable." He identifies the constraints, too. One of those constraints is time—the crisis will not pass soon, but he assures us that it will pass. Another constraint is what he characterizes as "recriminations and worn-out dogmas"—clearly people whose policies differ from his own, particularly those of the outgoing administration. But the very fact that such dogmatic policy positions still exist and that large numbers of people will continue to articulate them—one immediately thinks of former vice president Dick Cheney, for example—is a constraining factor. Later, he will specifically identify the market economy and national security policy as areas targeted for change. Yet another constraint is the inertia inherent in the system itself. Even some who wish Obama well are not convinced that any president can effect the kinds of structural changes he envisions. It is these people whom Obama identifies as "some who question the scale of our ambitions." A few lines later, he will label them "cynics." And some of them, he well knows, are in his own party. They are a constraining factor in his ability to carry through with the vision the inaugural articulates because they sit on congressional committees that must pass Obama's legislation and appropriate the monies for his programs. Finally, there is the constraint of business as usual, particularly in the economic realm. This may be the most difficult constraint of all, for it calls not just for change but for sacrifice. The temptation to keep on doing the same things in the same old ways is great, especially if it's not your job being shipped overseas, or your plant closing its doors, or your salary and benefits being cut. Obama addresses this issue by noting that "what is required is a new era of responsibility; a recognition, on the part of every American, that we have duties to ourselves, our nation, and the world." Indeed, I would argue that the ultimate success or failure of Obama's administration—and this speech that launched it—is the ability to overcome this most difficult of constraints, a constraint that is not so much physical or even psychological, as spiritual. It calls for a change of heart.

The audiences addressed are, for the most part, the ones we would normally expect in an inaugural—the American people, foreign allies, foreign foes, and what used to be called the nonaligned or Third World nations during the Cold War but whom Obama characterizes as "the people of poor nations," thus rhetorically transforming this audience from one based in ideology to one based in economic status. The only new audience is Obama's appeal "to the Muslim world," which is grounded in the exigence of ongoing wars in Iraq and Afghanistan and an international terrorist organization that claims justification for its actions in the teachings of an extreme branch of Islam. Those exigencies would be more than enough to justify an appeal to the Muslim world, but the fact of Obama's upbringing in a Muslim culture, what Stephen Mansfield calls his exposure to the "folk edge of Islam,"[43] as well as the fact that Obama's father was born into a Muslim family, would have made avoidance of this audience unthinkable, not to mention unwise.

Yet, as accurate and as illuminating as generic and situational analyses are, neither succeeds in fully penetrating to the rhetorical heart of Obama's inaugural address. For that, we must turn to his Narrative Signature.

Narrative Signature in the Inaugural Address

As we have seen, Obama's Narrative Signature is composed of a grammar, a rhetoric, and a dialectic that runs through virtually all of his major speeches from 2002 to 2008. The basic grammar is composed of twenty-four vocabulary terms, while the rhetoric is a persuasive narrative based on Judeo-Christian myths of the journey toward the Promised Land and the birth-death-rebirth cycle grounded in nature and made manifest most prominently in the life of Christ. The dialectic is an internal logical system that helps Obama justify ideas, test claims, create knowledge, and make distinctions. By applying the idea of a Narrative Signature to the inaugural address, we learn why the address was only partially successful and why some critics found it somewhat disappointing as rhetoric, while still holding the event itself as momentous, historical, and possibly a turning point in the American experiment.

To begin, it is useful to note that of the twenty-four grammatical terms that form the bedrock of Obama's signature, eighteen appear in the inaugural address, some of them multiple times. It is interesting to observe, however, that one of the terms that does not appear in the address is a term that was central in structuring Obama's mythic appeal—dreams.[44]

Indeed, the case could be made that the front part of Obama's address is more akin to a nightmare than a dream. Terms such as "storms," "crisis," "war," "hatred," "greed," "failure," "threaten," "fear," "decline," "conflict," and "discord" appear in the first three minutes alone. This is unusual in an Obama speech, which often opens with references to the dream or the journey. Instead, the first two terms of his Narrative Signature to make an appearance are "sacrifice" and "moments." He refers to the "sacrifices borne by our ancestors," thus linking the past with the present. He goes on to note: "At these moments, America has carried on not simply because of the skill or vision of those in high office, but because we the people have remained faithful to the ideals of our forebears, and true to our founding documents." The speech is thus located as happening within the dispensation of one of these moments when the people demonstrate how "faithful" and "true" they have been. But notice, in this speech the faithfulness is to "ideals" and to "our founding documents." Here the ideals and the documents take the place of the dream, thus underscoring the collective nature of the occasion.

Yet, neither the ideals nor the documents are referenced in the next six paragraphs. Instead, the term that is featured is "crisis." "That we are in the midst of a crisis is now well understood," Obama says. Here, too, is a change in his Narrative Signature. Almost without exception, when Obama speaks of a "moment" in his earlier speeches, those moments are times of progress and achievement. They are special precisely because good things happen to people. But in this telling, the moment holds only crisis. "Our nation is at war. . . . Our economy is badly weakened. . . . Homes have been lost; jobs shed; businesses shuttered," Obama observes. This is hardly the kind of "moment" that inspires. Throughout this litany of woes, the only other term in the signature to appear is "measure," which appears twice. In the first usage, Obama says, "These are the indicators of crisis, subject to data and statistics. Less measurable but no less profound is a sapping of confidence across our land, a nagging fear that America's decline is inevitable, that the next generation must lower its sights." Here Obama uses "measurable" in one of the standard ways associated with his signature—as a form of reason that makes empirical judgments. But this dialectic is measuring the "sapping of confidence" and a "nagging fear," hardly the kind of measurements that support a dream—which may be another reason that the term "dream" is nowhere to be found. The second usage of "measure" comes toward the end of the opening section when Obama says,

> The time has come to reaffirm our enduring spirit; to choose our better history; to carry forward that precious gift, that noble idea passed on from generation to generation: the God-given promise that all are equal, all are free, and all deserve a chance to pursue their full measure of happiness.

Here, "measure" means portion. To have a "full measure" also connotes completeness, and when read in the context of echoing the Declaration of Independence, it clearly seems directed to those for whom equality and freedom have not always led to a "full measure" of happiness. It could easily be argued that the term "promise" functions in this context as a substitute for dream, because the idea that "all are equal, all are free, and all deserve a chance" has, in fact, been the substance of the dream articulated by Obama from the beginning. But there is a problem. Just two lines earlier, Obama made reference to "false promises," thus tagging that term with a negative valence. Even if we read it as a positive term in the present context—which it clearly is—there is still the sense that the term can do double duty. It is not as unequivocally positive as "dream."

It is not until the tenth paragraph of the text that Obama introduces the terms "journey" and "path." These terms are often found together in his Narrative Signature and sometimes one substitutes for the other. "Our journey," Obama says, "has never been one of shortcuts or settling for less. It has not been the path for the faint-hearted." Here the basic metaphor that animates the entire Narrative Signature is introduced for the first time. But notice that it is initially defined in terms of what it is not—not one of shortcuts and not for the faint-hearted. It is only with the second use of "path," celebrating those "who have carried us up the long, rugged path towards prosperity and freedom," that the journey metaphor returns to its normative usage. At this point the audience knows that it is on a journey, following a path at a special moment that leads toward "prosperity and freedom," the ostensible destination of the journey, although the term "destiny" has not yet made an appearance.

Obama follows this setup with what is clearly the most eloquent passage of the speech, using his trademark anaphora to begin each series with "For us." Each member of the series implies a journey in which people "traveled across oceans," "settled the West," and "fought and died" in faraway places. This is clearly consistent with his earlier uses of the journey metaphor, which almost always imply that our journey is part of a larger historical journey that began before we came on the scene and will continue after we have left. Our part of this journey is the "moment," but it is a part, not the whole. This section is also important for the way it speaks to an important part of the audience—African Americans.

It would be wrong to think of African Americans as a separate and distinct audience for the speech, though the temptation to do so is great. But the whole logic of this speech and of Obama's Narrative Signature as a whole is that we are all "one people," a phrase that does not appear in the inaugural but whose spirit informs the entire speech. Even so, references to enduring "the lash of the whip," working until "their hands were raw," and the struggle being "greater than all the differences of birth" could not have been missed by African American listeners. Although we are all on a journey toward the same destination, our experiences along the path have been different, and Obama seeks throughout the address to recognize some of those differences even while proclaiming our unity of purpose and direction. "This is the journey we continue today," he instructs.

But no sooner has he reinforced the journey metaphor than he once again—for the third time—reminds the listeners that we are in crisis. "Our workers are no less productive than when this crisis began," he asserts. He then links this assertion to time. Not to the special "moment" that functions as sacred time in his Narrative Signature, but to profane time. "But our time of standing pat, of protecting narrow interests and putting off unpleasant decisions," Obama says, "that time has surely passed." Obama uses the distinction between the profane time of the past and the sacred moment of the present to distinguish both the direction in which the country should go and the destination it should be striving to reach.

"Starting today," said the president, "we must pick ourselves up, dust ourselves off, and begin again the work of remaking America." The cliché apparently originated in a 1936 depression-era film called *Swing Time,* but it evoked a tremendous round of applause from the immediate audience. Obama then went into his statement of political and policy objectives, which included the line, "We will restore science to its rightful place." The commentators immediately latched onto this statement as a not-so-subtle attack on the outgoing Bush administration. And so it was. But it was more than that. In his Narrative Signature "science" is closely linked to reason and measurement as a dialectical instrument of investigation and analysis. To "restore" means to return to the proper kind of analysis, and that kind, as Obama will shortly note, is what can be shown by empirical (measured) means to "work."

Obama then moves immediately to attack "some who question" his ambitious agenda. "Their memories are short," he asserts. "For they have forgotten what this country has already done; what free men and women can achieve when imagination is joined to common purpose, and necessity to courage." Here Obama introduces three more terms of his Narrative Signature—"imagination," "common purpose" (also called "common good"), and "courage." All three are linked to achievement—to movement toward the destination. The "common purpose" points toward the goal, but actual achievement of the goal depends on the use of "imagination" to conjure the means of ascent and the summoning of "courage" to follow through in the face of impediments. Such impediments are almost always imaged in his Narrative Signature through use of the terms "cynics" and "cynicism," and the inaugural follows the same pattern. Obama immediately follows the introduction of these new terms with the statement, "What the cynics fail to understand is that the ground has shifted beneath them." The "cynics" are those who lack the imagination and the courage to move forward. They are also those who employ the wrong means of measurement. "The question we ask today," says Obama, "is not whether our government is too big or too small, but whether it works." If it works, the president says, "we intend to move forward."

At this point in the speech, almost at the halfway point, Obama has set up the basic outline of his Narrative Signature, though without recourse to the dream. But no sooner is the basic outline of the narrative established than Obama—for the fourth time—inserts the rhetoric of crisis. Referring to the market economy, Obama notes that "its power to generate wealth and expand freedom is unmatched, but this crisis has reminded us that without a watchful eye, the market can spin out of control." Although "crisis" is a part of Obama's Narrative Signature, it has seldom been a featured term. Indeed, over the course of the twenty-six speeches surveyed, the term "crisis" appears only twenty-two times—and fifteen of these twenty-two usages come in only four speeches. In short, Obama's signature is not known for featuring "crisis" as a major or recurring term. By making "crisis" a central term in his inaugural, Obama interrupts the rhetorical design for which he had become known, thus making the myth harder to sustain.

In the Narrative Signature the weaving of the myth is almost always accompanied by numerous rhetorical devices—anaphora, antistrophe, parallelism, antithesis, alliteration, and more. Yet the inaugural address seems to lack rhetorical energy. With the exception of the anaphora used early in the address, there are only two or three other lines that stand out. One of them is in this section when Obama notes that "a nation cannot prosper long when it favors only the prosperous." This was a judicious use of polyptoton because the speaker links it directly to the Narrative Signature by stating, "The success of our economy has always depended not just on the size of our gross domestic product, but on the reach of our prosperity; on our ability to extend opportunity to every willing heart, not out of charity, but because it is the surest route to our common good." Here Obama introduces opportunity and common good, two of the key terms in his Narrative Signature. In the narrative, "opportunity" is what happens (or is created) at those special moments along the path. It is what is necessary to reach the destination. Without opportunity, one never reaches the destination. It is, as Obama notes, "the surest route to our common good." If the destination is, in fact, a "common" good, then the opportunities to reach it must be shared by all.

The president then went into three lengthy paragraphs on what he called "our common defense," the most famous line of which is the first sentence: "As for our common defense, we reject as false the choice between our safety and our ideals." Again, this was immediately understood as a rejection of the Bush-Cheney administration's national security policies. And so it was. But it was also an example of one of the predominant uses of dialectic in Obama's Narrative Signature—the eschewing of "either/or" thinking. Indeed, Obama had used that dialectical device on precisely this subject numerous times, including in his speech of June 27, 2005, when he told the American Library Association, "This is an issue that Washington always tries to make 'either-or.' Either we protect our people from terror or we protect our most cherished principles. But this kind of choice asks too little of us and assumes too little about America."[45] The line was not simply a critique of Bush, it was also a marker of the mind—the thought processes—of Obama. The other thing to note about these three paragraphs, which are unremarkable save for the attempts to echo JFK ("the rights of man," "still light the world," "old friends and former foes," "generations") is that they are bereft of any terms associated with his Narrative Signature. It is as though the journey stopped at the ocean's edge.

Obama concluded this section with a stark warning to terrorists: "for those who seek to advance their aims by inducing terror and slaughtering innocents, we say to you now that our spirit is stronger and cannot be broken; you cannot outlast us, and we will defeat you." This line brought loud applause from the immediate audience and led directly into his assertion that "our patchwork heritage is a strength." Now back on the journey, Obama returned to the language of his Narrative Signature.

> We are a nation of Christians and Muslims, Jews and Hindus, and non-believers. We are shaped by every language and culture, drawn from every end of this Earth; and because we have tasted the bitter swill of civil war and segregation, and emerged from that dark chapter stronger and more united, we cannot help but believe that the old hatreds shall some day pass; that the lines of tribe shall soon dissolve; that as the world grows smaller, our common humanity shall reveal itself; and that America must play its role in ushering in a new era of peace.

Here the term "believe" is introduced for the first time. In the Narrative Signature, "believe/belief" is the term that appears most often—ninety-eight times over twenty of the twenty-six speeches—where it usually signals a positive set of beliefs or policy positions. Sometimes it is used, as in this case, as a signal of belief in a future state. During his keynote address at the 2004 Democratic National Convention, Obama married these two uses of "believe/belief" when he said:

> In the end, that is God's greatest gift to us, the bedrock of this nation; a belief in things not seen; a belief that there are better days ahead.
>
> I believe we can give our middle class relief and provide working families with a road to opportunity.
>
> I believe we can provide jobs to the jobless. . . .
>
> I believe that we have a righteous wind at our backs, and that we stand on the crossroads of history.[46]

For Obama, to "believe" is both to have faith in the future and to hold specific beliefs that are grounded in the pursuit of our "common humanity." Although clearly addressing himself to all Americans, as well as the world at large, Obama's words seem carefully crafted to send a subtle message that would be particularly important to African Americans. Note that the belief is that old hatreds "shall some day pass" and that the lines of tribe "shall soon dissolve." Clearly, not all the "swill"—a term connoting waste that is unfit for human consumption—has yet dissipated. Those who think that Obama's is a postracial mind-set, and by that term mean to indicate that for Obama race is no longer a relevant factor in American life, need to read his inaugural more closely. Neither in the inaugural nor in his Narrative Signature more generally does Obama indicate that race, or inequality, or discrimination, or lack of opportunity are things of the past. They will be things of the past only when we reach the end of our journey, reach that destination where "our common humanity shall reveal itself."

Obama then turns, once again, to the world at large, addressing short paragraphs to "the Muslim world" and "the people of poor nations." Once again, the terms of the Narrative Signature disappear, although one of the chief terms of the campaign appears when Obama concludes by observing, "For the world has changed, and we must change with it." The transition between foreign lands and America are "those brave Americans who, at this very hour, patrol far-off deserts and distant mountains." Obama immediately returns to his Narrative Signature by using a substitute term for "path" when he observes, "As we consider the road that unfolds before us." He refers to the "fallen heroes" and "guardians of our liberty" before concluding, "And yet, at this moment—a moment that will define a generation—it is precisely this spirit [of service] that must inhabit us all." As should be clear by now, one of the problems with the inaugural address is that the journey begins and ends several times, and the moments appear and disappear without warning. The coherence of the Narrative Signature is considerably less in this address than in many of Obama's earlier speeches, even though the inaugural is teeming with the narrative terminology.

Obama introduces another part of the narrative grammar when he argues, "For as much as government can do and must do, it is ultimately the faith and determination of the American people upon which this nation relies." "Faith," in the Obama lexicon, is that which is required to keep us on the path and headed in the right direction. It is an attribute possessed by the people and often linked with "courage" and "hope" as the primary traits necessary to reach the end of the journey. As the president noted, "It is the firefighter's courage to storm a stairway filled with smoke, but also a parent's willingness to nurture a child, that finally decides our fate." Note that our fate, or destiny, is in our own hands. In many mythic journeys it is God or chance that controls one's fate, but not in Obama's narrative. For Obama, the people on the journey control their own fate by virtue of their individual and collective actions.

The president points to those values and actions in the next few lines when he speaks of "hard work and honesty, courage and fair play, tolerance and curiosity, loyalty and patriotism." "These things are old," Obama proclaims. "These things are true." Here, for the first time, "truth" is introduced. In Obama's Narrative Signature, truth is both an objective state ("These things are true") and the object of our pursuit ("truth isn't about who yells the loudest, but who has the right information"), as Obama noted when speaking to the American Library Association in June 2005.[47] In his Narrative Signature, truth is often aligned with progress, as it is in the inaugural address when Obama says in reference to these things that are true, "They have been the quiet force of progress throughout our history. What is demanded then is a return to these truths." Our values are true, and by remaining true to them we can pursue the truth that lies before us. "This," the president concludes, "is the price and promise of citizenship." The price is to recognize the truth, to tell the truth, and to believe in the promise that we shall someday find the truth at the conclusion of our journey. Hence, Obama completes the thought unit: "This is the source of our confidence: The knowledge that God calls on us to shape an uncertain destiny."

Only here, in the fourth paragraph from the end of the speech, does Obama introduce the idea of the "call," an idea that is central to his Narrative Signature. Although the call is identified explicitly as coming from God (which is not the case in most of Obama's speeches), the idea of the audience actively shaping "an uncertain destiny" is a standard part of his Narrative Signature. Obama often speaks of the need to "write our own destiny" (November 16, 2005), to move toward "an unknown destiny" (May 30, 2005), or to "forge our own destiny" (June 14, 2006).[48] Unlike the standard interpretation of American Exceptionalism that sees the nation's calling and destiny as predetermined and sure, Obama's sense of the calling usually comes from within history, not outside it, and is wholly dependent upon the actions of the people who are on the journey. Perhaps it was the need to fulfill the generic function of "putting the nation under God" that compelled a change in the standard narrative. But whether the call comes from God, history, or conscience, it bears the impress of a divine mandate—something that is both willed and spiritually compelling.

As Obama neared the end of his address, he offered his own interpretation of the calling:

> This is the meaning of our liberty and our creed, why men and women and children of every race and every faith can join in celebration across this magnificent mall, and why a man whose father less than 60 years ago might not have been served at a local restaurant can now stand before you to take a most sacred oath.

This is an interesting passage inasmuch as it is one of only two places in the address where Obama makes personal references. Since so much of his personal journey has revolved around the absence of his father and his own struggle to understand who he is—his identity in all its various dimensions—it is instructive to note how the personal ("father") is linked to the political ("might not have been served at a local restaurant") as a sign both of manhood ("now stand [as opposed to bow or kneel] before you") and acceptance ("take a most sacred oath"). It is not by accident that the very next words out of the president's mouth are these: "So let us mark this day with remembrance, of who we are and how far we have travelled," or, in other words, of our identity and our acceptance. Like the journey itself, Obama's words are both personal and communal; they are about the man, the communities from which he hails, and the destiny that hails him—and us.

Obama then goes into his peroration, which is built around the scene at Trenton and George Washington's order to read this passage to his frozen and demoralized troops: "Let it be told to the future world . . . that in the depth of winter, when nothing but hope and virtue could survive . . . that the city and the country, alarmed at the common danger, came forth to meet [it]." As an example of the American civil religious tradition that venerates Washington, Jefferson, and Lincoln, the quotation is unremarkable. Some commentators found it odd that Obama chose Washington rather than Lincoln, since the whole inaugural event had been advertised as "a new birth of freedom," and the parallels to Lincoln had been frequently emphasized. But it was far from the first time that Obama had quoted Washington, and the "icy currents" and "storms" of the peroration were doubtless meant to round out the "gathering clouds" and "raging storms" of the introduction. To the immediate audience, standing for hours in below freezing temperatures, the references to "icy" and "winter" must have seemed apropos.

But the really interesting aspect of the peroration is the way in which, even at the very end of the address, the tensions that have been present throughout between the rhetoric of crisis and the rhetoric of hope, as represented in the Narrative Signature, continue to play themselves out. While Obama speaks in the final sentences about "hope" and refusing "to let this journey end," he is simultaneously drawing the audience's attention to the words spoken by Washington. But they are not Washington's words; they are Thomas Paine's words from his first in a series of pamphlets called *The Crisis*. And without actually employing the term "crisis," the call to "brave once more the icy currents" and "endure what storms may come" certainly evokes something like crisis. Just as the speech began with a reference to "crisis," so it ended with an allusion to the same.

Conclusion

To fully appreciate Obama's inaugural address, we need the resources of generic, situational, and Narrative Signature approaches. The generic approach helps us see how the address conforms to or departs from type. In this case Obama conforms almost perfectly to the generic expectations. He unifies the audience at the beginning of the speech, rehearses communal values in a moving section distinguished by its employment of anaphora, articulates the new administration's political principles, in part by contrasting them to the outgoing administration's, recognizes the limitations of the office by putting it under God, and accomplishes all of this through epideictic discourse that asks the audience to look upon and affirm the American experiment. The only slight change is the source Obama uses to proclaim the nation's unity—moments of crisis. While this choice is not unique, it is unusual. Even FDR, in the midst of the Great Depression, used the term "crisis" only once in his 1932 inaugural address. Ronald Reagan used the term twice in his 1981 inaugural. Obama uses it four times.

The decision to structure the speech around the idea of crisis is proof positive of the influence of the situation on the process of rhetorical invention. Absent the financial and banking collapses of October 2008 and the weeks following, it is doubtful that Obama's address would have featured the term "crisis" as much as it did. Obama and his advisers must have felt that the situation was so overwhelming that the crises needed to be the focus of the inaugural address. Although inaugural addresses are often informed—sometimes heavily informed—by the immediate historical, political, or economic situations into which they enter, they are not often structured around those situations. And this, it seems to me, is the key difference—the difference between being *informed* by the immediate situation and being *structured* by that situation. As instances of epideictic discourse, inaugural addresses are offered for contemplation, not action. To contemplate a crisis without an equal—and equally compelling—vision of hope is to leave the audience more troubled than inspired, more focused on the problems than on the solutions. Obama's campaign speaking had always emphasized the rhetoric of hope. By comparison, the inaugural address placed a greater emphasis on the rhetoric of crisis.

Both hope and crisis were standard parts of Obama's Narrative Signature, though not in equal measure. The term "hope" occurred ninety-four times in twenty-five of the twenty-six speeches surveyed, while the term "crisis" occurred only twenty-two times across ten of the twenty-six speeches. By 2009 Obama had become known as an inspirational speaker who held out hope in even the darkest circumstances. But in the inaugural address the term "hope" appears only three times, with two of those mentions coming in the last four lines of the speech. Individual terms are not, of course, the only—or even necessarily the best—measure of how an audience experiences a speech. But they are one indication, and in this case both "crisis" and "hope" are indicators that are part of a larger narrative structure with which Obama had been identified since at least 2004.

Obama's Narrative Signature, composed of a grammar, a rhetoric, and a set of dialectical methods, was drawn from his life's story. Unlike generic analysis that depends on a fusion of form and function or a situational analysis that depends on a correct reading of exigencies, constraints, and audiences, the Narrative Signature depends on an understanding of the rhetor's personal history, autobiography, and character. The Narrative Signature is a rhetorical complement to approaches based in linguistic form or historical circumstance. It does not deny the influence of form or circumstance on rhetorical invention, but insists that for those who have a well-formed life story, the elements of that story, as they are condensed in the grammar, rhetoric, and dialectical methods of a Narrative Signature, are central to a proper understanding of such a person's persuasive discourses.

The analysis of Obama's Narrative Signature is meant both as a way of understanding and interpreting his discourses, including his inaugural address, as well as a nascent method of rhetorical criticism. To examine the Narrative Signature of a rhetor, the critic would follow a procedure similar to that described in this chapter. The first step is the selection of a representative group of speeches that span at least a five-year period. Every major speech should be included in this group. The second step is to subject the chosen speeches to a close reading that will reveal the grammatical terms that constitute the standard vocabulary that the speaker employs. Such terms may number as few as ten or as many as thirty. The third step is to re-create the "story" that lies at the heart of all the speeches, though the story may not be complete in any one speech. This story can take many different forms—quest, mission, revelation, personal growth, or transformation. Whatever the form of the story, there will be within it a strategic design that functions as a rhetoric—the persuasive story the speaker wants to tell. The fourth step is to discern the various dialectical methods employed by the speaker as ways of defining, delineating, or testing the central ideas of the story. Once the grammar, rhetoric, and dialectical dimensions of the Narrative Signature are determined, the critic will be in a position to use the signature as a critical tool to examine other instances of the speaker's discourse, using the signature as a normative instrument to probe how well and how completely the speaker has told the story that motivates his or her life and how well that telling is adapted to the needs of any given audience.

APPENDIX 1. THE TWENTY-SIX SPEECH DATASET

SPEECH	DATE	PLACE
"Dumb Wars: An Anti-Iraq War Speech"	October 26, 2002	Chicago, Illinois
"We Are One People!: Keynote Address to the Democratic National Convention"	July 28, 2004	Boston, Massachusetts
"Saving Social Security: A Speech at the National Press Club"	April 26, 2005	Washington, D.C.
"The Courage To Do Extraordinary Things: A Speech to the NAACP's Fight for Freedom Fund"	May 2, 2005	Detroit, Michigan
"Privacy and Freedom: A Speech to the American Library Association"	June 27, 2005	Chicago, Illinois
"Honoring America's Veterans: A Speech to the American Legion"	July 16, 2005	Springfield, Illinois
"If We Stand Together, We Rise Together: A Speech to the AFL-CIO National Convention"	July 25, 2005	Chicago, Illinois

"World-Class Education: Teaching Our Kids in the Twenty-First Century"
October 25, 2005 Washington, D.C.

"The Legacy of Robert F. Kennedy: The Robert F. Kennedy Human Rights Award"
November 16, 2005 Washington, D.C.

"The Coming Storm: The Newspaper Association of America"
April 3, 2006 Chicago, Illinois

"This Is Our Time! The 'Take Back America' Speech"
June 14, 2006 Washington, D.C.

"Politics and Faith: A Call To Renewal"
June 28, 2006 Washington, D.C.

"Embryonic Stem Cell Research: A Speech to the United States Senate"
July 17, 2006 Washington, D.C.

"The Voting Rights Act: A Speech to the United States Senate"
July 20, 2006 Washington, D.C.

"The Katrina Graduates: Commencement Address at Xavier University"
August 11, 2006 New Orleans, Louisiana

"An Honest Government, A Hopeful Future: A Speech at The University of Nairobi"
August 28, 2006 Nairobi, Kenya

"The Legacy of Dr. Martin Luther King, Jr.: A Speech at the Martin Luther King Memorial"
November 13, 2006 Washington, D.C.

"Withdrawal from Iraq: A Speech to the Chicago Council on Global Affairs"
November 20, 2006 Chicago, Illinois

"We Are All Sick Because of AIDS: The World AIDS Day Speech"
December 1, 2006 Lake Forest, California

"Our Past, Future, and Vision For America: Presidential Candidacy Announcement"
February 10, 2007 Springfield, Illinois

"Yes We Can: South Carolina Victory Speech"
January 26, 2008 Columbia, South Carolina

"A More Perfect Union"
March 18, 2008 Philadelphia, Pennsylvania

"Presumptive Nominee Speech"
June 3, 2008 St. Paul, Minnesota

"A World that Stands as One"
July 24, 2008 Berlin, Germany

"The American Promise: Acceptance Speech at the Democratic Convention"
August 28, 2008 Denver, Colorado

"Election Night Victory Speech"
November 4, 2008 Chicago, Illinois

APPENDIX 2. THE VOCABULARY OF OBAMA'S NARRATIVE SIGNATURE

TERM	CUMULATIVE FREQUENCY	COUNT/# OF SPEECHES
believe/belief	98	20/26
call/calling	25	11/26
common good	8	5/26
courage	30	12/26
crisis	22	10/26
cynics/cynicism	20	10/26
destiny	19	11/26
dream(s)	63	20/26
faith	55	13/26
hope	94	25/26
imagination	12	9/26
innovation	22	11/26
journey	13	8/26
measure	22	13/26
miracle	9	6/26
moment	56	13/26
one people	19	10/26
opportunity	57	20/26
path	28	12/26
perfect/perfecting	26	11/26
promise	63	16/26
rise/rise up	24	14/26
sacrifice	24	15/26
true/truth	25	12/26

NOTES

1. Although my analysis is based primarily on the written text of Obama's inaugural address, I also watched the visual coverage as it played out across several networks. After the inauguration, I studied the NBC production of *The Inauguration of Barack Obama,* which is available on DVD. The opening quotation is from Russell L. Riley, "Still Editing? A Few Words of Advice," *Washington Post,* January 18, 2009, http://www.washingtonpost.com/wp-dyn/content/article/2009/01/16/AR2009011602310.html.
2. Obama made a mistake at the opening of his address when he said that "Forty-four Americans have now taken the presidential oath." Although he was the forty-fourth president, only forty-three Americans have taken the oath. Grover Cleveland's two discontinuous administrations are counted separately, even though it was the same person taking the oath. Hence, forty-four presidencies, but only forty-three people who have served as president.
3. Robert D. King, "Franklin D. Roosevelt's Second Inaugural Address," *Quarterly Journal of Speech* 23 (1937): 433–439.
4. A computerized search utilizing the *Communication and Mass Media Complete* and *Communication Abstracts* databases yielded forty articles on inaugural addresses. Eight of those articles were on inaugurals in general, while thirty examined a single inaugural address. Two articles focused on a comparison of Jefferson's first inaugural with Reagan's first inaugural address. These forty studies covered eight different presidents and twelve different inaugural addresses. There are doubtless more studies of presidential inaugural addresses in book chapters. Chief among these are the chapters in Halford Ryan's *The Inaugural Addresses of Twentieth-Century American Presidents* (Westport, CT: Praeger, 1993), which contains twenty-four chapters on individual inaugural addresses from Theodore Roosevelt's in 1905 through Bill Clinton's first in 1993.
5. See Karlyn Kohrs Campbell and Kathleen Hall Jamieson, "Inaugurating the Presidency," *Presidential Studies Quarterly* 15 (1985): 394–441; Karlyn Kohrs Campbell and Kathleen Hall Jamieson, *Deeds Done in Words: Presidential Rhetoric and the Genres of Governance* (Chicago: University of Chicago Press, 1990). Campbell and Jamieson have recently released a second edition of their book titled *Presidents Creating the Presidency: Deeds Done in Words* (Chicago: University of Chicago Press, 2008). Their analysis of the generic dimensions of inaugural addresses has not changed, although their examples are updated. I am quoting from the original

edition, since this is the one that has influenced the field for almost twenty years.

6. Campbell and Jamieson, *Deeds Done in Words,* 15.
7. Ryan, *Inaugural Addresses,* xvii.
8. It is not my intention to enter into the theoretical debate over the proper classification of inaugural addresses. Unlike Professors Campbell and Jamieson, I do not believe that labeling all inaugurals as "epideictic" rhetoric is a sufficient response to their diversity. Nor do I believe that all inaugurals draw their sustenance from the past. As I noted in 1993, "Ike's First Inaugural looked forward, not back, and it was rooted in the historical exigencies of the moment." See Martin J. Medhurst, "President Dwight D. Eisenhower's First Inaugural Address, 1953," in Ryan, *Inaugural Addresses,* 153–154.
9. I chose these twenty-six speeches because they have already been anthologized and are thus available to a wide audience. The speeches appear in Maureen Harrison and Steve Gilbert, eds., *Barack Obama: Speeches* 2002–2006 (Carlsbad, CA: Excellent Books, 2007) and Barack Obama, *Words That Changed a Nation: The Most Celebrated and Influential Speeches of Barack Obama* (Seattle: Pacific Publishing Studios, 2009). The complete list of twenty-six speeches appears in appendix 1.
10. My notion of a Narrative Signature may remind some of the early "archetype and signature" studies of the 1970s and 1980s. Others may think of the Narrative Paradigm, as theorized by Walter R. Fisher in 1984. Both bear some resemblance to my idea about Narrative Signature, but neither is identical to it. A close comparison of these earlier studies with my own will, in fact, reveal some rather stark differences. See Anthony Hillbruner, "Archetype and Signature: Nixon and the 1973 Inaugural," *Central States Speech Journal* 25 (1974): 169–181; Dan F. Hahn, "Archetype and Signature in Johnson's 1965 State of the Union," *Central States Speech Journal* 34 (1983): 236–246; Walter R. Fisher, "Narration as a Human Communication Paradigm: The Case of Public Moral Argument," *Communication Monographs* 51 (1984): 1–22. For a complete frequency count of the twenty-four terms that constitute the vocabulary of Obama's Narrative Signature across all twenty-six speeches surveyed, see appendix 2.
11. To conduct a study using the Narrative Signature would require reading the public addresses of an individual over an extended period of time. No one has yet conducted such a study, but based on the extant scholarship several rhetors seem prime candidates for such analysis, including Malcolm X and Martin Luther King Jr. I base this conclusion on work that has already been completed and that reveals one or more elements of a Narrative Signature. On Malcolm X, see Robert

E. Terrill, *Malcolm X: Inventing Radical Judgment* (East Lansing: Michigan State University Press, 2004); Robert E. Terrill, "Protest, Prophecy, and Prudence in the Rhetoric of Malcolm X," *Rhetoric & Public Affairs* 4 (2001): 25–53; Robert E. Terrill, "Colonizing the Borderlands: Shifting Circumference in the Rhetoric of Malcolm X," *Quarterly Journal of Speech* 86 (2000): 67–85; Thomas W. Benson, "Rhetoric and Autobiography: The Case of Malcolm X," *Quarterly Journal of Speech* 60 (1974): 1–13. On Martin Luther King Jr., see Mark Vail, "The 'Integrative' Rhetoric of Martin Luther King, Jr.'s 'I Have a Dream' Speech," *Rhetoric & Public Affairs* 9 (2006): 51–78; Edward Berry, "Doing Time: King's 'Letter from Birmingham Jail,'" *Rhetoric & Public Affairs* 8 (2005): 109–132; Michael Osborn, "Rhetorical Distance in 'Letter from Birmingham Jail,'" *Rhetoric & Public Affairs* 7 (2004): 23–36; Drew D. Hansen, *The Dream: Martin Luther King, Jr. and the Speech That Inspired a Nation* (New York: HarperCollins, 2003); Richard Lischer, *The Preacher King: Martin Luther King, Jr. and the Word That Moved America* (New York: Oxford University Press, 1995); Carolyn Calloway-Thomas and John Louis Lucaites, eds., *Martin Luther King, Jr. and the Sermonic Power of Public Discourse* (Tuscaloosa: University of Alabama Press, 1993); Keith D. Miller, *Voice of Deliverance: The Language of Martin Luther King, Jr. and Its Sources* (New York: Free Press, 1992); Louis V. Baldwin, *There Is a Balm in Gilead: The Cultural Roots of Martin Luther King, Jr.* (Minneapolis: Fortress Press, 1991); Richard P. Fulkerson, "The Public Letter as a Rhetorical Form: Structure, Logic, and Style in King's 'Letter from Birmingham Jail,'" *Quarterly Journal of Speech* 65 (1979): 121–136.

12. For works that touch on elements of Reagan's Narrative Signature, see Stephen Vaughn, *Ronald Reagan in Hollywood: Movies and Politics* (Cambridge: Cambridge University Press, 1994); Kurt Ritter and David Henry, *Ronald Reagan: The Great Communicator* (Westport, CT: Greenwood Press, 1992); William Ker Muir Jr., *The Bully Pulpit: The Presidential Leadership of Ronald Reagan* (San Francisco: Institute for Contemporary Studies, 1992); Lou Cannon, *President Reagan: The Role of a Lifetime* (New York: Simon and Schuster, 1991); Martin J. Medhurst, "Ronald Reagan and the Cinematic Candidacy," *Pennsylvania Speech Communication Annual* 45 (1989): 29–37; William F. Lewis, "Telling America's Story: Narrative Form and the Reagan Presidency," *Quarterly Journal of Speech* 73 (1987): 280–302; Craig Allen Smith, "MisteReagan's Neighborhood: Rhetoric and National Unity," *Southern Speech Communication Journal* 52 (1987): 219–239; Paul D. Erickson, *Reagan Speaks: The Making of an American Myth* (New York: New York University Press, 1985); Martin J. Medhurst, "Postponing the Social Agenda: Reagan's Strategy and

Tactics," *Western Journal of Speech Communication* 48 (1984): 262–276; Walter R. Fisher, "Romantic Democracy, Ronald Reagan, and Presidential Heroes," *Western Journal of Speech Communication* 46 (1982): 299–310.

13. For works that touch on elements of William F. Buckley's Narrative Signature, see Michael J. Lee, "WFB: The Gladiatorial Style and the Politics of Provocation," *Rhetoric & Public Affairs* 13 (2010): 217–250; Edward C. Appel, "Burlesque Drama as Rhetorical Genre: The Hudibrastic Ridicule of William F. Buckley, Jr.," *Western Journal of Communication* 60 (1996): 269–284; John C. Hammerback, "William F. Buckley, Jr. on *Firing Line:* A Case Study in Confrontational Dialogue," *Today's Speech* 22, no. 3 (Summer 1974): 23–30; Thomas F. Mader, "Agitation over Aggiornamento: William Buckley vs. John XXIII," *Today's Speech* 17, no. 4 (November 1969): 4–15.
14. For works that touch on elements of the Reverend Jeremiah Wright's Narrative Signature, see Clarence E. Walker and Gregory D. Smithers, *The Preacher and the Politician: Jeremiah Wright, Barack Obama, and Race in America* (Charlottesville: University of Virginia Press, 2009); Stephen Mansfield, *The Faith of Barack Obama* (Nashville: Thomas Nelson, 2008), esp. 49–67, 133–141; Mark A. Noll, *God and Race in American Politics: A Short History* (Princeton, NJ: Princeton University Press, 2008); Barack Obama, *Dreams from My Father* (New York: Crown Publishers, 1995), 272–295.
15. Obama has been using the journey metaphor for many years. It plays a prominent role in his first book, *Dreams from My Father.* For an early study of Obama's journey metaphor, see James Darsey, "Barack Obama and America's Journey," *Southern Communication Journal* 74 (2009): 88–103.
16. Obama has described slavery as America's "original sin" at least since his November 13, 2006, speech at the groundbreaking for the Martin Luther King Jr. Memorial. His most famous usage of the phrase is, of course, in his speech "A More Perfect Union," delivered on March 18, 2008, in Philadelphia—what has become known as his "race" speech. For an analysis of the March 18 speech and its implications for race relations, see David A. Frank, "The Prophetic Voice and the Face of the Other in Barack Obama's 'A More Perfect Union' Address, March 18, 2008," *Rhetoric & Public Affairs* 12 (2009): 167–194; Robert E. Terrill, "Unity and Duality in Barack Obama's 'A More Perfect Union,'" *Quarterly Journal of Speech* 95 (2009): 363–386.
17. Barack Obama, "Privacy and Freedom: A Speech to the American Library Association," in *Barack Obama: Speeches 2002–2006,* 44 (emphasis added).
18. Barack Obama, "If We Stand Together, We Rise Together: A Speech to the

AFL-CIO National Convention," in *Barack Obama: Speeches 2002–2006,* 56 (emphasis added).

19. Barack Obama, "The Legacy of Robert F. Kennedy: The Robert F. Kennedy Human Rights Award," in *Barack Obama: Speeches 2002–2006,* 72 (emphasis added).
20. Barack Obama, "Dumb Wars: An Anti-Iraq War Speech," in *Barack Obama: Speeches 2002–2006,* 12.
21. Obama, "Privacy and Freedom," 37, 40, 42.
22. Barack Obama, "Politics and Faith: A Call to Renewal," in *Barack Obama: Speeches 2002–2006,* 107.
23. Barack Obama, "We Are All Sick Because of AIDS: The World AIDS Day Speech," in *Barack Obama: Speeches 2002–2006,* 161.
24. Obama, "Privacy and Freedom," in *Barack Obama: Speeches 2002–2006,* 38.
25. Barack Obama, "World-Class Education: Teaching Our Kids in the Twenty-First Century," in *Barack Obama: Speeches 2002–2006,* 62.
26. Obama, "We Are All Sick Because of AIDS," in *Barack Obama: Speeches 2002–2006,* 158.
27. Barack Obama, "We Are One People! Keynote Address at the Democratic National Convention," in *Barack Obama: Speeches 2002–2006,* 16.
28. Obama, "World-Class Education," in *Barack Obama: Speeches 2002–2006,* 63.
29. Barack Obama, "An Honest Government, a Hopeful Future: A Speech at the University of Nairobi," in *Barack Obama: Speeches 2002–2006,* 136.
30. Barack Obama, "The Legacy of Dr. Martin Luther King, Jr.: A Speech at the Martin Luther King Memorial," in *Barack Obama: Speeches 2002–2006,* 141.
31. Obama, "Politics and Faith," in *Barack Obama: Speeches 2002–2006,* 106.
32. Barack Obama, "A More Perfect Union," in *Words That Changed a Nation,* 41.
33. Obama, "If We Stand Together, We Rise Together," in *Barack Obama: Speeches 2002–2006,* 55.
34. Barack Obama, "This Is Our Time! The 'Take Back America' Speech," in *Barack Obama: Speeches 2002–2006,* 93.
35. For a theoretical treatment of these terms, see Chaim Perelman and Lucie Olbrechts-Tyteca, *The New Rhetoric: A Treatise on Argumentation,* trans. John Wilkinson and Purcell Weaver (Notre Dame: Notre Dame University Press, 1969).
36. Barack Obama, "The Courage to Do Extraordinary Things: A Speech to the NAACP's Fight for Freedom Fund," in *Barack Obama: Speeches 2002–2006,* 34.
37. Obama, "If We Stand Together, We Rise Together," in *Barack Obama: Speeches 2002–2006,* 52.

38. For a generic study of presidential acceptance addresses that examines dialectical opposites, see Martin J. Medhurst, "The Nomination Acceptance Address: Presidential Speechwriting, 1932–2008," in *The President's Words,* ed. Michael Nelson and Russell L. Riley (Lawrence: University Press of Kansas, 2010), 27–50.
39. Barack Obama, "The American Promise: The DNC Acceptance Speech," in *Words That Changed a Nation,* 90.
40. Barack Obama, "Election Night Victory Speech," in *Words That Changed a Nation,* 96.
41. This short paragraph was requested by journalist Tom Sabulis for an article he was preparing on the inaugural address for the *Atlanta Journal-Constitution.* The article ran on January 18, 2009, but my quotation was left on the cutting room floor. Other communication scholars—Mary Stuckey, Bruce Gronbeck, and Ekaterina Haskins—did have their paragraphs published. See Tom Sabulis, "Inauguration 2009: Voice of a New Era," *Atlanta Journal-Constitution,* January 18, 2009, http://www.ajc.com/metro/content/printedition/2009/01/18/inaugspeech0118.html.
42. All quotations from Barack Obama's inaugural address come from the version at http://www.presidency.ucsb.edu/ws/index.php?pid=44.
43. See Mansfield, *The Faith of Barack Obama,* 15.
44. The other terms of the Narrative Signature that do not appear in the inaugural address are "innovation," "miracle," "one people," "perfecting," and "rise up."
45. Obama, "Privacy and Freedom," in *Barack Obama: Speeches 2002–2006,* 38.
46. Obama, "We Are One People!," in *Barack Obama: Speeches 2002–2006,* 19.
47. Obama, "Privacy and Freedom," in *Barack Obama: Speeches 2002–2006,* 37.
48. Obama, "The Legacy of Robert F. Kennedy," in *Barack Obama: Speeches 2002–2006,* 75; Barack Obama, "Memorial Day Speech," in *Words That Changed a Nation,* 159; Obama, "This Is Our Time," in *Barack Obama: Speeches 2002–2006,* 96.

To Exist, You Need an Ideology: Alan Greenspan on Markets, Crisis, and Democracy

Robert Asen

Ideology operates best when it operates invisibly. Often obscuring the role of values and interests in society, ideologies render the particular as universal, decisions as givens, and constructs as natural. The circulation and comparative strength of competing ideologies shape deliberation and decision making in democratic polities, effectively constituting a "zone of reasonableness" that delineates public agendas, frames public debates, establishes presumption and burdens of proof, and secures first premises and normative frameworks. Even as ideologies may construct boundaries of public debate, they do not produce unthinking subjects who simply accept the precepts of a particular ideology wholly and without question. Indeed, in many societies, as David Zarefsky notes, people's worldviews may draw upon various—and sometimes opposing—ideologies. Zarefsky observes that, in the United States, "people may be fiscally conservative but socially liberal, for example. Or they embrace the future while feeling nostalgia for the past."[1] The copresence of potentially competing ideologies at the social and individual levels facilitates purposeful political action to challenge dominant ideologies, but we cannot escape ideology's influence.

Frustrating visions of a neutral realm of debate, ideology shaped the emergent institutions of democracy in the West. As publics assembled in modern Europe to challenge the Crown as the ultimate seat of political authority, they asserted a supposedly universal humanity that actually reflected the particular experiences of the bourgeoisie. In this way, as Jürgen Habermas has shown, the bourgeois public sphere perpetuated a conflation of property owner and human being. As tensions appeared in society that threatened its ideology, the bourgeoisie held firm to its putative universal standing. Exclusions in practice could be justified in theory so long as all members of society had the same opportunity to achieve the conditions of entry for the bourgeois public sphere. Even if these opportunities did not exist, the bourgeoisie believed that it still represented a universal interest because its members' standing as property owners especially motivated them to protect civil society as a sphere of individual liberty.[2]

In the contemporary West, and increasingly in other parts of the globe, a powerful ideology has emerged as the voice of the market.[3] Addressing issues ranging from municipal trash collection to international finance, market talk embraces markets as essential elements of human liberty, efficacious forces for financial gain, and superior governing structures.[4] As Thomas Frank observes, advocates of market talk insist that "markets are where we are most fully human; markets are where we show we have a soul. To protest *against* markets is to surrender one's very personhood."[5] Associating markets and personhood in this way advances a consequential set of claims about human psychology and agency, society and belonging, and democracy itself. Advocates of market talk tend to treat "market" and "democracy" as synonymous terms. Communication theorist George Cheney notes that a triumphant tone has accompanied this association in recent decades. Declaring an "end of history," advocates assert that the "market has triumphed over socialist and communist economies. With this position, capitalism is usually equated with democracy, such that mentioning one neatly accounts for the other."[6] Inevitability accompanies triumph, as advocates situate markets at the end of an evolutionary trajectory of economic and political maturity.

As an ideology, market talk presents these value claims as existential facts. Whereas "political" rhetorics betray the values and interests of their proponents, market talk simply describes the world as it truly is. Other participants in policy debates remain bound by social convention and influenced by special pleading, but advocates of market talk reject the mysteries and machinations of politics to speak directly, frankly, and without constraint. As James Arnt Aune notes, "realism is the default rhetoric for defenders of the free market." Market talk treats language as a veil over nature. Participants in policy debates may discover truth only by shedding their symbolic attachments and locating a nonrhetorical essence, which market talk has already achieved. Aune explains that "the realist economic style works by radically separating power and textuality, constructing the political realm as a state of nature, and by depicting its opponents as prisoners of verbal illusions."[7] This is enacted, in part, through the authoritative voice of the economist, who speaks as a cultural representation of objective knowledge. Portraying this authorial pose, Deirdre McCloskey elucidates how the economist disavows one's own advocacy: "It is not I the scientist who makes these assertions but reality itself."[8] In this way, market talk seeks to deny its status as rhetoric.

Yet market talk—like any ideology—cannot maintain this guise unproblematically, since all ideologies exhibit contradictions that may become manifest through social, political, and economic developments.[9] In particular moments, an invisible ideology may suddenly begin to flash brightly. This essay considers one such moment. On October 23, 2008, former Federal Reserve chairperson Alan Greenspan, an especially prominent proponent of market talk, testified before the House Committee on Oversight and Government Reform to address the sources of a worsening economic crisis: in the preceding few months, large investment banks had failed, credit had become increasingly difficult to obtain, the stock market had plummeted, and housing prices had collapsed. As committee chair Henry Waxman queried about whether Greenspan's promarket views had prevented him from taking corrective action as Federal Reserve chair, Greenspan conceded that "everyone has [an ideology]. You have to. To exist, you need an ideology."[10] By conceding the ideological basis of his economic views, Greenspan ceded the privileged position of market talk: it did not espouse a reality against which all other positions betrayed their textuality. Moreover, Greenspan confessed that his ideology was wrong: "I was shocked, because I had been going for forty years or more with very considerable evidence that it was working exceptionally well."[11]

This essay considers how Greenspan's testimony constituted a crisis rhetoric that holds potential for bolstering democratic deliberation. Typically, scholars view deliberation and crisis as conflicting. From this perspective, deliberation takes time, but crises demand immediate action. In the first main section of this essay, I discuss this apparent tension, arguing that if we dissociate crisis and control, we may open up possibilities for deliberation. In the second main section of this essay, I analyze Greenspan's testimony, which wavered between doubt and confidence, disorder and order, crisis and stability. Amid these tensions, Greenspan admitted his ideology, even as he sought to recuperate the privileged standing of market talk. He framed the crisis through the natural metaphor of a tsunami, but his explanation highlighted human action. I conclude by considering how his invocation of crisis may reconfigure topoi of agreement, soundness, and inclusion to make time for deliberation.

(No) Time for Deliberation

Deliberation takes time. It need not proceed leisurely—indeed, people may deliberate with a sense of urgency—but deliberation calls on participants to weigh premises and conclusions, assess evidence, and evaluate warrants. In these ways, participants in deliberation need time to render judgment. Fittingly, the temporal demands of deliberation have been recognized by rhetorical scholars for a long time. In the *Nicomachean Ethics,* Aristotle observed that people "deliberate a long time, and they say that one should carry out quickly the conclusions of one's deliberation, but should deliberate slowly."[12] However, a common theme in studies of crisis rhetoric is that the invocation of "crisis" frustrates judgment; rhetors advancing a crisis often claim that, since immediate action is necessary, an audience does not have the time—which is cast in these situations as a "luxury"—to discuss and reflect on matters. Instead, they must throw their unqualified support behind leaders who can resolve the crisis. As David Zarefsky explains, "by their nature, crises cannot be resolved through 'business as usual'; it is precisely the failure of normal processes to resolve a problem that transforms an ordinary issue into a crisis. Crises do not admit of time for reflective deliberation."[13] To be sure, Zarefsky and others recognize that crises do not exhibit a "natural" tempo; rather, rhetors articulating a crisis deploy a powerful frame to cast debates in ways that advance their interests. In this section, I discuss the time called for by deliberation and the "absence" of time in crisis to provide a perspective against which we may consider Greenspan's testimony as opening up the possibility for rethinking the relationship between deliberation, crisis, and time.

Deliberation takes time for several reasons: to enable participants to persuade each other of mutually agreeable outcomes; to produce sounder decisions; and to generate just decisions by facilitating wide-scale participation. In terms of persuading others, theorists of deliberation sometimes uphold the stringent standard of consensus. In his seminal essay on "Deliberation and Democratic Legitimacy," Joshua Cohen holds that "ideal deliberation aims to arrive at a rationally motivated *consensus*—to find reasons that are persuasive to all who are committed to acting on the results of a free and reasoned assessment of alternatives by equals."[14] If we uphold consensus as our ideal, then we can imagine potentially endless deliberation—hardly an appropriate decision-making technique for moments of crisis—as interlocutors attempt to persuade a stubborn holdout to ascribe to the majority will. Of course, even Cohen admits that consensus is not always possible, and he explains that deliberation and voting can work together to produce legitimate decisions. In the field of rhetoric, some critics have argued that consensus effectively operates as a kind of coercion that discounts minority views as "irrational" and enforces a conformist value system.[15] These critiques base their objections not on logistical but principled grounds—consensus advances an exclusionary ethics.

Yet even if we identify our ideal outcome as something short of consensus—say, a slim majority—we might not "speed up" deliberation, especially on contentious issues. Better still, we may move away from a primarily outcome-based approach and instead associate the persuasive qualities of deliberation with an attitude (e.g., an openness to alternative perspectives) and/or a process (e.g., an exchange of reasons).[16] Both of these approaches avoid the dangers of an effects-based definition (i.e., if a majority does not form, deliberation has not occurred), but they still refer to communicative practices that unfold over time. Indeed, attitude, process, and outcome all suggest the possibility of transformation, which cannot occur instantaneously. In this spirit, Amy Gutmann and Dennis Thompson write that "the very nature of the deliberative process of justification sends a signal that its participants are willing to enter into a dialogue in which the reasons given, and the reasons responded to, have the capacity to change minds."[17] If we are to retain some distinction between deliberation and aggregative decision-making techniques (e.g., voting without any discussion), then we have to acknowledge the potentiality of transformation and its temporal entailments.

A second reason that deliberation takes time is that it may produce sounder decisions by incorporating more perspectives and participants in decision-making processes. By considering a wider range of perspectives, participants presumably will examine more thoroughly the varying aspects of public issues. In this way, James Bohman maintains that "deliberation improves the quality of political justification and decision making by subjecting them to a wide range of possible alternative opinions."[18] Bohman acknowledges that errors and prejudices may be shared by members of a community and that experts sometimes may be better situated to render a judgment on complex issues. However, he retorts that even in these cases incorporating aspects of public deliberation into decisions bolsters soundness by improving the "epistemic quality of the justifications for political decisions." He holds that in deliberative forums, "public opinion is more likely to be formed on the basis of all relevant perspectives, interests, and information and less likely to exclude legitimate interests, relevant knowledge, or appropriate dissenting opinions."[19] Ultimately, Bohman argues, better reasons will produce better outcomes.

Taking the time to consider alternative perspectives serves as a primary quality of judgment itself. Drawing on Kant's notion of an "enlarged mentality," Hannah Arendt argues that judgment requires "the ability to see things not only from one's point of view but in the perspective of all those who happen to be present." Because it facilitates perspective taking, judgment, for Arendt, acts as a primary human capacity for creating a public sphere, since judgment enables people to orient themselves "in the public realm, in the common world . . . [j]udging is one, if not the most, important activity in which this sharing-the-world-with-others comes to pass."[20] Although our contemporary intellectual sensibilities may lead us to treat with skepticism Arendt's instruction that we "see things" from "the perspective of all those who happen to be present"—for this may assume that we can negotiate issues of cultural diversity and value pluralism unproblematically, transparently, and fully—we nevertheless may find common cause with her references to a jointly constructed world. Acting in this world, as Ronald Beiner notes, "cannot be a matter of spontaneous, immediate, intuition." Instead, "judgment requires time: the time in which to weigh one's judgment, time to think things over and reflect, the pause before the moment of decision."[21] Deliberation, then, promises to bring together multiple perspectives and to encourage individual participants to engage these perspectives thoughtfully to produce sounder decisions.

A third reason deliberation takes time is that it promotes inclusive communicative processes. Just as deliberation may invoke wide-ranging perspectives to produce sounder decisions, it may do so to produce more just decisions. On this point, Habermas argues that all theories of cognitive ethics, which maintain that people can reasonably adjudicate among competing value claims, incorporate some form of generalizability. He explains that "the moral principle is so conceived as to exclude as invalid any norm that could not meet with the qualified assent of all who are or might be affected by it." A maxim conceived along these lines expresses the intuition that "valid norms must *deserve* recognition by *all* concerned."[22] Of course, debates on important public issues may proceed without the full participation of potentially affected parties. Moreover, as scholarship on counterpublics has demonstrated, excluded individuals and groups often have to struggle to gain entry to restricted forums.[23]

Inclusion need not (and, in most cases, cannot) take the form of the actual physical participation of all potentially affected individuals. The economic issues Greenspan addressed in his testimony, for example, would likely impact all citizens of the United States, as well as many people across the globe. Moreover, as inclusion involves greater numbers of people into public debates, it may frustrate the goal of producing sounder decisions. As Darrin Hicks explains, "the more people that are included with full and equal speaking rights, the less influence anyone has, and, therefore, the less incentive anyone has to participate in an informed manner." Dissatisfied with this option, Hicks sees promise in proposals that "detach the idea of legitimacy from a head count of reflectively consenting individuals and, in its place, ground legitimacy in the resonance of decisions with the prevailing range of political discourses circulating in a popularly controlled public sphere."[24] Yet, as Hicks notes, even this proposal requires some kind of metadiscourse to demonstrate that the perspectives taken up in deliberative exchanges represent the range of opinions held by majority and minority groups across societies.

In their most frequent rhetorical frame, however, crises do not appear to have time for metadiscourses, nor for potentially endless attempts to persuade reluctant holdouts. Like any public problem, crises may be resolved through sound decisions, but, during these time-sensitive moments, members of a collective have to take as a matter of faith the view that their leaders have identified the appropriate response. After all, in these atypical situations, what else could we do? Lingering too long over alternative viewpoints may turn a potentially resolvable crisis into an unmitigated catastrophe. In many ways, this pattern seems natural; crises appear to arise outside of the realm of ideology. However, scholars have shown that crises are not "natural" events but rhetorical constructs that function strategically in public discourse. Amos Kiewe defines crisis as a "sociorhetorical construct" that "frames an issue, an event, or an occurrence as urgent, unusual, and in need of quick resolution for the resumption of normality."[25] Because of their extraordinary character, crises call for unity and sacrifice.

As strategic tools, however, crises do not appear independently of relations of power. As Murray Edelman explains, a "crisis is uneven in its impact, typically bringing deprivations for many, especially those who are politically and economically weak, and often bringing benefits to some who have the resources to deal with the new situation."[26] In this way, crises index competing ideologies and interests in pluralist societies. Recounting a litany of twentieth-century crises, Edelman argues that each reflected "the response of rational people to opportunities to make use of their economic and political resources."[27] In crisis situations, desired outcomes may be more achievable when deliberation proceeds along a prescribed route. Focusing on U.S. presidents, scholars have considered how they have sought to retain control over their crisis rhetoric: not only have presidents often announced crises, but they have insisted on their interpretation of events.[28]

Many scholars have noted that a common consequence of crisis rhetoric is that it forestalls deliberation. Referencing presidential rhetoric, Jim Kuypers holds that "by announcing the crisis, the president asks for his decision to be supported, not for debate upon what should be done. Thus, crisis rhetoric is a rhetoric that excludes discussion."[29] Over time, recurrent crises may encourage citizens to be less critical of public policies and government actions.[30] In post-9/11 U.S. political culture, for example, a seemingly constant sense of crisis related to the ongoing War on Terror has been invoked to justify a range of potentially controversial decisions. Exploring a range of time-based strategies legitimating the war, Roger Stahl argues that they all lead to the same conclusion: "Deliberation thus disappears as a possibility"; "The trope works to suspend public deliberation"; "No deliberation, only authority."[31] More studies could be added to this list, but the message is clear: many rhetorical scholars view crisis as antithetical to deliberation.

However, scholars' selection of cases used to illustrate crisis rhetoric may help explain its resistance to deliberation. Illustrating the quality of "control," scholars frequently have investigated situations where policymakers, typically presidents, utilize crisis to achieve particular goals, which often are connected to matters of foreign policy. In contrast, Greenspan's testimony encourages us to consider how policymakers may articulate crisis without control. Still a construct, crisis sometimes may circulate as a rhetoric that eludes policymakers' efforts to control it. In this spirit, Denise Bostdorff and Daniel O'Rourke identify the lack of control as a potential difference between domestic and foreign crisis rhetoric. In the realm of foreign affairs, presidents may implement their policies unilaterally. With respect to domestic issues, presidents must rely more on public persuasion. Bostdorff and O'Rourke observe that "although presidents might wish it otherwise, their discourse about domestic crises necessarily invites public deliberation over their preferred policy resolutions and thereby makes policy implementation more difficult for presidents to achieve."[32] Although not a president,

Greenspan has been regarded by policymakers, media commentators, and citizens alike as a "chief executive" of markets. His congressional testimony suggests how crisis sometimes may hold potential benefits for democratic deliberation.

The Problems and Promise of Markets

Greenspan's testimony effectively merged two testimonies: one expressed doubt and the other exhibited confidence; one discerned disorder and the other forecast order; one conceded contemporary crisis and the other reaffirmed historical stability. The first half of his testimony focused mainly on problems with financial markets, while the second half of his testimony primarily addressed the promise of markets. However, this sequencing of main points did not facilitate a logical, problem-solution development of his argument. He could not fully answer the questions he raised. Tensions persisted throughout his testimony as the contradictions of market talk as an ideology did not achieve resolution. Crisis appeared not as a singular event but as an ever-present danger. Once disclosed, Greenspan's market ideology could not recede softly into the background.

Tensions notwithstanding, Greenspan framed the economic crisis engulfing the nation as an extremely rare event. He had not witnessed such devastation during his career, nor, he suggested, had policymakers experienced a similar crisis: "We are in the midst of a once in a century credit tsunami. Central banks and governments are being required to take unprecedented measures. . . . [The crisis] has turned out to be much broader than anything I could have imagined."[33] This framing of events, especially Greenspan's use of a tsunami metaphor, held significant political and policy implications. As a catastrophic event, a tsunami is unexpected, fast, natural, unpreventable, and indiscriminately destructive. Likening these qualities to the economic crisis absolves policymakers and businesspeople. They did not create the crisis, nor could they be expected to fully alleviate suffering, since only evacuations can prevent harm once a tsunami has developed. In this way, the best investors could do was to withdraw any remaining assets from troubled accounts. Further, because a tsunami-like disaster connoted an atypical and unpreventable natural act, it did not necessitate rethinking economic policies, since even the strongest "seawalls" cannot mitigate large-scale damage.

Framing the economic crisis as a natural disaster also served as an incipient response to a spreading populist anger with the excesses of Wall Street executives and public reluctance to bail out faltering firms. The weeks preceding Greenspan's late-October 2008 testimony saw an increasing financial commitment by the federal government to saving Wall Street firms from bankruptcy.[34] Initially, in mid-September, federal officials stood by as the prominent securities firm Lehman Brothers declared bankruptcy and Merrill Lynch submitted to a sale. However, just a few days later, the federal government agreed to lend $85 billion to the troubled insurance firm American International Group (AIG), which many observers characterized as "too big to fail." By October, the Treasury Department announced the creation of a Troubled Assets Relief Program (TARP) to provide firms with hundreds of billions in additional funds to prevent further bankruptcies.[35] During this same period, reports surfaced that some bailed-out firms continued to spend lavishly on corporate perks and executive bonuses. In particular, citizens and politicians alike expressed outrage upon learning that AIG had spent nearly a half-million dollars on an executive retreat at a luxury California resort after the firm received bailout money. Framing the economic crisis as a tsunami presented a means of blunting populist anger by suggesting that its indiscriminate destruction impacted large and small investors similarly. Both types of investors suffered; both saw their portfolios dwindle. Indeed, when a tsunami strikes, the square footage of one's beach house does not matter, since large and small homes alike are leveled.

Striking quickly, the speed of the economic tsunami exhibited a quality common to crises. Many crises happen fast and call for immediate action. Without fast action, a leader may insist, a collective could be ruined. Although the economic crisis may not have permitted careful reflection, it appeared to prompt Greenspan to confront his core beliefs, as he expressed shock repeatedly throughout his testimony. During the question-and-answer session, he admitted that a "critical pillar to market competition and free markets did break down. And I think that, as I said, shocked me. I still do not fully understand why it happened."[36] These moments in Greenspan's testimony foregrounded a sense of doubt that contrasted sharply with his frequent media representations as a market oracle.

Yet speed itself was not detrimental to the economy, since a common refrain of market talk characterizes markets as quick and nimble and governments as slow and plodding. Representative Tom Davis, the Oversight Committee's ranking member, stressed this point during his opening statement. He maintained that "free markets are constantly evolving and innovating. Regulators, by law, bureaucratic custom or just bad habit tend to remain static. Modernization to federal regulatory structures have to take account of the new global dynamics to restore transparency, confidence, and critical checks and balances."[37] As Davis's references to "innovation" and "dynamism" suggest, markets move purposely to achieve creative, ameliorative ends. The problem with the economic tsunami, then, was not speed, but rather who—or what—was moving so quickly. According to market talk, in a properly functioning market, the uncoordinated actions of innumerable individuals—Adam Smith's "invisible hand"—produce positive social outcomes. By contrast, in an economic tsunami, a larger force *acts upon* individuals, thus undermining the individual agency necessary for the invisible hand to do its work. However, even as Davis and others reiterated the mantras of market talk, Greenspan's analysis of the crisis called into question the ethics implied by the invisible hand—namely, that in working for oneself, a market actor promotes the good of others.

Greenspan conceded that investors seeking quick and easy returns played an important role in the crisis. He revealed that "those of us who have looked to the self-interest of lending institutions to protect shareholders' equity, myself especially, are in a state of shocked disbelief. Such counterparty surveillance is a central pillar of our financial markets state of balance."[38] From the perspective of market talk, "self-interest" is all the regulation markets need. Self-interest encourages investors to do their homework, making sure that they are buying sound assets and that the returns on their investments are proportionate to the risks involved. Self-interest presumably also pushes producers—in this case, mortgage lenders and investment banks—to offer sound goods, since they possess an interest in attracting repeat customers. In this market scenario, a bad reputation could lead to a firm's bankruptcy.

The economic tsunami revealed another kind of self-interest, however. The lure of quick money overwhelmed the careful scrutiny that self-interest supposedly promoted. Investment bankers believed that they could generate considerable profits by selling a new product—mortgage-backed securities—that bundled together higher-risk ("subprime") mortgages as investment vehicles. Investors, for their part, valued the high rates of return and seemingly low risks that these securities offered, which was facilitated by a housing bubble that inflated home prices and masked the inability of many borrowers to pay their mortgages. Mortgage lenders contributed to the crisis by responding to the increased demand for mortgage-backed securities by placing many people in homes they could not afford. Greenspan held that this confluence of events confused ostensibly sophisticated investors: "To the most sophisticated investors in the world, they [mortgage-backed securities] were wrongly viewed as a steal."[39]

As demand for these securities increased, the various parties involved in these transactions increasingly dispensed with any sense of caution. Greenspan explained that "demand became so aggressive that too many securitizers and lenders believed they were able to create and sell mortgage-backed securities so quickly . . . [that] they did not have the incentive to evaluate the credit quality of what they were selling." Similarly, he noted that "uncritical acceptance of credit ratings by purchasers of these toxic assets has led to huge losses."[40] Speed influenced these decisions and the larger credit crisis: investment bankers and mortgage lenders believed they could sell their products quickly, and investors believed they could make a quick buck. All parties believed they were acting in their self-interest, yet their actions did not produce a greater good, and even harmed their individual situations. In this way, the market for mortgage-backed securities operated like a Ponzi scheme—an appellation that market advocates often associate with government programs—since only those investors who withdrew their money early avoided losses.

Greenspan's explanation of the crisis also challenged the implications of his tsunami metaphor. Unlike the natural disaster of a tsunami, specific actors contributed to the credit crisis and thus deserved blame for its devastation: lenders approved mortgages that families could not afford; investment bankers packaged and sold these high-risk mortgages as securities; and investors did not investigate fully their purchases. If self-interest failed as a sufficient regulator of markets, then the crisis called for policy interventions. The self-interest (manifest as a desire for easy money) driving these interactions also reopened the possibility for a populist critique, since the creation and sale of mortgage-backed securities were not transactions undertaken by ordinary folk. Further, if self-interest could produce positive or negative outcomes, then the devastation wrought by the economic crisis indicated that positive outcomes required market actors to act ethically. This circumstance meant, contrary to the conceit of market talk, that markets expressed *values*.

Although Greenspan admitted that he operated with an ideology, he sustained a view of economics as scientific discovery. At these moments, his testimony moved toward recuperating the privileged standing of market talk. Greenspan admitted that mortgage-backed securities were not priced properly—that is, sellers and buyers understated the risks associated with these instruments. However, he insisted on the basic soundness of the system: "In recent decades, a vast risk management and pricing system has evolved, combining the best insights with mathematicians and finance experts, supported by major advances in computer and communications technology."[41] Against the current crisis, this characterization reasserted a stable, progressive view of markets as evolving over time toward an optimal end. Whereas the crisis disoriented investors and cast markets as erratic, unpredictable realms, the basic system still promoted purpose and direction, recapturing the sense of innovation that Representative Davis expressed in his opening statement. A sound system also served to depoliticize a market made tendentious by "bad" self-interest. Under this influence, markets, like governments, function as sites of power struggles where leverage, coercion, and special pleading—rather than good decision making—carry the day; the various parties looking to make quick money on mortgage-backed securities displayed the same behaviors as politicians who make decisions to reward friends and punish enemies.

Greenspan's references to "mathematicians," "finance experts," and "advances in computer and communications technology" reclaimed the supposedly scientific basis of economics. From this perspective, time unfolds along a clear, predictable path rather than an erratic, discordant accumulation of individual actions. Along this timeline, the invisible hand resumes its ameliorative role. Underscoring the system's soundness, Greenspan remarked that "a Nobel Prize was awarded for discovery of the pricing model that underpins much of the advance in derivatives markets."[42] To be sure, this remark invoked the prestige of the Nobel Prize to assist in the rehabilitation of market talk. In addition, by framing this feat as a "discovery," Greenspan dissociated the pricing model from human activity: the model—like, perhaps, some rare species of bird—exists in our environment whether or not we encounter it. As scientists, economists do not construct models from their personal preferences or ideological commitments. Instead, they "discover" the properties of markets. Just as this model, then, "underpins" derivatives markets, it also reestablishes the realist style of market talk.

Throughout the crisis, while the pricing model remained sound, human actors inputted incorrect data. Greenspan held that "the whole intellectual edifice, however, collapsed in the summer of last year, because the data inputted into the risk management models generally covered only the past two decades, a period of euphoria."[43] This explanation retained the independence of the model from human activity: analysts can input good or bad data into the model, but the model itself does not change. As the economic crisis unfolded, investors operated with too limited a historical perspective, mistaking the long-run bull market for a permanent condition. In their haste to make quick money, they neglected a longer trajectory. According to Greenspan, had the model "been fitted more appropriately to historic periods of stress, capital requirements would have been much higher, and the financial world would be in far better shape today."[44] Incorporating the disorder of the crisis into a stable timeline, this assertion implied that, at any moment in time, markets may seem erratic and capricious, but over time they exhibit clear patterns. If observers considered only the housing bubble, credit constriction, and stock-market declines, then the economy appeared in ruins. However, by placing this temporary crisis into a longer history, investors could regain confidence in the self-correcting capacity of markets.

Greenspan maintained that investors would learn from the current crisis and that markets would be stronger in the long run. He argued that "whatever regulatory changes are made, they will pale in comparison to the exchange already evident in today's markets. Those markets for an indefinite future will be far more restrained than with any currently contemplated new regulatory regime."[45] Although markets and investors both exhibited progress, their development operated according to different temporal trajectories. The search for pricing models and other structures represented a continuous process of discovery. Economic scientists did not pace their search to current human capacities, nor should they. Sometimes their discoveries directly addressed ongoing needs and interests; at other times their discoveries outpaced human imagination. However, Greenspan insisted that investors would learn to use the models appropriately—the dynamism and innovation of markets demanded no less. He predicted that "the financial landscape that will greet the end of the crisis will be far different from the one that entered it a little more than a year ago. Investors, chastened, will be exceptionally cautious."[46] In the current crisis, the lure of quick money short-circuited investors' judgment. Exuberance fostered impatience, as investors did not take the time to input correct data into their models. Greenspan's contrast of a "regulatory regime" to "restrained" markets and "chastened" investors also implied that policy interventions would not work as effectively because government actions served as external motivators while the lessons of money lost acted as an internal incentive. In this way, self-interest would resume its properly regulatory role.

Other recent events, most notably the dot-com crash of 2000–2001, dampened Greenspan's optimism, but his appeal to investor learning recuperated these events, too, within a longer time frame. These other bubbles suggested that the lure of quick money was hard to resist: if investors saw an opportunity to obtain a sizable return before a bubble burst, they would do so. But, from Greenspan's perspective, this interpretation relied on an incorrect temporal frame. Although crises appeared to lack direction and sweep away established structures and practices, they represented only temporary downturns in a longer positive trajectory. If crisis caused Greenspan to acknowledge and question his ideology, a longer view enabled him to regain his confidence in the value-free, nonpolitical character of markets. He insisted that "this crisis will pass, and America will reemerge with a far sounder financial system."[47] Yet Greenspan's testimony evidenced a temporal trajectory at odds with this concluding statement. Rather than resolving the conflicts he articulated, Greenspan wavered back and forth between crisis and stability. Almost as soon as he ended his prepared remarks with this confident pronouncement, he returned in the question-and-answer session to raising questions about the role of self-interest. He conceded that "I made a mistake in presuming that the self-interest of organizations, specifically banks and others, were such that they were capable of protecting their own shareholders and their equity in the firms."[48] But what appeared as a lingering problem for market talk holds the possibility of a benefit for democratic deliberation.

Making Time for Deliberation through Crisis

Theorists of deliberation often imagine a particular context for its practice. In this scenario, interlocutors gather to reason together—assessing evidence, premises, and conclusions—to determine mutually agreeable and potentially efficacious outcomes to common concerns. Construed in these terms, deliberation occurs as a purposeful, coordinated activity in which participants recognize and consciously sustain their mutual roles.[49] In this way, participants make time for deliberation. Rhetorical scholars need not look far to find various examples of these deliberative contexts, from policymakers attending a committee meeting to resolve differences in the details of legislation to community members attending a town hall meeting in the hopes of developing a shared judgment about a local issue. In these situations and others, potential participants may anticipate a deliberative exchange; they may arrive at a town hall meeting, for instance, knowing that arguments will be advanced and a decision will be reached.

Greenspan's testimony illuminates how the invocation of crisis may engender unexpected and "accidental" opportunities for deliberation. Given the typically confident pronouncements of market talk, Greenspan's authoritative public persona, and the market-affirming aspects of his testimony, we may reasonably conclude that Greenspan did not testify with the purpose of questioning the norms of market talk, even as he may have been open to modest and temporary changes to economic policy. Yet crisis unsettles, raising questions that do not appear as agenda items circulated prior to a meeting. These questions may challenge how prevailing but invisible ideologies frame public debates. Undermining the strength of a particular frame, crisis may draw attention to alternatives.

Deliberation still takes time, but crisis may make time for deliberation. Indeed, as scholars of argumentation and rhetoric, we ought to insist on the temporal quality of deliberation even as we rethink its relationship to crisis, since time bolsters critical judgment. To the extent to which deliberation involves participants in inferential processes of reasoning, it necessarily includes a temporal component as the connections that arguers make between, say, premises and conclusions unfold over time.[50] Deliberation may proceed slowly or quickly, ploddingly or adroitly, but it must *proceed* rather than register instantaneous responses. John Dewey touched on the importance of making connections in his famous thesis about the public's eclipse. For Dewey, efficacious public engagement required that citizens perceive the consequences of their interactions. However, his assessment of contemporary society led Dewey to the judgment that "many consequences are felt rather than perceived; they are suffered, but they cannot be said to be known, for they are not, by those who experience them, referred to their origins."[51] A felt consequence indicates awareness absent understanding; it may produce an aggravated response to a grievance—such as registering immediate like or dislike to the statements of candidates in a presidential debate, which some television networks have simultaneously presented in their broadcasts—but inference exceeds an instant. Insisting on time for deliberation constitutes an act of critical resistance. To appreciate more fully how Greenspan's testimony intimates a refiguration of the relationship among deliberation, crisis, and time, we need to reconsider my previously mentioned topoi of deliberative decision making.

Often, deliberation takes time because interlocutors seek to persuade each other of a mutually agreeable outcome. The default contextual setting for this temporal topos is a town hall meeting, where citizens assemble in the hope of gaining adherents for their favored positions. To the extent to which it may rush decision making, crisis appears in this context as a potential threat. However, Greenspan's identification of an economic tsunami did not serve the end of a strategically developed plan to persuade others of a distinct position. Rather, this metaphor signaled Greenspan's own struggles with determining appropriate public policy in response to current economic events. In this way, crisis did not forestall deliberation by rushing judgment but invited judgment by unsettling seemingly settled issues. Whereas Greenspan, in his previous public statements, frequently expressed a confidence that blunted questioning of his policy directives, his lack of confidence invited critique.[52]

In this spirit, Greenspan acknowledged that human actions—his tsunami metaphor notwithstanding—contributed to the economic crisis. As scholars of economic rhetoric have explained, proponents of market talk frequently depict themselves as scientists discovering natural laws. Greenspan's reference to the "discovery" of a pricing model illustrated this rhetorical quality. However, at other moments, he conceded that self-interest drove bankers and investors to understate the risks associated with mortgage-backed securities. This explanation promised to recover a sense of agency elided by the "scientific" pose of market talk. If natural laws guide the economy, then human agents are limited in their choices about economic policy: we can only suffer (silently) when recessions happen, and we cannot craft policies to direct our economic future. Greenspan's testimony suggested that economic failures and successes are events that humans create, and public policies can—and should—regulate the economy to achieve desired outcomes.

Deliberation also takes time to produce sound decisions, requiring participants to consider alternative perspectives when debating an issue. Adhering to this topos, we may conclude that the more thoroughly we investigate alternatives—including the values and assumptions attending arguments—the more soundly we may reach decisions. Yet, as Greenspan's admission that "to exist, you need an ideology" implies, ideology informs our investigations, frustrating the idea of an ideology-free deliberative context. Moreover, by sustaining a "zone of reasonableness," ideology may render some potential objects of investigation as "natural" or "commonsensical," thus circumscribing our critique and fostering an incomplete sense of exhaustiveness. If we cannot escape ideology and if public debates always utilize frames, then we cannot hope to consider alternative perspectives from a neutral vantage point. In some situations, then, the invocation of crisis may promote deliberation by shifting deliberative frames and recasting previously regarded common sense as appropriate subjects of investigation.

Along these lines, Greenspan's testimony shifted presumptions and burdens of proof in debates about economic policy. Typically, many policymakers and citizens "defer" to the market in these debates, asserting that markets operate more effectively than governments and that proposals to "intervene" in markets ought to be regarded skeptically.[53] This presumption places a greater burden of proof on advocates proposing more progressive policies. Further, it sustains an artificially limited public agenda by declaring particular economic topics and perspectives as "off-limits." In contrast, acknowledging the human basis of markets creates a more level playing field for public debates, indicating that markets and governments both may be subjected to rigorous debate. Rejecting the dichotomy that associates values with government and neutrality with markets, this view retorts that both affirm values. Through public deliberation, then, citizens may identify and prioritize their shared values, and they may insist that public policies reflect these values.

Proponents of deliberative democracy have held that deliberation not only produces sound decisions, but just decisions, too, by including more perspectives. Recognizing that participant lists and procedures alone will not achieve inclusive deliberation, scholars have attended to the important roles of reciprocity and perspective taking.[54] To reach mutually agreeable decisions about matters of common interest, participants in deliberation must conduct themselves with an openness to considering alternative perspectives.[55] Without this approach, deliberative outcomes may reproduce social, economic, and political inequalities. Yet the means of inculcating this attitudinal approach among interlocutors remains an open question. Crisis may serve this end by unsettling a stubborn commitment to self-interest that may lead interlocutors to dismiss alternative perspectives. Crisis may challenge a hubristic refusal to hear the counsel of others, delivering a shock to the system that leads participants to seek collaborative solutions to common concerns.[56]

Market talk has valued self-interest, but Greenspan's testimony challenged the view that self-interest always produces positive public outcomes. Throughout his appearance, he expressed shock that this ostensibly sufficient regulator turned out to be inadequate. Intimating the need for a more expansive ethics from market actors, Greenspan's testimony suggested that reciprocity and perspective taking may be crucial for markets, too. When acting in markets and, more generally, formulating economic policy, policymakers and citizens should consider a range of alternative perspectives. In this spirit, a "deliberative economy" may accompany renewed commitments to deliberation and democracy.

NOTES

1. David Zarefsky, "Strategic Maneuvering in Political Argumentation," *Argumentation* 22 (2008): 323.
2. Habermas holds that the bourgeoisie's assertion that it represented a universal interest was true as a specific historical claim. He writes that "class interest was the basis of public opinion. During that phase, however, it must also have been objectively congruent with the general interest, at least to the extent that this opinion could be considered the public one, emerging from the critical debate of the public, and consequently, rational." Jürgen Habermas, *The Structural Transformation of the Public Sphere: An Inquiry into a Category of Bourgeois Society,* trans. Thomas Burger (1962; reprint, Cambridge: Massachusetts Institute of Technology, 1989), 87.
3. On the global rise of market-based politics and policies, see Pierre Bourdieu, *Acts of Resistance: Against the Tyranny of the Market,* trans. Richard Nice (New York: New Press, 1998); M. Lane Bruner, "Taming 'Wild' Capitalism," *Discourse and Society* 13 (2002): 167–184; Helga Leitner, Jamie Peck, and Eric S. Sheppard, eds., *Contesting Neoliberalism: Urban Frontiers* (New York: Guilford, 2006); Alfredo Saad-Filho and Deborah Johnston, eds., *Neoliberalism: A Critical Reader* (London: Pluto Press, 2005).
4. In my book *Invoking the Invisible Hand,* I identify market talk as a "discourse," which I define as "bodies of rhetoric that serve as publicly articulated ways of collectively understanding and evaluating our world that propagate and enforce social norms with material consequences." In this essay, I refer to the ideological standing of market talk to comport my analysis with Greenspan's testimony. Conceptually, discourse, as I have defined it, is the broader term that explains the various functions of market talk. All discourses carry ideological weight, which is the focus of this essay. Robert Asen, *Invoking the Invisible Hand: Social Security and the Privatization Debates* (East Lansing: Michigan State University Press, 2009), 11–12.
5. Thomas Frank, *One Market Under God: Extreme Capitalism, Market Populism, and the End of Economic Democracy* (New York: Doubleday, 2000), 29, xiii.

6. George Cheney, "Arguing About the Place of Values and Ethics in Market-Oriented Discourses of Today," in *New Approaches to Rhetoric,* ed. Patricia A. Sullivan and Steven R. Goldzwig (Thousand Oaks, CA: Sage, 2004), 74.
7. James Arnt Aune, *Selling the Free Market: The Rhetoric of Economic Correctness* (New York: Guilford Press, 2001), 40. Aune draws on the work of Robert Hariman, who has authored an instructive book on political style. Robert Hariman, *Political Style: The Artistry of Power* (Chicago: University of Chicago Press, 1995).
8. Deirdre N. McCloskey, *The Rhetoric of Economics,* 2d ed. (Madison: University of Wisconsin Press, 1998), 9. See also Willie Henderson, Tony Dudley-Evans, and Roger Backhouse, eds., *Economics and Language* (New York: Routledge, 1993); Arjo Klamer, Donald N. McCloskey, and Robert M. Solow, eds., *The Consequences of Economic Rhetoric* (New York: Cambridge University Press, 1988).
9. Identifying contradiction as a primary quality of ideologies, James Aune argues that the "mediating and synthesizing function of rhetorical practice" may serve as a "coping mechanism" or a source of critique. James Arnt Aune, "An Historical Materialist Theory of Rhetoric," *American Communication Journal* 6 (2003), http://acjournal.org/holdings/vo16/iss4/mcmcgee/aune.htm.
10. House Oversight and Government Reform Committee, *The Financial Crisis and the Role of Federal Regulators,* 110th Cong., 2d sess., 2008, 36.
11. Oversight, *Financial Crisis,* 37.
12. Aristotle, *Nicomachean Ethics,* trans. W. D. Ross (Oxford: Clarendon Press, 1908), bk. 6, sec. 9.
13. David Zarefsky, *President Johnson's War on Poverty: Rhetoric and History* (Tuscaloosa: University of Alabama Press, 1986), 13.
14. Joshua Cohen, "Deliberation and Democratic Legitimacy," in *Deliberative Democracy: Essays on Reason and Politics,* ed. James Bohman and William Rehg (Cambridge: Massachusetts Institute of Technology Press, 1997), 75.
15. See Cindy L. Griffin, "The Essentialist Roots of the Public Sphere: A Feminist Critique," *Western Journal of Communication* 60 (1996): 21–39; Kendall R. Phillips, "The Spaces of Public Dissension: Reconsidering the Public Sphere," *Communication Monographs* 63 (1996): 231–248. For responses arguing that Phillips, in particular, overstates the reliance on consensus in public sphere scholarship, see G. Thomas Goodnight, "Opening Up 'the Spaces of Public Dissension'," *Communication Monographs* 64 (1997): 270–275; Gerard A. Hauser, "On Publics and Public Spheres: A Response to Phillips," *Communication Monographs* 64 (1997): 275–279.
16. For a discussion of various approaches to defining argument, see David Zarefsky,

"Product, Process, or Point of View?" in *Proceedings of the Summer Conference on Argumentation, 1979,* ed. Jack Rhodes and Sara Newell (Washington, DC: National Communication Association/American Forensic Association, 1980), 228–238.

17. Amy Gutmann and Dennis Thompson, *Why Deliberative Democracy?* (Princeton, NJ: Princeton University Press, 2004), 20.
18. James Bohman, *Public Deliberation: Pluralism, Complexity, and Democracy* (Cambridge: Massachusetts Institute of Technology Press, 1996), 26.
19. Ibid., 27.
20. Hannah Arendt, *Between Past and Future* (New York: Penguin Press, 1961), 221.
21. Ronald Beiner, *Political Judgment* (Chicago: University of Chicago Press, 1983), 105.
22. Jürgen Habermas, "Discourse Ethics: Notes on a Program of Philosophical Justification," in *Moral Consciousness and Communicative Action,* trans. Christian Lenhardt and Shierry Weber Nicholsen (Cambridge: Massachusetts Institute of Technology Press, 1990), 63, 65.
23. See Daniel C. Brouwer, "Communication as Counterpublic," in *Communication as . . . Perspectives on Theory,* ed. Gregory J. Sheperd, Jeffrey St. John, and Ted Striphas (Thousand Oaks, CA: Sage, 2006), 195–208.
24. Darrin Hicks, "The Promise(s) of Deliberative Democracy," *Rhetoric & Public Affairs* 5 (2002): 227–228.
25. Amos Kiewe, "The Crisis Tool in American Political Discourse," *Politically Speaking: A Worldwide Examination of Language Used in the Public Sphere,* ed. Ofer Feldman and Christ'l De Landtsheer (Westport, CT: Praeger, 1998), 80.
26. Murray Edelman, *Political Language: Words that Succeed and Policies that Fail* (New York: Academic Press, 1977), 45.
27. Edelman, *Political Language,* 46.
28. See, for example, Jim A. Kuypers, *Presidential Crisis Rhetoric and the Press in the Post-Cold War World* (Westport, CT: Praeger, 1997), 18; Kiewe, "Crisis Tool," 80.
29. Kuypers, *Presidential Crisis,* 17.
30. Edelman, *Political Language,* 48–49.
31. Roger Stahl, "A Clockwork War: Rhetorics of Time in a Time of Terror," *Quarterly Journal of Speech* 94 (2008): 82, 85, 90.
32. Denise M. Bostdorff and Daniel J. O'Rourke, "The Presidency and the Promotion of Domestic Crisis: John Kennedy's Management of the 1962 Steel Crisis," *Presidential Studies Quarterly* 27 (1997): 345.
33. Oversight, *Financial Crisis,* 15.

34. See Andrew Ross Sorkin, "Lehman Files for Bankruptcy; Merrill Is Sold," *New York Times,* September 15, 2008, http://www.nytimes.com/2008/09/15/business/15lehman.html?pagewanted=all; Matthew Karnitschnig, Deborah Solomon, Liam Pleven, and Jon E. Hilsenrath, "U.S. to Take Over AIG in $85 Billion Bailout; Central Banks Inject Cash as Credit Dries Up," *Wall Street Journal,* September 16, 2008, http://online.wsj.com/article/SB122156561931242905.html.
35. U.S. Treasury Department, "Treasury Announces TARP Capital Purchase Program Description," http://www.treas.gov/press/releases/hp1207.htm.
36. Oversight, *Financial Crisis,* 34.
37. Ibid., 8.
38. Ibid., 17.
39. Ibid., 17–18.
40. Ibid., 18.
41. Ibid.
42. Ibid.
43. Ibid., 18–19.
44. Ibid., 19.
45. Ibid.
46. Ibid., 20.
47. Ibid.
48. Ibid., 33.
49. Writing to a nonspecialist audience, John Gastil answers the question of what deliberation means this way: "when people deliberate, they carefully examine a problem and arrive at a well-reasoned solution after a period of inclusive respectful consideration of diverse points of view." John Gastil, *Political Communication and Deliberation* (Thousand Oaks, CA: Sage, 2008), 8.
50. In referencing "premises" and "conclusions," I am invoking a propositional model of argument but not a universal model of argument. Others have explored how visuality and performance may be incorporated into our models of argument. See, for example, Catherine Helen Palczewski, "Argument in an Off Key: Playing with the Productive Limits of Argument," in *Arguing Communication and Culture,* ed. G. Thomas Goodnight (Washington, DC: National Communication Association, 2002), 1–23.
51. John Dewey, *The Public and Its Problems* (1927; reprint, Athens, OH: Swallow Press, 1954), 131.
52. For an analysis of some of Greenspan's previous public statements, see Michelle C.

Bligh and Gregory D. Hess, "The Power of Leading Subtly: Alan Greenspan, Rhetorical Leadership, and Monetary Policy," *Leadership Quarterly* 18 (2007): 87–104.

53. See James K. Galbraith, *The Predator State: How Conservatives Abandoned the Free Market and Why Liberals Should Too* (New York: Free Press, 2008).

54. See, for example, Joshua Cohen, "Democracy and Liberty," in *Deliberative Democracy*, ed. Jon Elster (Cambridge, MA: Cambridge University Press, 1998), 196–197; Amy Gutmann and Dennis Thompson, *Moral Disagreement: Why Moral Conflict Cannot Be Avoided in Politics, and What Should Be Done About It* (Cambridge: Harvard University Press, 1996).

55. See Robert Asen, "A Discourse Theory of Citizenship," *Quarterly Journal of Speech* 90 (2004): 189–211.

56. Crisis may elicit fear, which, Michael William Pfau argues, sometimes may facilitate deliberation. Pfau conceptualizes "civic fear" as a way that a rhetor may draw an audience's attention to an underappreciated issue that is constructed as contingent rather than necessary and subject to deliberation over a range of actions that may redress the issue. See Michael William Pfau, "Who's Afraid of Fear Appeals: Contingency, Courage, and Deliberation in Rhetorical Theory and Practice," *Philosophy and Rhetoric* 40 (2007): 216–237.

Contributors

Robert Asen is professor of rhetoric in the Department of Communication Arts and an affiliate at the Institute for Research on Poverty at the University of Wisconsin–Madison. His research explores the connections between political and economic inequalities, public deliberation, and public policy. He is the author of *Visions of Poverty: Welfare Policy and Political Imagination* and *Invoking the Invisible Hand: Social Security and the Privatization Debates*. He has also coedited two books.

Denise M. Bostdorff is professor of communication at the College of Wooster in Wooster, Ohio. She is the author of *The Presidency and the Rhetoric of Foreign Crisis* and *Proclaiming the Truman Doctrine: The Cold War Call to Arms*, which won the 2010 Bruce E. Gronbeck Political Communication Research Award, as well as scholarly and pedagogical essays related to political rhetoric. She wishes to thank Abbey Smanik, Class of 2011 at the College of Wooster, who served as a research assistant on this project.

Karlyn Kohrs Campbell is professor of communication studies at the University of Minnesota. She is the author or coauthor of seven books, including the groundbreaking two-volume work *Man Cannot Speak for Her: A Critical Study of Early Feminist Rhetoric*. She is the recipient of a Shorenstein Center fellowship from Harvard University's Kennedy School, the National Communication Association Distinguished Scholar Award, the Lauren Ecroyd outstanding teacher award, and the Woolbert Award for scholarship of exceptional originality and influence, and she was named the 2002 Distinguished Woman Scholar in the humanities and social sciences at the University of Minnesota.

G. Thomas Goodnight is professor of communication at the Annenberg School for Communication and Journalism at the University of Southern California. His areas of interest include rhetorical theory and practice, public address, and argumentation, particularly in instances of post-traumatic cultures across time.

James Jasinski is professor of communication at the University of Puget Sound in Tacoma, Washington. He is the author of *Sourcebook on Rhetoric: Key Concepts in Contemporary Rhetorical Studies* and various essays and book chapters in rhetorical criticism and American public address. He currently serves as editor of *Rhetoric Society Quarterly*.

Michael Leff was professor and chair of the Department of Communication at the University of Memphis. At the time of his death in 2010 he was president of the Rhetoric Society of America. He was named a Distinguished Scholar by the National Communication Association and received the Distinguished Research Award from the International Society for the Study of Argumentation. Much of his scholarship in rhetorical criticism illustrates the approach of close textual reading, which he pioneered in the field of rhetoric and public address.

Martin J. Medhurst is distinguished professor of rhetoric and communication and professor of political science at Baylor University in Waco, Texas. He is the author or editor of thirteen books, most recently *Words of a Century: The Top 100 American Speeches, 1900–1999* (with Stephen

E. Lucas). His interest areas include presidential rhetoric, civil-religious discourse, and the rhetoric of the Cold War. He is also the founder and editor of the interdisciplinary quarterly *Rhetoric & Public Affairs*.

John M. Murphy is associate professor of communication at the University of Illinois. His research has appeared in the *Quarterly Journal of Speech, Rhetoric & Public Affairs, Presidential Studies Quarterly*, and elsewhere. His teaching interests include the history of American public address, the U.S. presidency, and rhetorical criticism. He is a recipient of the National Communication Association's Golden Anniversary Monograph Award.

Kathryn M. Olson is professor of communication at the University of Wisconsin–Milwaukee (UWM) and director of UWM's Rhetorical Leadership Graduate Concentration/Certificate Program. Her research interests include rhetorical criticism and theory, argumentation, and contemporary public address. Her scholarship has appeared in journals such as *Quarterly Journal of Speech, Presidential Studies Quarterly, Rhetoric & Public Affairs, Journal of Applied Communication Research, Philosophy and Rhetoric*, and *Argumentation and Advocacy*. She has won numerous awards for her research, including two National Communication Association Golden Anniversary Monograph Awards.

Michael William Pfau is associate professor of communication at the University of Minnesota, Duluth. His book, *The Political Style of Conspiracy: Chase, Sumner, and Lincoln*, was published by Michigan State University Press in 2005. His scholarship has appeared in a number of journals, including *Rhetoric & Public Affairs, Quarterly Journal of Speech, Philosophy and Rhetoric*, and *Argumentation and Advocacy*.

Benjamin Ponder is an executive in the educational software industry. He is also the author of *American Independence: From Common Sense to the Declaration* (2010).

Kirt H. Wilson is associate professor and graduate program officer in the Department of Communication Arts and Sciences at Pennsylvania

State University. A critic and theorist of U.S. public discourse, he focuses his research on mid to late nineteenth-century political rhetoric and African American civil rights struggles. He has won several national awards, including two honors from the National Communication Association for his book *The Reconstruction Desegregation Debate: The Politics of Equality and the Rhetoric of Place, 1870–1875*.

David Zarefsky is Owen L. Coon professor emeritus of argumentation and debate and professor emeritus of communication studies at Northwestern University, where he served as dean of the School of Speech from 1988 to 2000. He is the author of *Lincoln, Douglas, and Slavery: In the Crucible of Public Debate* and *President Johnson's War on Poverty: Rhetoric and History*. He is the author or editor of seven additional books and more than 100 scholarly articles. He is a former president of the National Communication Association, the Rhetoric Society of America, and the Central States Communication Association.